# THE BUSINESS OF NETWORKS

T0362251

# The Business of Networks

Inter-firm interaction, institutional policy and the TEC experiment

ROBERT HUGGINS
*Cardiff University*

Routledge
Taylor & Francis Group

LONDON AND NEW YORK

First published 2000 by Ashgate Publishing

Reissued 2018 by Routledge
2 Park Square, Milton Park, Abingdon, Oxon, OX14 4RN
711 Third Avenue, New York, NY 10017, USA

*Routledge is an imprint of the Taylor & Francis Group, an informa business*

A Library of Congress record exists under LC control number: 00130122

ISBN 13: 978-1-138-71604-9 (hbk)
ISBN 13: 978-1-138-71602-5 (pbk)
ISBN 13: 978-1-315-19721-0 (ebk)

# Contents

# List of Tables

# 1 Introduction

## Business Networks in the UK

Network concepts have evolved into important instruments for theorising and describing contemporary organisational relationships, in particular the linkages, exchanges and interaction that take place between firms. These relationships are often termed inter-firm, or business, networks, and their study has been increasingly connected to explanations of industrial competitiveness and economic development. In particular, inter-firm networks have been studied specifically in the context of facilitating economic development and growth at local and regional levels. Subsequently, there has been growing public policy interest in stimulating inter-firm networks in a number of states and regions throughout the world.

In the United Kingdom (UK) context, most studies have focused on finding evidence and evaluating the prevalence of existing inter-firm networks within localities and regions. These studies have reported very mixed and differing results. For example, Sweeting's (1995) study of manufacturing industry in the North West found that strong and effective networks were being developed by managers of regional firms; and Bryson et al.'s (1993) work found networks to be a vital and inherent part of the UK business services sector. In contrast Baker's (1995) study of Hinckley and Penn's (1992) work on the Rochdale economy both argued that they found little evidence of local inter-firm relations. Furthermore, Crewe's (1996) findings of a critical mass of linked firms in the Nottingham Lace Market conflicts to an extent with Hardill et al.'s (1995) survey of the East Midlands, which argued that business linkages did not form an important part of the local socio-economic fabric. Garnsey and Cannon-Brookes's (1993) study of the computing and software complex at Cambridge, which it is often argued is the UK's best example of a local economy consisting of significant inter-firm networks, has also cast doubts on the extent to which local linkages exist. They argue that most companies in the area are more pre-disposed to network and nurture links with firms at the global rather than the local level (Garnsey and Cannon-Brookes, 1993).

These studies all have their merits, with the differing results often due to the range of definitions of networks or networking applied to empirical work. However, the overall situation in the UK, as recognised by

1

Hirst and Zeitlin (1989), appears still to consist of a general absence of a supportive inter-firm culture. It has also been suggested that the common factor differentiating relatively innovative and entrepreneurial localities in the UK from those with low levels of innovation is the operation of relatively effective networks (Bennett and McCoshan, 1993). Bennett and McCoshan (1993) have further argued that there are limitations on the extent to which network capacity can, to any considerable degree, organically permeate the business community in the UK. Therefore, from the assumption that networks have the potential to contribute to economic growth, it can be suggested that public policy action is required.

Policy intervention in the UK has, so far, concentrated on extending the 'interactivity' of existing groups, as well as catalysing and forming new networks, primarily aimed at small and medium-sized enterprises (SMEs) at the local and regional level, via the facilitation of intermediary policy support organisations. This has been prompted by an increased awareness among policy-makers in the UK that competitiveness and innovation are connected to co-operative and long-term relationships between businesses, with a number of recent developments being promoted by organisations involved in policy intervention (Sako, 1992; Joyce et al. 1995). In particular, it is Training and Enterprise Councils (TECs) in England and Wales (Local Enterprise Companies in Scotland), operating as local public-private partnership organisations, that have taken an endogenous policy approach to the process of encouraging inter-firm network formation, as part of an overall strategy of attempting to become institutions that are increasingly referred to as 'civic entrepreneurs'.

The introduction of TECs was to a large extent related to a recognition by the Conservative Government of the time that the most effective economic development policies, aimed specifically at the business community, are provided by institutions that themselves act like entrepreneurial businesses (Gibb and Manu, 1990; Gibb, 1993; Bennett, 1995a). Institutions acting in such a manner are said to be operating as 'policy' or 'civic' entrepreneurs, introducing policy change and innovation that are new to the locality or region adopting it (Mintrom, 1997). Clarke and Gaile (1997) label such a policy system as one of 'entrepreneurial mercantilism', based on aims for more diversified growth within new and expanded exogenous markets, through mobilising local initiatives and indigenous assets providing greater benefits for economic development. According to Harvey (1989) this 'new entrepreneurialism' has as its centrepiece the notion of public-private partnerships, in which 'traditional local boosterism' has become integrated into activities that are entrepreneurial precisely because they are speculative in execution and design. It is such a public-private partnership role that the previous

Conservative Government attempted to vest in TECs. This book investigates how TECs in the UK have attempted to act as civic entrepreneurs in a bid to generate networks, particularly of an inter-firm form, within their localities, and to further analyse how the effectiveness of the instruments adopted have aided economic development.

## Civic Entrepreneurship

It is in the United States (US) that civic entrepreneurship has received the most attention. According to Leicht and Jenkins (1994) entrepreneurial approaches have formed one of three main sub-national economic development strategies in the US; the other two concerning industrial recruitment and deregulation approaches. Leicht and Jenkins (1994) further argue that entrepreneurial policies are directed at qualitative growth, defined by the promotion of high value–added production, through processes that state governments can facilitate by assuming entrepreneurial functions. These functions include launching new enterprises, creating new technologies and products, and identifying new markets for these products, typically through public-private ventures. The first detailed academic discussion of entrepreneurial policies stemmed from the work of Eisinger (1988), which argued that traditional local supply-side incentives directed at the attraction of large industrial concerns during the 1970s and early 1980s merely served to move productive capital around the US. Eisinger (1988) suggested that during the mid 1980s a shift occurred whereby economic development grew from being a relatively marginal item on the political agendas of state and local officials to becoming a central and even pivotal issue among prevailing concerns, and that certain social development goals could be best achieved through the enhancement of local businesses, rather than in disbursing public resources in an effort to attract the rare mover.

This change was coupled with the rise of entrepreneurial bureaucrats in the US, who attempted to propel dynamic policy change by creating or exploiting new opportunities to push forward their ideas, often via targeted firms or sectors that they believed were best positioned to respond to market opportunities identified or legitimated by the state (Eisinger, 1988; Teske and Schneider, 1994). These approaches were further popularised in the work of national government policy advisers Osborne and Gaebler (1992), who conveyed a message that mayors and governors throughout the US were 're-inventing government' by embracing public-private partnerships and developing alternative ways to deliver services through creation of catalytic governance that acted to 'steer' rather than 'row'. One example of the creation of these 'steering' organisations cited by Osborne and Gaebler (1992) were the Private Industry Councils (PICs), set up under the federal Job Training Partnership Act to bring local public and private sector leaders together to manage job training activities within their region, and which were the original model upon which TECs were based.

Osborne and Gaebler (1992) have undoubtedly highlighted a trend in US policy-making, however they have been criticised as presenting a rather lop-sided view of such economic development approaches. For example, Kobrak (1996) has argued that although Osborne and Gaebler's (1992) emphasis on the need to create a market-oriented system of governance implies the need for important public choice innovations, it says little, if anything, about the relation of risks to rewards. DeLeon (1996) has also argued that the primary reason behind many of these initiatives was the pressure to 'do more with less', resulting in the road to re-invention becoming 'littered with bashed bureaucrats, dashed hopes, and political casualties'. Entrepreneurial approaches have been further criticised within the academic literature of the US for promoting economic development policies that are opposed to democratic accountability, participation, openness, and stewardship (Bellone and Goerl, 1992). Others have suggested that empirical analysis of entrepreneurial local economic development activity in the US does not actually reflect a clear shift to demand-side activities, directed at stimulating indigenous business and promoting economic base diversity (Reese and Malmer, 1994). Interestingly, Eisinger (1995) has more recently argued that the commitment to active economic intervention by sub-national government in the US, exemplified by the entrepreneurial programmes of the 1980s, is beginning to flag in the face of doubts about the efficacy and political viability of many initiatives.

To an extent these arguments undermine the ethos of widespread successful civic entrepreneurship within the US. Nevertheless, the interpretation of academics in the UK has stuck very much to the literature acknowledging its success in the US, in the attempt to assess the replication in the UK which was undoubtedly a feature of Conservative Government policy - as Rhodes (1997) indicates, the Conservative Government often cited Osborne and Gaebler (1992) to justify its policies. It has been suggested that one of the problems in analysing policy replication imported from the US was the assumption that while the policy development situation in both countries seemed to be similar, they were in reality quite different. For instance, as Fasenfest (1993) argues, while the US administration attempted to remove federal government from maintaining an array of local programmes, the Thatcher Government in the UK sought to impose greater control over the day-to-day actions of local government.

The most detailed work on policy change in the UK is that of Rhodes (1997), which argues that there has been a shift from government to governance at a local level typified by there being no one policy centre; but multiple centres forming an amalgam of organisations drawn from the public, private and voluntary sector, involved in delivering local services and interacting within inter-organisational policy networks. Rhodes (1997) refers to this entrepreneurial governance as 'new public management', stressing the introduction of private management methods to the public sector, and highlighting TECs as the nodal points in local policy networks co-ordinating multiple stakeholders.

As both Rhodes (1997) and Axford and Pinch (1994) indicate, the introduction of TECs has given rise to a chorus of complaints about the loss of democratic accountability. TECs have further been seen as undermining the role of local government authorities, with the 'hidden' agenda consisting of public spending cost-cutting exercises through the tightening of local government expenditure (Rhodes, 1997). Hall and Hubbard (1996) argue that although the changes that have taken place in the UK have led many commentators to define the emergence of models of governance and economic development as entrepreneurial, it is nevertheless difficult to assess whether the shift to entrepreneurial modes is actually supplanting or merely supplementing traditional approaches. They further suggest that the reality has proved rather mundane, with the key change involving local business leaders being co-opted into local politics through the boards of new non-elected local agencies, particularly TECs (Hall and Hubbard, 1996). Indeed, with regard to mobilising small firms and developing networks between such companies in the UK, Gibb (1993) argues that many of the challenges facing the 'new institutions' will need to be faced through still better management of both the environment of support for the growth of firms and the institutional assistance environment as a whole.

The call for better management between and within these new institutions resonates with Bennett et al.'s (1994) concept of the 'perverse policy syndrome', which states that more resources alone will change nothing; and indeed more resources may make matters worse by strengthening the power of the institutions allocating those resources. Bennett et al. (1994) argue that the only way to break out of this syndrome is to radically move away from the institutional priorities and economic values of the past, and to develop new institutional goals and systems of economic support. The introduction of TECs was, as Bennett et al. (1994) further contend, a bid to contribute to this institutional break, meeting the challenges highlighted by Gibb (1993), through the facilitation of: (1) new leadership; (2) a focus on the performance of programmes; (3) emphasis on customers over producers; and (4) local flexibility. The following section considers in more detail the recent evolution of economic development policy in the UK leading towards a 'network approach' and the introduction of TECs.

## The Evolution of Network Approaches to Economic Development

In the UK, recent economic development strategies directed at the indigenous business community have largely evolved from the Conservative Government's policies on small firm development, predominantly designed during the 1979-1990 Thatcher administration. Of course, small business policy was not solely an invention of the Conservative Government at that time and its roots should properly be placed in the Bolton Committee of Inquiry on Small Firms, established by a Labour Government in 1969 and which reported in 1971 (Bolton, 1971). The major impact of the report concerned its finding that little was known at the time on the role that small firms played in the national economy, thus recommending the establishment of a small firms division within the Department of Trade and Industry (DTI) (Robertson, 1996a). The change of Government in 1979 quickly increased the policy momentum surrounding small firms by placing them near the head of the political agenda (Goss, 1991). The Government perceived the decline in the competitiveness of UK economy to be a direct result of a pervading 'dependency' culture, within which individuals were unwilling to take, and subsequently benefit from, commercial risk-taking (Storey and Strange, 1992). Therefore, policies were designed to create a shift to a more dynamic 'enterprise culture' through a wave of measures in the 1980s, aimed at directly and indirectly fostering the formation and growth of small business, within three broad categories: finance; legislation and administration; and information and advice (Goss, 1991). Burrows (1991) has suggested that this discourse of an 'enterprise culture' has been one of the major articulating principles of the recent age.

The emergence of network approaches to business support policies can be traced to 'softer' measures concerning the provision of information and advice services to SMEs. Initiated by already existing bodies such as the Small Firms Service (established in 1973), these services increasingly acted in a 'referral' and 'signposting' capacity to other agencies, rather than being directly involved in business support. By 1992, the Government had explicitly identified networks and the interaction between small firms, and their intermediaries, as being an area of particular importance in any new small firm policy measures (DoE, 1992). This growth of public policy interest in small firms, and of their inter-relationships and interdependence in the business community, was coupled with an increasing fascination for local approaches towards increasing competitiveness and promoting economic regeneration (Curran and Blackburn, 1993). An increased awareness in the 1980s that the predominant markets for a large proportion of businesses were locally-based led to public intervention being increasingly channelled towards locally delivered initiatives (Storey, 1994). Also, specific small business policy in the 1980s, administered through the DTI's Enterprise Initiative (EI), was delivered more and more by organisations such as local enterprise agencies. Keeble and Bryson (1996) show that it is the peripheral regions of the UK that made the most use of the EI, with approximately 50 per cent more firms in these regions, as compared to areas such as the South East of England, using the services offered through EI; while nearly four times as many periphery-based firms reported approaching and receiving advice from enterprise agencies. This was undoubtedly partly due to peripheral regions receiving a greater endowment of Government resources for the development of such support services.

The introduction of local TECs between 1990 and 1991 (and subsequently Business Links) was an attempt to make such support more systematic, by levelling the playing field between core and peripheral areas, with regard to the availability of services, and co-ordinating other local actors and support users through partnerships and networks. A marked shift in approach also appeared to be emerging whereby intervention that initially had been put in place purely for small firms was extended to the wider community of SMEs, particularly those that were considered to have 'growth potential' (Curran and Blackburn, 1991 Chittenden et al., 1995). At the same time the economic development agenda of the Government gave great emphasis to achieving 'competitiveness', with 'human resource development' becoming a recurring and key component of this theme (GHK, 1995). This led to small business policies in the UK becoming gradually subsumed in wider economic development strategies, advocating a broader support framework through public and private sector partnerships and networks. For instance, development and enterprise agencies are increasingly focusing on promoting 'soft support' and company 'aftercare' initiatives, via networked approaches of sustained and consistent interaction involving multiple parties (Bennett, 1995a).

The evolution from a specific small business policy to more diffuse economic development, based on an implicit networked support approach, is best manifested by the role envisaged for TECs. TECs were implicitly developed to act as brokers and intermediate nodes of information and expertise, serving an enterprise culture which itself became a pervasive social phenomenon going beyond its link with small business activity

(Ploszajska, 1994). One implication of this approach is the emergence of a culture whereby public sector intervention consists of intermediary agencies that seek to bring together companies seeking mutually beneficial support through collaboration - in other words, the formation of inter-firm networks. These policies were most coherently set-out in the Conservative Government's 'Competitiveness White Papers' (HM Government, 1994b; 1995). The 'White Papers' advocate economic development strategies, many of which were initially 'piloted' in peripheral areas, based on catalysing local networks that encourage partnerships between and among local firms and institutions. Within this framework, TECs have become the key policy agent for intervention that has attempted to implant a culture of competitiveness through co-operation.

The Labour Government has indicated, within its own 'Competitiveness White Paper' (HM Government, 1998), that it wishes to continue and strengthen this agenda. In particular, its policy focus consists of the development of localised networks of sector-related companies or 'clusters'. This agenda is to be carried forward in the future by the Small Business Service and the new Learning and Skills Councils and Regional Development Agencies (RDAs) in England, and the Community Consortia for Education and Training (CCET) and Business Connect in Wales (with Scotland most probably retaining its Local Enterprise Companies). By 2001 the Small Business Service and the Learning and Skills Councils (CCETs in Wales) will replace TECs, although the reality is that they will share many features with their predecessors. The most important difference being that Learning and Skills Councils and CCETs will incorporate responsibility for training activity within the further education sector. It is hoped that the Small Business Service (and the revamped Business Connect in Wales) will further facilitate a business culture within which entrepreneurialism is engendered through a co-operative and networked environment. Given these changes it is vital that the policy lessons from the UK's experiment with TECs in the 1990s are both fully learnt and acted upon.

**This Book: Objectives and Structure**

This book examines the extent to which TECs have acted as facilitators and catalysts for inducing companies within their localities increasingly to collaborate and co-operate through inter-firm networks. The key hypothesis is that significant positive benefit can be gained through public policy support that facilitates network approaches to economic development, particularly those initiatives directed towards the business community. The focus of the book is whether - and how - network building, particularly of an inter-firm nature, offers an alternative to traditional forms of local economic development in the UK. It aims to make a contribution both to the theoretical discourse of inter-firm networks and public policy debates concerning support for their development. In particular, it assesses and explores:

- the role that TECs have assumed within their localities as cultivators of inter-firm networks
- the awareness among public sector institutions and private companies, particularly SMEs, in the UK of the concept of inter-firm networks
- the relative effectiveness of the instruments and initiatives employed to generate networking
- the effect of changing Conservative Government policies in the 1990s on local economic development strategies
- the practicalities and problems of actually applying network approaches to economic development
- the strengths and weaknesses of inter-firm networks as a public policy resource
- the success and failure of differing inter-firm network initiative models

The book is structured as follows. Chapter 2 analyses, and attempts to add some coherence and focus to, the numerous discourses that have emerged in relation to inter-firm network theory. The chapter assesses whether it is possible to identify any underlying convergence of thought, concentrating on: the influence and criticism of neo-classical economic thinking; the influence of sociological models of interaction and exchange; the value and importance of factors concerning 'trust' and 'social capital' to inter-firm networks. It is argued that the seemingly opposing views within the logic of economic and sociological debates, centred on the 'rationality' and 'norms' of inter-firm networks, as well as economic behaviour in general, can be significantly drawn together if economic action is viewed as a function of economic and/or social rationality.

In chapter 3 the contribution of economic geography is discussed in an analysis of spatial elements, such as the locally or regionally defined boundaries that are often associated with many inter-firm network forms. Also, attempts to implant and catalyse inter-firm networks through public policy intervention are assessed. The work of economic geographers is found to be grounded in a socio-economic approach, principally concerned with the study of networks of learning, knowledge and innovation. In particular, it is the study of the 'industrial districts' of the northern Italian region of Emilia-Romagna that have highlighted the potential for specific localities to contribute to economic development. This chapter further argues that publicly induced or implanted networks cannot implicitly be said to reduce transaction costs in the short-term, as the activities of firms in such networks are usually additional and new to their normal operations. However, if the activities of such networks are continued over a significant period, it is suggested that their cessation may result in increased transaction costs for participants, as they attempt to substitute the outputs of the networks via a non-networked market or hierarchical approach.

TECs were introduced in England and Wales to assist the regeneration of local economies through an emphasis on training and enterprise development. Chapter 4 reviews the relevant literature in order to contextualise the role of TECs as facilitators of local economic development, particularly during the early years of their establishment, and how this was approached through the creation of local networks. It is found that key to the emergent system of local governance in the UK has been a focus on new mechanisms for development undertaken by a wide range of individuals and organisations. Within this system the local economic development role of TECs is primarily to create enabling and stimulating infrastructure for regeneration. TECs were introduced by the Conservative Government with a vision of them becoming hybrid local support organisations operating on commercial terms and acting as facilitators of training and enterprise support. However, this chapter shows that an almost inevitable gap opened between the rhetoric and the actual practices of TECs. The under-efficiency of TECs meant that they continued to rely heavily on central government funding, which weakened their potentially powerful role as agents of local regeneration.

Chapter 5 empirically analyses the role of TECs as cultivators and catalysts of inter-firm networks in their respective localities. The chapter focuses on the awareness among TECs of inter-firm networks, and the effectiveness of the instruments used by TECs to generate such networks. It evaluates the consequential outputs of, and barriers to, networking, the level of involvement encountered, and existing regional disparities. The chapter finds that the success and effectiveness of those networks which have been generated by TECs has often fallen short in terms of the TECs' own criteria. This lack of success is due to a number of factors, the most considerable being that network involvement was hampered by a lack of managerial and staff time among local firms. A lack of awareness and perception of the benefits of networking by firms was also seen as an important barrier, with TECs arguing that there is a need for marketing strategies which highlight that the necessary time and costs can prove to be an investment if chosen wisely. TECs pointed out that most firms are looking for 'quick fix' solutions rather than the long term benefits that are normally associated with inter-firm networks. Other demand side barriers concerned a fear by firms of compromising competitive position, with a lack of trust among firms seen as a deep-rooted problem in many localities.

Chapter 6 assesses how the concept of networking has actually been practically applied to the evolving economic development policies of TECs within a framework of a dual capacity: (1) to act as a catalyst for the generation of new networks, predominantly of an inter-firm nature; (2) to create partnerships and communication networks between themselves and other local institutions and businesses. It is shown that the approach adopted by TECs, based on developing networks with other partners, has suffered in many circumstances due to the Governmental restrictions placed on them, in particular the necessity to constrict activities to arenas that are often overly localised. Also, a key outcome of the reduction in TEC budgets and the introduction of a funding regime based on a bidding process has been to limit the ability and capacity of TECs to tackle economic development on their own. This has resulted in the concept of networking, through the generation of local partnerships, becoming an even more important component within the economic development landscape.

Whereas chapters 5 and 6 have viewed policy developments from the perspective of TECs, as the key facilitators, chapters 7 and 8 focus on an analysis of the performance of these policies from the view-point of participating companies. Chapter 7 is an evaluation of the inter-firm network initiatives operated by TECs and their partners. The chapter confirms that inter-firm network initiatives have faced a number of problems which has severely limited the number of firms that have benefited from participation, as well as the overall level of economic impact on growth and development. More positively, it is shown that the initiatives have resulted in substantial gains for albeit a small number of participating companies. Also, it is assessed that the cost of the jobs created through network initiatives have not been overly expensive to the public exchequer. The small number of companies achieving substantial benefits were most often those involved in initiatives that were able to formalise sustainable networks.

The processes and causes of network success and failure are examined in more depth in chapter 8 - defined in terms of the ability of the network to become a sustained and valued form of business activity for its members. The chapter examines four different case-study network initiatives as follows: (1) a failed informal 'new entrepreneurs network'; (2) a successful informal 'local cluster group'; (3) a failed formal 'defence contractors network'; (4) a successful formal 'small-firm technology group'. It is found that the success or failure of networks is closely linked to the level of trust and social capital that is fostered between participants, and the means by which a favourable environment facilitating co-operation is generated. In particular, network sustainability was gained where 'free-loaders' and 'free-riders' were eliminated and where power within groups was relatively evenly distributed. It is shown that networks in business are often consciously developed and maintained by those managing directors who have recognised the importance of co-operative activities for achieving competitive advantage for their companies. The best network support consisted of brokers who are able to mix and overlap the 'hard' business and 'softer' social interests of participants. The case-studies indicate that it is formal groups which are the most potent form of inter-firm network, but that it is through an initially informal structure that they are best facilitated.

Chapter 9 looks at some of the theoretical conclusions and policy recommendations that can be made regarding both the institutional position of the agents involved in economic development, and the fostering of inter-firm networks as a contributory tool for sustaining the regeneration of local business communities. In particular, it is emphasised that as TECs have increasingly taken a strategic role they have come to realise that their impact relies more and more in mobilising the activities of others, if economic development strategies are to be translated into effective support delivery mechanisms. It is argued that this approach has emphasised the importance of networking and networks within this framework, with TECs increasingly focusing on trying to bring local businesses closer together through the building of inter-firm networks. Such an approach is, in itself, an innovative shift away from the 'traditional' concerns of economic development, such as area promotion and the provision of land and buildings, to policies more concerned with 'soft' support and business 'aftercare'.

# 2 The Socio-Economics of Networks

## Introduction

The current vogue for the 'network' metaphor within the social sciences is reflected by the interest and popularity of theoretical perspectives concerning notions such as the 'network paradigm' (Cooke and Morgan, 1993; Karlsson, 1994) and the 'network society' (Castells, 1996), as well as the emergence of a field of study labelled 'network economics' (Karlsson and Westin, 1994). This spread in the appeal of network concepts has not, generally, been accompanied by any consensus or single-stream approach to analysis or parsimony in the theoretical constructs deployed. One area where this has been evident is in debates concerning networks involving businesses, or what have been termed, and are now commonly referred to, as 'inter-firm networks'. The growth of academic interest in inter-firm networks as organisational forms, and the accompanying study of business co-operation, can be related to a number of factors, two of which have been particularly influential. Firstly, the acknowledgement and increasing pre-occupation with the study of the restructuring processes that most large corporations have been involved with in recent years. This restructuring, typified by process terms such as 'outsourcing', 'down-sizing', 're-engineering' and 'lean production', has taken place at a global level, often involving multinational enterprises, and has been intrinsically linked to the increasing prevalence of forms of inter-firm networks defined as strategic alliances. Furthermore, as some corporations have down-sized they have spun-off units to serve as independent entities, and instituted more collaborative relationships with suppliers (Indergaard, 1996).

Secondly, but equally influential and inter-related to the above, has been the academic popularisation of spatially defined 'industrial districts' that are seen to resemble those first studied by Alfred Marshall in the late nineteenth century. Such districts are said to be typified by small and medium sized enterprises (SMEs) involved in highly interactive collaborative networks that act as localised productive systems and which stimulate economic prosperity (Piore and Sabel, 1984). The study of such districts has been intrinsically linked to arguments concerning an apparent

13

paradigm shift in global production methods from a so-called traditional Fordist regime of large firms producing goods for mass markets, to a post-Fordist structure within which SMEs are the key proponents of 'flexibly specialised' approaches to producing a wide range of goods for niche markets. In part, the flexible specialisation debate contends that companies are increasingly benefiting from mobilising the resources of other firms through networks of co-operation. Therefore, as Powell (1996) argues, the upsurge of academic interest in inter-firm networks has been primarily due to changing perceptions concerning the shifting strategic focus of firms in the light of factors such as shortened innovation cycles and the increasing rapidity of technological change, which have resulted in the necessity for increasing access to both new markets and new skills.

The study of inter-firm networks has taken a very eclectic form, becoming established in a multi-disciplinary and overlapping arena, primarily involving economics, sociology and geography (the spatial implications are analysed in chapter 3). This chapter discusses, and attempts to add some coherence and focus to, the numerous discourses that have emerged in relation to inter-firm network theory. The chapter seeks to assess whether it is possible to identify any underlying convergence of thought, or the emergence of common ground, between the differing discourses discussed, as well as their relative influence on inter-firm network theory as a whole. One of the problems entailed in the multi-disciplinary approach has been the general vagueness about what exactly inter-firm networks involve, and a subsequent proliferation of definitions (Powell and Smith-Doerr, 1994). Indeed, a review of the literature reveals many definitions of networks, varying in their degree of simplicity or complexity, that are applied to inter-firm forms within the relevant text. Some examples of the alternatives include: individuals and agencies that are linked around certain types of relationships which presume some form of mutual orientation and usually obligation (Amin and Thrift, 1995); unbounded or bounded clusters of organisations that permit interactions of exchange, concerted action and joint production (Alter and Hage, 1993); firms that regularly collaborate over a long time period (Powell and Smith-Doerr, 1994); a collection of firms bound together in some formal and/or informal ways (Granovetter, 1994); linkages among firms based on material input-output links, a traditional focus of production systems, or on information and technology flows (Malecki and Tootle, 1996); a set of two or more connected business relationships in which each exchange relation is between firms that are conceptualised as collective actors (Anderson et al., 1994). This range of differing definitions is a reflection of the fact that the study of inter-firm networks not only involves those networks that are consciously constituted as such by the individuals and firms participating in them, but also those that are the analytical and theoretical constructs of academic studies (Staber, 1996a). Nevertheless, the above indicates that inter-firm networks are usually acknowledged to consist of companies that are connected or bound together through some form of sustained interaction, within which there is necessarily a degree of commonality. Therefore, a suggested 'hybrid' of these definitions is that inter-firm networks consist of two or more firms pursuing common objectives or working towards solving common problems through a period of sustained interaction.

As with the variations in definition, there are also numerous taxonomies and typologies that exist with regard to inter-firm networks, and, as Szarka (1990) states, any inventory of these may prove interminable. A number of these typically take a bifurcated route, with a distinction made between informal and formal inter-firm networks, generally based on whether or not the network is governed by contractual or 'dotted-line' agreements (Ibarra, 1992). Rosenfeld (1996) extends this dichotomy by suggesting that networks may take the form of formal 'hard' networks involving firms joining together to co-produce, co-market, co-purchase, or co-operate in product or market development; and more informal 'soft' networks of firms joining together to solve common problems, share information, or acquire new skills. A distinction is also usually made between vertical networks within which firms at different stages of the same production chain join together, in the type of input-output relationship highlighted by Malecki and Tootle (1996), and horizontal networks of firms at similar stages in the production process with similar needs and/or objectives (Bosworth and Rosenfeld, 1993). In general, horizontal networks consist of a higher level of competition and are often more likely to break up than vertical networks, although many of the greatest gains from networks appear to be significantly related to the stimulation of collaboration through horizontal networks (Sydow, 1996). Another typology that is utilised in varying formats consists of information, knowledge and innovation networks, within which interaction becomes increasingly intense and sophisticated, and therefore is an increasingly complex undertaking (Huggins, 1997). Other more detailed classifications include the identification of seven types of inter-firm network within which the extent of interdependence becomes increasingly binding: (1) industry association; (2) innovative industry association; (3) learning collaboration; (4) shared resource; (5) joint marketing; (6) customer-supplier; (7) co-production (Bosworth, 1995; Malecki and Tootle, 1997).

It is not the aim of this chapter to delve even deeper into issues of definition and typology, but rather to make sense of the existing literature relating to inter-firm networks, predominantly from the abundance generated in the 1990s, from a more over-arching and inclusive point of view. The following sections of this chapter concentrate on: (1) the influence and criticism of neo-classical economic thinking on the development of inter-firm network theory, from the point of view of differing economic theories of the firm (in particular transaction costs-based, resource-based and knowledge-based views of the firm); (2) the influence of sociological models of interaction and exchange that attempt to explain the importance of social and non-economic factors within economic activity, with a discussion of constructs such as 'embeddedness', 'structural holes' and 'brokerage'; (3) the value and importance of factors concerning 'trust' and 'social capital' to inter-firm networks; this is explored from the starting point of game theoretic models, in particular the 'prisoner's dilemma' variant. In conclusion, it is suggested that the seemingly opposing views within the logic of economic and sociological debates, centred on the 'rationality' and 'norms' of inter-firm networks, as well as economic behaviour in general, can be significantly drawn together if economic action is viewed as a function of economic and/or social rationality. The key difference between these two forms of rationality being whether the action is motivated by behaviour that seeks to accumulate economic or social capital.

## Neo-Classical Economics

### A Transaction Costs-Based Theory of the Firm

As an influential OECD publication has made clear (OECD, 1992), there is no fully-fledged economic theory of networks. Most studies couch networks somewhere between markets and hierarchies, within the framework of Coase (1937) and Williamson's (1975; 1985) theories of markets and hierarchies. However, one of the key reasons for the lack of a such a network theory is the dependence that would be necessary on one of the numerous discourses and interpretations concerning the theory of the nature of the firm, of which the Coase-Williamson framework is one. This theory, first advocated by Coase (1937), argues that firms emerge due to the 'transaction costs' involved in entering markets, such as negotiating for goods and services and enforcing contracts. According to Coase (1937), if the cost of carrying out a transaction in the market is higher than the cost of carrying out the same transaction within the firm, firms will internalise the transaction in order to lower costs - thus firms emerge and grow precisely when they are more efficient than the market.

Coase's (1937) theory of transaction costs has been elaborated upon by Williamson (1975; 1985). He presents a dichotomous view of 'markets' and hierarchies' (i.e. firms), with decisions to enter one or the other based on minimising transactions costs (or 'friction costs') and promoting efficiency through a focus on the costs of devising, monitoring, and carrying out economic transactions between or within firms. Williamson's (1975; 1985) theoretical building blocks are well known and consist of: (1) 'bounded rationality' - a weak form of rationality within which actors are conceived as seeking to make rational decisions, but with their ability to do so constrained by limits on their capacity to receive, process, store and retrieve information (McGuiness, 1991); (2) 'opportunism' - or the ability to act dishonestly or deviously in order to 'make a quick buck' (Coulson, 1997); (3) 'asset specificity' - or the investments required that are specific to a particular relationship (Christensen et al., 1990). Therefore, 'transaction cost economics' argues that under certain conditions of high asset specificity, market transactions become subject to higher levels of opportunism and bounded rationality, making them more costly to govern, and that it is the role of the firm to regulate such costs (Fligstein and Freeland, 1995).

Although Williamson (1975) originally presented a dichotomous route of either 'market' or 'hierarchy', he later modified this position in order to take account of contractual arrangements in the 'middle range' between the poles of markets and hierarchies. Williamson (1985; 1991) has tried to explain more complex forms of contracting, in particular inter-firm networks, by arguing that such forms of contracting economise on transaction costs where there is genuine interdependence between organisations but not enough to merit full-scale merger (Fligstein and Freeland, 1995). In this later approach, Williamson presented four alternative forms of economic governance: (1) markets (classical); (2) trilateral governance (involving mediating third parties); (3) bilateral governance (relational contracting); (4) hierarchies (organisations) (Lundvall, 1993). Although both trilateral and bilateral governance imply a form of networking, Williamson stops short of conceding 'networks' to be a distinctive third mode of governance. Instead, Williamson along with others (for example: Thorelli, 1986) has defined inter-firm networks as an 'intermediate' or 'hybrid' framework for organising economic activities with respect to markets and firms (Grandori and Soda, 1995).

Williamson's thesis is very much set in the premises of the 'new institutional economics', within which it is argued that the organisational forms that prevail are those that deal most efficiently with the cost of economic transactions (Grabher, 1993). As DiMaggio and Powell (1991) argue, a transaction costs approach, and 'new institutional economics' as a whole, has contributed to adding a degree of realism to standard economic theory, within which it is assumed that individuals rationally attempt to maximise their behaviour over stable and consistent preference orderings, by acknowledging factors such as cognitive limitations, incomplete information, and difficulties in monitoring and enforcing agreements. Therefore, the contributions of Coase and Williamson have added an important correction to a classical and neo-classical economic tradition that had tended to neglect all costs except production costs, and also in viewing firms not as the production function described in neo-classical micro-economic theory, but as a governance structure of transactions (Christensen et al. 1990; McGuiness, 1991; Lundvall, 1993).

Despite ceding a more institutional approach to economic action, transaction costs theory has been extensively debated and widely criticised in both economics and sociology. In particular, so-called 'neo-institutionalists' have criticised transactions cost theory for accepting the neo-classical assumption that the most efficient institutional form will 'survive', as well as its 'unrealistic' assumptions about the difference between markets and hierarchies (Johanson and Mattsson, 1985). It is argued that transaction costs theory, despite institutional appearances, is embedded in a neo-classical framework focused on achieving the conditions for stable equilibrium, and making the assumption that observed markets are either in, or approaching, some form of equilibrium (Clark and Staunton, 1989; Fligstein and Freeland, 1995). In particular, the neo-classical economic paradigm conceives of ideal conditions for perfect competition, and is criticised for its fundamental assumption that economic actors are rational and autonomous, and seek their self-interest independent of social relations or characteristics (Biggart and Hamilton, 1992). As Lundvall (1993) further indicates, neo-classical economists have taken a rationalist and instrumentalist approach to the design of institutional governance systems, such as inter-firm networks, arguing that actors view the choice among institutional arrangements as part of an overall optimisation problem that is subject to efficiency pressures and information-processing limitations.

*Non-Economic Frameworks*

Although the neo-classical perspective on inter-firm networking is consistent with a transaction cost reasoning of economic action, it takes little account of more sociologically informed institutional discourses that focus on the cognitive and normative frameworks that give meaning and legitimacy to economic choice (DiMaggio and Powell, 1991; Staber and Aldrich, 1995; Staber, 1996a). Such discourses question whether humans actually act as individual utility maximisers, rather than viewing themselves as a part of larger socially influenced structures, and has led to arguments concerning the extent to which firm-based theories can explain the existence of inter-firm networks (Biggart and Hamilton, 1992). The most influential sociological work in this area is that of Granovetter (1985), who argues that economic action is not the aggregate of the actions of isolated individuals but is further 'embedded' in social relationships. In this respect, 'embeddedness' refers to the fact that all actions, whether economic or social, are affected by the dyadic relations of actors and the overall structure of their 'network' of relations.

Grabher (1993), drawing heavily on Granovetter's (1985) embeddedness approach, argues that there is a need to balance both under and over socialised assumptions of economic behaviour, as well as the need to avoid the 'atomisation' of economic actors as narrow utilitarian pursuers of self-interest. Social ties are seen to be infused with non-economic notions such as equity, loyalty, and tradition, which from a standard economic perspective are viewed as constraints on efficient exchange (Staber, 1996b). In general, sociological approaches to the firm are a progression away from efficiency principles, towards a more diffuse set of political and cultural explanations (Fligstein and Freeland, 1995). However, what the actual balance is between 'rationality' models and 'cultural' or 'societal' interpretations is, unsurprisingly, unclear. Fukuyama (1995) has contended, somewhat arbitrarily, that it might be approaching the following order:

> 'We can think of neoclassical economics as being, say, eighty percent correct: it has uncovered important truths about the nature of money and markets because its fundamental model of rational, self-interested human behaviour is correct about eighty percent of the time. But there is a missing twenty percent of human behaviour about which neoclassical economics can give only a poor account. As Adam Smith well understood, economic life is deeply embedded in social life, and it cannot be understood apart from the customs, morals, and habits of the society in which it occurs. In short, it cannot be divorced from culture.' (Fukuyama, 1995, p. 13).

Whether or not Fukuyama (1995) is near the mark, the neglect of non-economic influences within neo-classical accounts has led to the proposition that inter-firm network models should be viewed as a distinct form of economic organisation, with their own characteristics and properties, and which are qualitatively different from those of both markets and firms (Grandori and Soda, 1995). This proposition has been most notably, and convincingly advocated by Powell (1990), who argues that networks involve neither the 'explicit criteria' of the market, nor the 'familiar paternalism' of the hierarchy, with the basic assumption of network relationships being that one party is dependent on resources controlled by another, and that there are gains to be had by the pooling of resources.

Taking the position of Powell (1990) further, Cooke and Morgan (1993; 1998) contend that as transactions between Williamson's poles are not only more prevalent than he originally conceded, and that as network relationships are an increasingly common organisational form at both the inter- and intra- firm level, networks should be viewed within the parameters of an emerging and new economic paradigm. If such a paradigm shift is taking, or has taken, place it can, according to Clark and Staunton (1989), be typified by the notion of opportunism within transaction costs being replaced by the notion of trust as the outcome of the long-term investment by sets of firms in developing interdependency, and giving the formation of knowledge and expertise precedence over concepts of bounded rationality. However, one of the key problems in proving that such a shift is taking place is that it is empirically difficult to distinguish between different types of relationships - social, informational, business - occurring when economic actors interact. In other words, assessing the importance of non-economic influences, such as trust, is problematic precisely due to their embedded nature.

Nevertheless, Cooke and Morgan's (1993; 1998) bold thesis is supported by the discourse of a school of Swedish scholars in the field of industrial marketing, who attempt to connect the economic and sociological elements of long-term buyer-seller relationships in the exchange of industrial goods (Hakansson, 1982; 1989; Axelsson and Easton, 1992; Hakansson and Johanson, 1993; Forsgren et al., 1995; Mattsson, 1995; Johanson and Mattsson, 1985; 1987). Their approach to analysing and understanding economic governance is based on the argument that co-ordination between firms takes place in networks within which product price and associated costs are just one of a number of influencing factors, along with others such as trust, confidence and complementarity. In this sense market forces are at work, with firms free to choose customers and suppliers, but access to external resources has to be built up over time through networks demanding effort and investment (Christensen et al., 1990).

The Swedish school view inter-firm relationships, or the mutual orientation of two firms towards each other, as being set within two closely related interactive processes: exchange and adaptation (Hakansson, 1989; Forsgren et al., 1995; Mattsson, 1995). In defining and explaining exchange processes they draw principally on the 'social exchange theory' associated with Blau (1964). This argues that social relations evolve in a slow and incremental manner from 'minor transactions' - which require little trust due to the lack of risk involved - whereby partners can prove their trustworthiness, to deeper relationships through which they may engage in 'major transactions'. The essential proposition is that Blau's (1964) 'trying out' processes can be equally applied to corporate relationships. The other side of the interaction, adaptation processes, refers to the various ways in which parties adjust to each other in their attitudes, strategies and overall knowledge-base (Forsgren et al., 1995). As with Cooke and Morgan (1993; 1998), this more socially focused analysis does not regard opportunism as a basic characteristic of actors, but rather highlights the importance of its opposite - trust. However, the Swedish thinkers make no secret of the fact that their concepts, and their application, are still being applied in a rather crude manner, due to a number of key theoretical and empirical gaps (Ford, 1994). One of these gaps concerns the relative importance and mechanisms whereby adaptations take place, in particular the acquisition and application of knowledge. Secondly, the relative neglect of non-economic exchange in theoretical work on economic behaviour, as highlighted by Easton and Araujo (1992), and the wider importance and inputs of sociological thinking in attempts to explain inter-firm networks are problematic. These themes form the basis for discussion in the following sections of this chapter.

## Networks and the Pursuit of Knowledge by Firms

The emergence of schools of thought on the 'strategic management of firms' within economics has had the effect of spawning new contributions to the theory of the firm, building primarily on transaction costs theory and integrating 'organisational approaches' (Grant, 1996). The most influential of these contributions has been the 'resource-based' view of the firm, which focuses on the characteristics of the resources, and the strategic factor markets from which they are obtained, in order to explain firm heterogeneity and sustainable competitive advantage (Oliver, 1997). Within this view the firm is seen as a 'unique bundle of idiosyncratic resources and capabilities', through which management aims to maximise value by optimally deploying existing resources and capabilities, as well as developing the firm's future resource base (Grant, 1996). In essence, firms are considered to be a collection of 'sticky' and difficult-to-imitate resources, whereby sustainable competitive advantage is critically determined by the capacity to transfer these resources and capabilities in an effective and efficient manner (Penrose, 1959; Barney, 1986; Mowery et al., 1996).

As Oliver (1997) makes clear, resource-based views of firms are still very much rooted in rational-cognitive assumptions about management and organisational effects on decision-taking and economic choice making. However recent development in the theory of 'knowing and doing' has led to a school of management discourse that focuses more on institutional activities, whereby firms normatively make rational choices that are shaped by the social context of the firm, in particular the application of 'knowledge' residing within individuals (Blackler, 1993; Grant, 1996; Oliver, 1997). This emerging 'knowledge-based' view of the firm focuses on knowledge as the key competitive asset, emphasising the capacity to integrate tacit knowledge, or 'knowing how', as distinct from explicit knowledge or 'knowing about' (Grant, 1996; Mowery et al., 1996). As Blackler (1993) argues, such knowledge is very much an institutional asset due to its indeterminate nature and the active nature of the processes through which it is managed. Within this framework, a focus on knowledge application by the firm has, Grant (1996) argues, implications for the determinants of the horizontal and vertical boundaries of the firm.

Kogut and Zander (1996) contend that firms are organisations that represent the social knowledge of co-ordination and learning, with the communication of knowledge being facilitated through networks of interacting firms. Furthermore, Powell et al. (1996) argue that as the knowledge base of industries becomes increasingly expansive and dispersed, the locus of innovation - which in this case can be said to be the capacity to access knowledge that can be applied to make competitive change - will be found in 'networks of learning', rather than in individual firms, whereby learning occurs within the context of membership of a 'community'. Therefore, if the argument that knowledge is the most fundamental resource of firms is taken seriously, it can be suggested that networking behaviour, as a learning mechanism, is one of the most important processes undertaken by firms (Lundvall and Johnson, 1994; Lundvall, 1994). Kogut et al. (1993) suggest that more knowledge leads to more network relations as:

> '.....know-how operates at several levels of analysis, from the individual, to the group and organisation, and ultimately to the network itself. Information of the network consists of identifying who will co-operate and who has what capabilities. Know-how is the knowledge of how the capabilities of individual firms might be harnessed through co-operation.' (Kogut et al., 1993, p.77).

The growing importance of the economics of knowledge and learning has been further recognised by a school of 'evolutionary economists', who focus their attentions on the necessity for firms to undertake technical and organisational innovation in order to overcome uncertainty and instability, within Schumpeter's (1934) framework of the evolutionary nature of capitalism arising from within economic life (Nelson and Winter, 1982; Dosi, 1988; Dosi et al., 1988; Freeman, 1994). Evolutionary economists, or 'neo-Schumpeterians' as they are often referred to, conceptualise the firm in a similar manner to the resource-based view, in this case as differentiated organisations that use differentiated inputs for production (Dosi, 1988; Cooke 1998). However, evolutionary thinking has essentially emerged as a critique of the neo-classical perspective, by placing considerable emphasis on the 'social institutions' into which firms are integrated, giving particular emphasis to history, routines and their influence on the evolution of firms and the trajectory of their development (Cooke, 1998; Morgan, 1997). As Cooke (1998) indicates, within evolutionary economics it is knowledge that plays one of the fundamental institutional roles, with the knowledge possessed by the firm founder or entrepreneur acting as the key 'creation' catalyst. This new knowledge is seen as being best developed through learning processes which are mediated through heterarchical, or network, relationships based on social institutions concerning trust, reputation, custom, reciprocity, etc (Cooke, 1998). In other words, innovation is facilitated by the pursuit of knowledge and its application, which is itself conditioned by the ability to 'learn-by-interacting'. Gregersen and Johnson (1997) sum-up this 'evolutionary' economic process by stating that:

> 'Put in a very simple way we regard innovations as 'learning results'. Learning leads to new knowledge and entrepreneurs of different kinds use this knowledge to form innovative ideas and projects and some of these find their way into the economy in the form of innovations. This means that there is a distinction between the production of knowledge and the utilisation of knowledge.' (p. 481).

Therefore, despite the traditional dominance of neo-classical perspectives within economics, it appears that spread of interest in the network metaphor has been most rapid in those fields where evidence about the interdependence of firms and an acknowledgement of the existence of imperfect operating conditions is strong (Antonelli, 1996). Interestingly, Lado et al. (1997) have recently developed a so-called 'syncretic model' within which competition and co-operation are conceptualised as distinct but inter-related dimensions. The model incorporates many of the notions outlined above that have attempted to act as the 'paradigmatic bridge' between the polar perspectives of neo-classicicism and institutional sociology (Lado et al., 1997). This nexus of thinking is often referred to as 'socio-economics' and, as Amin and Thrift (1995) contend, emphasises the 'power' of networks, and the accompanying collective agency, as being the mainstay for the facilitation of learning, innovation, knowledge formation and information exchange as contributors to economic success and adaptability. Indeed, socio-economics is an acknowledgement that in the search for competitive advantage firms require both 'resource capital' and 'institutional capital' (Oliver, 1997). It is interesting to note that Williamson (1994) has recently suggested that economic and sociological approaches to economic organisation have reached a state of 'healthy tension' with genuine give-and-take, as compared to an earlier state of affairs where the two camps were largely 'disjunct' and hence ignored one another.

## Sociological Approaches

The growing influence of socio-economic and institutional theory highlights the importance of looking further at sociological conceptions of economic organisational structures. The basic premise of most sociological thought is that individuals are motivated to comply with external social pressures, and that the tendency of firms, therefore, is towards conformity with predominant norms, traditions, and social influences (Oliver, 1997). As Amin and Thrift (1995) suggest, the effect of these inputs from 'non-economic' disciplines is an attempt to redefine the nature of economics, and what is regarded as 'economic'. In relation to inter-firm networks, sociological thought emphasises the hypothesis that firms should be conceptualised as collective actors whereby the 'connectivity' between firms is based on trust, reciprocity and mutual interdependence (Larson, 1992; Anderson et al., 1994).

### Social Exchange Theory

The key insight from sociological thinking on economic behaviour can be summed-up as the importance of social exchange between individuals. As referred to earlier, the social exchange theory developed by Blau (1964) aims to contribute to the understanding of social structure on the basis of analysing the processes that govern the relations between individuals and groups. Put simply, Blau (1964) argues that it is social exchange that acts as the central principle of all behaviour and from which other complex social forces are derived. Blau's (1964) analysis emphasises the 'primitive' baseline at which behaviour can be analysed, and in this respect it is important to acknowledge the work of social anthropologists as being instrumental in developing the field of social exchange theory, and the overlapping field of network analysis, focused on exploring how actual human ties, rather than their institutional structure, influence behaviour, i.e. there is less emphasis on the study of the 'role' of individuals and more on their patterns of actions, transactions and exchange (for example: Barnes, 1954; Bott, 1957; Mitchell, 1969; 1973). Mitchell's (1969, 1973) work, in particular, highlights networks as being specific types of relations linking a defined set of persons, objects or events within a framework of three overlapping content types: exchange, communication and social.

Social network analysis has been further developed by sociologists. The key behavioural assumption being that any actor typically participates in a social system involving any other actors who are significant reference points in each other's decisions (Knoke and Kuklinski, 1982). The nature of the relationships a given actor has with other system members may, therefore, affect that focal actor's perceptions, beliefs and actions, and analysis must take into account both the relations that occur and those that do not exist (Knoke and Kuklinski, 1982). With regard to inter-firm co-ordination, social network analysis has been applied to the emergence and change of informal economic structures (including network boundaries), the process of corporate co-optation, and the patterns and importance of relations among small firms (see later section on 'entrepreneurship') (Hakansson and Johanson, 1993). Also, as highlighted by Murdoch (1995), social network analysis seeks to understand economic structures as the outcomes of attempts to construct and maintain power relations, rather than purely as the determinants of economic activity.

Returning to social exchange theory, the model has two key mechanistic variables to explain behaviour. Firstly, trust and the processes by which exchange evolves over time as actors mutually and sequentially demonstrate their trustworthiness. Secondly, power, which is best associated with the work of Emerson (1962) and refers to the relative dependence between two actors in an exchange relationship. Power deriving from having resources that the other needs and from controlling the alternative sources of these resources (Hallen et al., 1991). Later, Blau (1977) has extended the model to include concepts such as 'in-group bias' and 'opportunities for contact' to explain inter-group relation. Blau (1977) argues that rates of interaction are a function of the preference to associate with 'similar alters', and the restrictions of the available population in terms of its 'similarity' to the individual (Baker, 1992). Although, the exchange model is but one possible sociological source for 'grounding' the development of a theory of inter-firm networks (Cook, 1982), it has acted as the catalyst for the most well known sociological model to explain inter-organisational behaviour - the resource-dependence model.

## The Resource-Dependence Model

The resource-dependence model elaborated and generalised to an organisational level the argument within exchange theory that the structural potential power of one actor in a relationship can influence the other to comply with the former actor's needs (Hallen et al., 1991). Best associated with Pfeffer and Salancik (1978), the basic principle of the resource-dependence model is that organisations operate in turbulent and uncertain environments over which they attempt to gain control, and because critical resources are often controlled by other organisations they must find ways to ensure a smooth and predictable flow of resources from these other organisations (Mizruchi and Galaskiewicz, 1994). To an extent, this thesis resembles the resource-based view of the firm put forward by economics, sharing the core assumption that control structures arise from economic exchange in order to offset uncertainties (Lincoln et al, 1992). However, while the resource-based approach highlights the importance of pursuing competitive advantage, the resource-dependence framework stresses the influence of 'power shifts' due to changes in resource-dependence.

The model focuses on three key 'bridging' strategies that organisations use to control their environments. One strategy is to co-opt the source of the dependence; another is to use one's ties to leverage resources from the other organisation; a third is to make alter dependent on ego (Cook, 1977). Once an inter-organisational strategy has been pursued, a network of relations is created that may constrain the subsequent behaviour of actors, with 'centrality' in the network being correlated with relative power (Mizruchi and Galaskiewicz, 1994). In this sense, power refers to the 'set of resources that actors (could) mobilise through their existing set of social relationships' (Galaskiewicz, 1979, p. 151). Resource-dependence strategies refer to adaptive and incremental adaptations that stop short of internalising exchange into a corporate hierarchy, and as such can plausibly be said to account for the formation of inter-firm networks. That is, as firms try to influence each other, primarily through interactions and counter-actions, every exchange can be regarded as a series of questions and answers involving 'personal contact' (Hakansson, 1989; Lincoln et al., 1992). However, Fligstein and Freeland (1995) suggest that despite some empirical data not enough evidence has been gathered to determine whether such network arrangements reflect resource dependencies that can be sufficiently differentiated from certain market or hierarchical dependencies.

## The Strength of Ties, Embeddedness and Structural Holes

The most important commentary within sociology - or more exactly economic sociology - on inter-firm networks is that of Granovetter (1973; 1982; 1985; 1992; 1994), who has developed two key concepts: the 'strength of weak ties'; and the 'embeddedness' concept referred to earlier. The strength of weak ties argument lies in Granovetter's (1973; 1982) assertion that relatively 'weak' interpersonal ties serve the important function of acting as 'bridges' that indirectly connect actors or member of different groups. Granovetter's (1973) argument elaborates on the social network analysis of Bott (1957), which suggests that the crucial 'tie variable' is whether one's friends tend to know one another ('close-knit' network) or not ('loose-knit' network). Granovetter (1973) defines the strength of a tie as a combination of the amount of time, the emotional intensity, the intimacy, and the reciprocal services which characterise the tie. The strength of weak ties has become associated in the economic world with avoiding business stagnation and institutional 'lock-in', i.e. where firms and individuals are unable to adjust to change due to limited knowledge and awareness of activity beyond their own specific interactive arena (Arthur, 1988; 1989; Grabher, 1993; Grabher and Stark, 1997). However, it appears that Granovetter's (1973) argument has often been misconstrued as suggesting that actors should create weak ties to the exclusion of strong ones. Granovetter (1982) addresses this falsification in a later article:

> 'Lest readers [of the original 1973 article] ditch all their close friends and set out to construct large networks of acquaintants, I had better say that strong ties can also have some value.........I have not argued that all or even most weak ties serve the functions described in [the original article] - only those that act as bridges between network segments. The importance of weak ties is asserted to be that they are disproportionately likely to be bridges, as compared to strong ties, which should be underrepresented in that role. This does not preclude the possibility that most weak ties have no such function.' (p. 113).

Indeed, Granovetter's (1985) second important concept, that of embeddedness, stresses the role of 'concrete' personal relations and structures (i.e. networks) in generating trust and 'discouraging malfeasance' within society. With regard to business relations and networks, Granovetter (1985) recognises that there will be more variability in the 'degree of confidence' individuals have in each other, due to the existence of obvious economic factors, but that nevertheless the key motivating variable as to whether or not economic interaction and exchange occur is the strength of personal concrete relations, based on the identity and past history of the individual transactors. However, while Granovetter (1973; 1985) has argued that both strong direct 'embedded ties' and weaker indirect 'linking ties' have important socio-economic functions to play, others have more recently suggested that it is primarily the strong ties that have the instrumental effect on the economic prosperity of both firms and individuals. For example, Meyerson (1994) argues that it is principally the strong ties developed by the managers of firms that are most closely correlated to increases in the size of the firm.

Other sociological work has indicated that less direct weaker ties also have an important economic role. Marsden (1982), for example introduces the concept of brokerage behaviour in restricted exchange networks, which recognises that intermediate actors can control the messages passing through indirect channels. The essence of what is involved in brokerage behaviour is the functional equivalence of indirect ties to direct ones, with the mechanism being one in which actors lying on indirect channels between other actors, lacking access to one another, arrange exchanges for the latter in return for payments in the form of resource commissions (Marsden, 1982). This notion is further elaborated and more fully defined by Burt's (1992) concept of 'structural holes', which can be most simply defined as a lack of contact between two actors with whom a third actor – the main actor – is connected. According to Burt (1992), a structural hole is the separation between 'non-redundant' contacts, whereby non-redundant refers to the fact that contacts do not share the same information. Therefore, it is argued that structural holes are a standard feature of social structure, but are of particular importance in the process of economic competition, as those who compete to sell their products and services most often direct their attention at the same particular actor (i.e. the buyer) without being in direct contact with one another (Burt, 1992).

Burt (1992) suggests that those actors with a large number of structural holes not only fill them, and in doing so expect a degree of profit, but can mobilise them by precluding knowledge exchange between unconnected actors to create competitive advantage for themselves i.e. strategically located firms and/or individuals can restrict the flow of information in markets. Burt's (1992) emphasis on creating opportunities for brokering and entrepreneurialism is almost neo-classical in its outlook, and his concepts build on the resource-dependence arguments of centrality and power, emphasising that even when firms and individuals do operate in networks there is the dilemma of whether to take a competitive/exploitative stance or a co-operative/facilitating one. Significantly, Burt's (1992) assumption of playing people off against one another has been criticised by other sociologists who argue that while the structure that Burt employs generally holds in a competitive market place context, it ignores the content of ties formed. For example, Podolny and Baron's (1997) recent study of workplace mobility indicates that Burt overlooks the primary base of 'social identity' that conveys a sense of collective belonging and clear normative expectations, and highlights the advantages of more cohesive networks than those described by Burt.

It is worth noting, that while the work of Burt and Granovetter has usually been perceived as theoretically compatible, there is one significant dividing point. That is, where Granovetter highlights the benefits that all actors, essentially in terms of reciprocal exchanges, can accrue through networks and the development of trustworthy interactions, Burt's works concentrates on the distribution of power, control and the ability to competitively exploit networks. Nevertheless, Burt's (1992) work does raise further important debates concerning trust, and in particular notions such as 'free-riders' and 'suckers-payoff', which will be discussed later, as well as highlighting that, despite the rhetoric of co-operation within inter-firm networks, power is rarely symmetrically distributed (Staber, 1996a).

*Actor-Network Theory*

So far, all the sociological literature has highlighted the actor within networks as being the individual or an the individual residing within a particular institution. However, a more radical school of sociological thought is that of 'actor-network theory', which has sought to undermine the divide between human and non-human actors within networks, arguing that each should be treated symmetrically. The principle of actor-network theory, best associated with the work of Callon, Latour and Law (for example: Callon, 1986; 1991; Latour, 1986; 1991; Law, 1991; 1994), is that actors define each other through interaction and via the intermediaries they put into circulation, where such intermediaries are usually defined as: embodied subjects; texts; machines and money (Amin and Thrift, 1995). These intermediaries are viewed as active agents that can be used to build networks through which actors can exert power, and whereby actors continually attempt to 'enrol' both human and non-human entities (Amin and Thrift, 1995).

The core proposition of actor-network theory is that in order to analyse technologies they must be viewed as being essentially equivalent to social or human actors within networks (Sverisson, 1994). In particular, the 'sociology of translation', introduced by Callon (1986), addresses how both human and non-human resources are made available for the construction and reproduction of techno-economic networks. 'Translation' refers to the processes involved in turning an idea, identified by a problem or opportunity, into reality through a series of moves, or 'passage points', through which actors become enrolled and locked into a project (Knights et al., 1993). Furthermore, Callon's (1991) concept of a techno-economic network consists of a co-ordinated set of heterogeneous actors which interacts to develop, produce, distribute and diffuse methods for generating goods and services. The power distribution within such networks is dependent on the strength of the associations between actors, which is in turn reliant on the ability to use the network to 'enrol the force of others' (Amin and Thrift, 1995), which interestingly resonates with resource-dependent models of exchange. The most enlightening and detailed critique of actor-network theory is that of Murdoch (1995; 1997) which describes the theory as arguing that:

> 'in order for new networks to be constructed, the enrolling actors or strategic centres have to draw upon materials, actors, and intermediaries, which will already be inserted in established networks. We must 'follow' the actors through the network as they build and shape its contours, and we cannot specify in advance where their efforts will take them. The behaviour, definition, roles, and interests of actors are negotiated within the network. There is, therefore, no theory or model of the actor or the network that can be specified a priori....[and]....[I]t is only in retrospect that we can understand how actors and networks have coevolved and how these coevolutions were maintained or undermined.' (Murdoch, 1995, p. 752).

Therefore, the priority is to allow the actors to teach the theorists the causes of the success or failure of network building, and how actors seeking to enrol other actors 'stabilise and channel' the behaviour of these enrolling actors in the desired direction (Murdoch, 1995).

Actor-network theory attempts to tackle themes such as innovation (and its related concepts such as 'path dependency' and 'lock-in'), with Callon's work, in particular, crossing-over with that of the school of evolutionary economics (Murdoch, 1995; Wilkinson, 1997). Although actor-network theory is very much an abstract method of conceptualising economic behaviour, notions such as the sociology of translation - i.e. the process of building networks - does highlight a real world tendency for actors, in particular firm-managers, to be encouraged to 'acquire a knowledge of themselves as network builders, and to understand their visibility and success in this activity as critical both for their personal advancement and for the strategic development of their industry/firm/department etc' (Knights et al., 1993, p. 990). Also, as Grabher and Stark (1997) make clear, whatever the conceptual differences between actor-network theory's 'passage points', and the 'weak ties' and 'structural holes' associated with Granovetter and Burt respectively, each demonstrates that connecting actors in relatively isolated groups is crucial for the adaptability of networks.

## Game Theory, Trust and Social Capital

Game theory is a well established modelling approach that can be used to specify the optimal decisions that 'rational' individuals will choose, pre-supposing that the strategic character of action of one actor's decisions will be directly influenced by those of other relevant actors (Cable and Shane, 1997; Wilkinson, 1997). The growing acknowledgement of sub-optimum equilibrium assumptions, such as imperfect information and knowledge restrictions, has pushed game theory in the direction of rule formation, with increasing recognition of co-operative activities among actors opening up more institutional forms of analysis (Wilkinson, 1997). In particular, the 'prisoner's dilemma' variant of formal game theory has become a well-known metaphor used in psychological, sociological, and economic studies to model situations of conflict between two or more interdependent actors (Cable and Shane, 1997).

In the original prisoner's dilemma a pair of accomplices are held in-communicado, with each being told that if he alone implicates his partner he will escape scot-free, but if he remains silent, while his partner confesses, he will be punished especially severely. If both remain silent both will be let off lightly, but as they are unable to co-ordinate their stories each is better off 'squealing' no matter what the other does (Putnam, 1993). Therefore, the prisoner's dilemma game consists of two players with each having two choices: co-operate or defect. Each player must make the choice without knowing what the other will do, and no matter what the other does defection yields a higher payoff than co-operation. However, the dilemma is that if both defect, both will do worse than if both had co-operated; i.e. both actors are collectively better-off and receive higher rewards if they co-operate (Axelrod, 1984).

Prisoner's dilemma research into decision making processes is now fairly well established, with it popularity owing much to the fact that it is applicable to the reward structures of many real-life settings (Cable and Shane, 1997). Previous prisoner's dilemma research has indicated the following factors concerning 'co-operate or not' decision processes: (1) the greater the time pressure to reach an agreement, the more likely parties are to reach a co-operative solution; (2) co-operation can be enhanced by increasing payoffs for co-operation; (3) co-operation is enhanced when information about the co-operative strategy of one party can be gathered easily by the other; (4) social relationships increase co-operation; (5) co-operation is easier to develop and maintain if the other party is viewed as similar to oneself; (6) the more equal the power balance between the two parties the more likely they are to co-operate; (7) the longer people interact the more likely they are to co-operate (Cable and Shane, 1997). These findings all highlight some of the key factors necessary for the development of inter-firm networks, and in particular the need for continuing interaction, which makes possible co-operation based on reciprocity to be stable (Axelrod, 1984).

As Putnam (1993) makes clear, failure to co-operate does not necessarily signal ignorance or irrationality, as in the absence of a 'credible mutual commitment' each party may rationally expect the other to defect, and become a 'free-rider' or 'free-loader', while leaving them with the 'suckers pay-off'. Within an inter-firm network context, a 'free-rider' or 'free-loader' would consist of a firm that reaps the benefits of the activities of other network members without actually committing any resources or undertaking any co-operative activities themselves (Telser, 1987). In other words, 'free-loaders' are the equivalent of the 'opportunists', highlighted by transaction costs theory, who profit by acting dishonestly or deviously. Hence, the prisoner's dilemma indicates that a key ingredient which is often necessary for sustainable co-operative activity is, as has already been highlighted by other institutionally informed literature, trust.

Although the concept of trust has seldom been a central focus of sociological theory, it has, in recent years, come more to the fore due to the increasing prominence that has been attached to factors such as globalisation and the increased level of risk taking by individual and institutions (Giddens, 1990; Beck, 1992; Miztal, 1996). Even within so-called rational perspectives, trust has increased in relevance as it has become recognised that declining trust in long-term exchange relationships increases transaction costs, resulting in actors being less willing to take risks (Tyler and Kramer, 1996). This resonates strongly with arguments concerning the increased prevalence of network practices in modern economic behaviour (for example: Powell, 1990; Cooke and Morgan, 1993). Indeed, it could be argued that generating and securing trust through inter-firm networks is one of the most potent examples of Beck's (1992) notion of the 'risk society'. As Granovetter (1992) contends, some degree of trust is a basic necessity for the normal functioning of economic actions and institutions, and that the trust element, and the conditions for building up trust relations, are embedded in a network approach, i.e. without trust relations there could be no networks.

Arrow (1974) argues that virtually all commercial transactions have within themselves an element of trust. Gambetta (1988) defines such trust as being a situation whereby it is highly probable that someone will perform an action that is beneficial enough, or at least not detrimental, to consider engaging in co-operation. The undermining of this trust results in distrust, which is extremely difficult to reverse. Any doubts concerning the trustworthiness of others are likely to end in the breakdown of the 'tacit' agreement to co-operate (Lorenz, 1992). As Bradach and Eccles (1991) suggest, trust arises out of the social context and norms of transactions, and in a business setting out of the personal relationships that overlap with economic exchange activities. Trust is an expectation that alleviates the fear of opportunism, and only truly being in operation if this risk of opportunism is present. Therefore, one of the key advantages of trust, as Arrow (1974) indicates, is that it is a lubricant of efficient social systems as 'it saves people a lot of trouble to have a fair degree of reliance on other people's word' (p. 23).

The most detailed work on the relationship of trust with business action is that of Sako (1992), who suggests that if it were not for the existence of factors such as imperfect information, bounded rationality, risk and uncertainty, then trust would have no function to fulfil in business transactions as reckoned by economists (interestingly, Williamson (1993) has defined trust as a calculation of the likelihood of future co-operation). According to Sako (1992), trust between trading partners results in increases in the predictability of mutual behaviour, through the honouring of commitments made and behaving or responding in a mutually acceptable manner. Sako (1992) argues that this predictability in behaviour exists for different reasons, and allows for the distinguishing of three composite types of trust: (1) 'contractual trust', whereby trading partners mutually adhere to specific written or oral agreements and 'keep promises'; (2) 'competence trust' whereby partners expect each other to have the managerial and technical competence to perform their trading role; (3) 'goodwill trust', which is a more diffuse property and refers to mutual expectations of open commitment to each other through the willingness to do more than is formally expected. Although contractual and goodwill trust appear to be fairly robust concepts, it is debatable whether competence trust is in fact a trust variable, and perhaps should otherwise be viewed within Luhmann's (1988) distinction between trust and confidence, in that they are different ways of asserting expectations which may end up in disappointment.

An important 'type' of trust that has been identified by Sabel (1992; 1994) is the concept of 'studied trust', which suggests that trust can be generated in personal and business relations through a systematic process of learning how and why to trust, based on actors studying their 'collective past' in order to seek features such as compatible motives. Sabel (1994) further argues that this trust is maintained and secured through processes of 'monitoring', which acts as a facility for routinising and systematising trust and allowing for adjustments to be made to relationships. These processes of studying and monitoring imply that trust is by no means 'cheaply' acquired, and, as Sako (1992) found, despite beneficial aspects trust may be detrimental to achieving total organisational efficiency in the short run, due to the high set-up costs incurred in investing into various types of trust to obtain open-ended and difficult-to-appropriate benefits. For example, initial search costs identifying suppliers to enter long-term trading may be considerable, with durable trust only being created through frequent and intense communication, which is often resource diverting (Sako, 1992). However, as Meyerson et al. (1996) have recently suggested, as organisations move away from formal hierarchical structures to more flexible and temporary groupings (i.e. networks), often based around particular projects, such groups often exhibit behaviour that presupposes trust, without having any of the traditional sources of trust - i.e. familiarity, shared experience, reciprocal disclosure, threats and deterrents, fulfilled promises and demonstrations of the non-exploitation of vulnerability. Meyerson et al. (1996) resolve this seemingly paradoxical situation by suggesting that a characteristic of these groups is that they have developed methods for acquiring 'swift trust', which involves a series of hedges in which people behave in a trusting manner but also hedge to reduce the risks of betrayal. Swift trust centres around the competent and faithful enactment of clear roles and their associated duties, echoing Sako's (1992) notion of 'competence trust' or Luhmann's (1988) 'confidence'.

'Trust models' of interaction within sociology differ from the 'power models' of resource-dependence and structural holes, within which actors are portrayed pursuing a position of 'centrality' in a network that appears to have more in common with neo-classical economic perspectives. Indeed, these 'power perspectives' form part of the rational-choice model of the individual, which is generally associated with a particular school of political science and sociology, and whose assumptions bear a close resemblance to those attached with neo-classical theory. Based in the 'utilitarian' tradition associated with Locke, Hume and Mill, rational-choice theory brings a viewpoint of unsentimental realism to analysing policy issues (Collins, 1994). The rational-choice model assumes that people are motivated to maximise their personal gains and minimise their personal losses in social interactions and react to others (including: individuals; organisations; authorities and rules) from a self-interested and instrumental perspective (Tyler and Kramer, 1996). As with neo-classical theory, it has been argued that the rational-choice perspective ignores the larger social framework within which interaction occurs (Tyler and Kramer, 1996). Trust models, on the other hand, go back to original theory of social exchange, from which it will be remembered resource-dependence models evolved, that emphasises both trust and power as key variables within exchange behaviour.

One of the most perplexing arguments arising from sociological thinking is whether or not 'power' and 'trust' are compatible behavioural traits, i.e. can actors maintain trustworthy relations as they seek power and centrality, and is trust concomitant with actors 'knowing their position'? Superficially, it would appear that the two are incompatible and cannot be sought simultaneously, as trusting behaviour necessarily consists of actions that increase an actor's vulnerability to those whose behaviour is not under their control - in other words, the increase in risk reduces power (Lorenz, 1991; Powell, 1996). However, it should be remembered from the prisoner's dilemma that trust does not typically consist of 'goodwill', or the good inclination of the mind or disposition of the spirit, but a repeated game within which everyone is able to gain (Brusco, 1996). The type of trust defined by game theorists - or 'Axelrod (1984) style' as Sako (1992) refers to it - instrumentalises the position whereby the absence of opportunistic behaviour stems not from internalised moral commitment, but from the fear of external sanctions where the penalty suffered for abusing trust would lead to actors regretting their actions (Lorenz, 1991; Sako, 1992). Therefore, as Sako (1992) suggests, trust is, in effect, an uneasy cross between a capital asset in which people invest for self-interest and a social norm. As Powell (1996) states, trust should not be seen to imply blind loyalty, but should in fact be deliberate, or in Sabel's (1992) words 'studied', and can therefore be pursued as a mode of power accumulation as long as it does not abuse the position of others. For example, politicians can be viewed as being accumulators of power, while simultaneously claiming to have trusting relationships with their communities at large.

Putnam (1993) has argued that the supply of trust increases with use, and as the stock of social capital is built up. As Powell and Smith-Doerr (1994) suggest, trust and other forms of social capital are particularly interesting because they are what Hirschman (1984) describes as 'moral resources', operating in a fundamentally different manner to physical capital. A strong and successful networking culture has increasingly been tied to the concept of social capital, which Putnam (1993) defines as the features of social organisation such as networks, norms and social trust that facilitate co-ordination and co-operation for mutual benefit through collective action. North (1990), referring to these social features as the institutions of society, argues that they have important consequences for economic development. In other words, networks themselves are institutional, and as such the social relations they are built upon are embedded within social and economic life (Granovetter, 1985). Amin and Thrift (1995) argue that the 'institutional thickness' of this 'associationist' networking is the key to unlocking forms of exchange that facilitate the enhancement of factors that can contribute to economic success. Similarly, Flora and Flora (1993) suggest that with local economies facing increasing responsibilities to provide for their own well-being and development, 'entrepreneurial social infrastructure' is a necessary ingredient for successfully linking local business communities, particularly as people often appear to learn more from like-minded individuals.

Burt (1992) has suggested that an actor brings three kinds of capital to the business arena: financial; human; and social capital. He argues that, of these, it is social capital that is the final arbiter of competitive success. Taking this proposition further, Fukuyama (1995) has argued at length that there is a direct correlation between the social capital endowed in particular societies and their overall economic prosperity, highlighting Japan, Germany, and particular regions of Italy - as opposed to those weak social capital countries which he designates as France and China. Whether or not Fukuyama's (1995) propositions are empirically sound, one of the consequences of the mainstreaming of the social capital concept is, as Wilson (1997) suggests, that it essentially flies in the face of two of the central tenets of mainstream economics: (1) the assumption of scarcity - social capital is free, it requires no natural resources, no machines, no bricks and mortar, no advanced degrees, and no paid labour; (2) the idea of 'economic man' - instead of the concept of the individual separate self rationally calculating the costs and benefits of his every action on the basis of self-interest, social capital lends legitimacy to the idea of the individual-in-community, whereby each person is defined not just alone but in relationship to others.

Drawing on systems theory, Wilson (1997) argues that it is social learning practices, such as informal task-oriented action groups, that have the greatest relevance for empowering both individuals and communities alike through the production of social capital that is dependent on 'learning to listen to one another'. Utilising Putnam's (1993) definition of social capital, Wilson (1997) suggests that it is precisely business networking that adds to a community's productive potential, not only due to social learning factors but also because such networks promote faster information flows and more agile transactions, as well as the sharing of equipment and services. Wilson (1997) proposes that catalysing such actions may require the involvement of a change agent or facilitator who encourages, guides and assists the process, and develops a rapport within groups that is conducive to mutual learning. Such an agent could be termed a 'civic entrepreneur', acting in a fashion similar to the role that certain municipal and regional governments have assumed in helping to establish business networks (Wilson, 1995). These agents bear a strong resemblance to the informal and catalytic 'community entrepreneurs' that Cromie et al. (1993) describe as the linchpins in creating social networks, through forging associations between individuals and organisations within the process of business creation and development.

## Conclusions

Despite the traditional dominance of neo-classical and rationalist perspectives on economic behaviour there is increasing recognition that such behaviour is not purely the result of the decisions of profit maximising individuals and firms, but is also the result of the social relationships within which economic actors are embedded. This recognition has been particularly influenced by an acknowledgement that inter-firm networks represent a mode of economic governance significantly distinct from either market-based or hierarchical firm-based transactions. This new socio-economic perspective on economic behaviour and networks has itself come to the fore as 'knowledge' has become recognised as one of the most valued resources held by firms, and its exchange and transfer a key mode for facilitating innovation and achieving competitive advantage.

Whether inter-firm networks that facilitate the exchange of knowledge and other resources are a distinctive third mode of governance, or a hybrid or intermediate of markets and hierarchies, appears to be partly a problem of definition. That is, it is still a matter of contention as to whether economic interactions such as joint ventures, sub-contracting and other forms of relational contracting are sufficiently distinctive from the two traditional transaction modes. However, due to the increasing complexity of business activities and modes of interaction such 'fuzziness' is virtually impossible to resolve, and in any case adds little to the actual understanding of business relationships.

Sociological approaches to the firm and networks have injected an important progression away from efficiency-maximising principles towards a more diffuse set of cultural and political explanations. Although sociological models of resource-dependence explain why firms may pool resources, they also highlight that networks may be used to exploit a 'power position' such as in the 'structural holes' interpretation. The voluntary nature of relations in most inter-firm networks is such that significant variations in structures of power and control are to be expected (Johannisson, 1995; Staber, 1996a). According to Powell and Smith-Doerr (1994), the persistent concern of sociologists with 'power' marks one of the key points of divergence between themselves and economists who study firms essentially as rent-seeking organisations, i.e. revenue and profit-maximising. In this sense, it appears that economists have overlooked the 'power games' that businesses appear to continually play.

The analysis has highlighted variables concerning 'trust' and its acquisition as being inherently linked to inter-firm network building. Trust can be seen both as a rational profit maximising asset in which individuals and firms invest for self-interest, such as the type of trust highlighted by the prisoner's dilemma, and as a social norm resulting from institutional and cultural environments. It has been further shown that trust, whatever its form, is under-girded by social capital, or what has been referred to as the 'favour bank' (Putnam, 1993). Interestingly, Powell (1996) has recently asked three pertinent questions concerning trust: (1) Can co-operation come about independently of trust? (2) Can trust be a result rather than a pre-condition of co-operation? (3) Is co-operation a strategic, self-interested calculation? Although it is difficult to answer such questions definitively, the following suggestions can be made. Firstly, co-operation cannot be said to come about independently of trust if notions such as Sako's (1992) concept of competence trust is accepted. Secondly, trust can be a result of co-operation if Putnam's (1993) argument that the supply of trust increases rather than decreases with use is accepted.

Powell's (1996) third question is highly philosophical, and those institutional analysts and critics of neo-classical theory, who draw on arguments concerning the 'embeddedness of economic behaviour in social life', would undoubtedly argue that co-operation is not always a strategic and self-interested calculation. However, it is suggested that the answer may be yes, and that as well as acting in an economically rational manner individuals also act in a 'socially rational manner', whereby they perceive of their own interactions as being strategic and self-interested not always for any direct economic gain but as a means of increasing their particular stock of social capital. This argument closely resembles the approach taken by Blau (1964) whereby social capital, and the ability to interact with and relate to others, can be utilised by both the individual and those they wish to endow it upon. The 'beauty' of social capital being that endowing elsewhere actually results in increases to the individuals own stock, and, therefore, need not necessarily be viewed as a 'goodwill' or 'altruistic' gesture.

The poles of rational and institutional thinking can be drawn together if it is accepted that economic life is embedded in the customs, morals, and habits of social life - factors which are themselves the result of socially rational behaviour. That is, non-economic concepts such as equity, loyalty and tradition are based on social rationality. For example, it can be argued that the decision to enter institutions such as marriage and friendship, or the joining of 'social clubs', are based on social rationality and that such decisions are not to the detriment of the other actors involved, in terms of the 'winning and losing' that is associated with rational opportunism. However, even social rationality will be 'bounded' by the limits of the capacity of individuals to retrieve and process information.

The concept of social rationality differs from typical sociological-instrumental rational-choice perspectives, which argue that individuals seek to maximise personal gains and minimise their personal losses in social interactions. A socially rational perspective views individuals as pursuing social capital that has different non-utility maximising or material accumulation motives. For example, group/community acceptance or other communal undertakings within which individuals may be willing to forgo what could be considered to be obvious personal gain, or be willing to absorb certain actual 'transparent' losses, in an effort to enhance the positive effects on their overall personal and common good. In other words, by serving the interests of others, individuals rationally serve their own - or, 'what's good for me, is good for you'. If people are not operating rationally (or even opportunistically) in economic terms then they can be said to be operating in a socially rational manner. The decision to join inter-firm networks, therefore, is based on economic and/or social rationality. Socially rational forces can curb and check thoughts of opportunistic behaviour and are key proponents in the forging of trust. This is not to suggest that economic and social rationality work in conflict, but in a balance reminiscent of Granovetter's (1985) neither over- or under-socialised interpretation of economic action. Such action is based on the accumulation of economic and/or social capital, resembling Oliver's (1997) assertion that in the search for competitive advantage firms require both resource and institutional capital. Therefore, as Fukuyama (1995) contends, social capital is critical to prosperity and competitiveness.

It is suggested that the decision to enter an inter-firm network resembles the decision-making processes associated with other business transactions, being the result of weighing-up the risks based on ones economic and social rationality, and are therefore subject to the same speculation and variability. However, expectations in terms of 'uncertainty' may, as Powell (1996) suggests, be radically different from market or intra-firm transactions. In many ways, socially rational behaviour is a particularly strong factor in network development, as it echoes the often long-term nature of interaction and relationships, as opposed to the short-term exposure traditionally associated with market-based interaction. Socially rational behaviour also highlights the motive of 'learning-by-doing' within networks, as well as the general principles of evolutionary economic behaviour, whereby individuals make on-going decisions based on their knowledge and past experiences. Within this evolutionary framework, it is interesting to note Schumpeter's own distinction between creative action and rational action has recently been drawn upon in the development of a theory of the social rationalisation of the economy (Dahms, 1995).

# 3 Space, Place and Policy Intervention

## Introduction

The previous chapter concentrated on theoretical explanations for economic behaviour and inter-firm networks, with little mention of evidence concerning the actual existence of network forms. In general, there is an obvious disparity between the glut of theoretical and abstract literature, and the dearth of actual on-the-ground examples. However, there is a growing core of literature, based on empirical research, that has attempted to analyse existing inter-firm networks within differing formats and settings. This chapter focuses on further analysing some of this research, in order to assess the importance of the spatial and place-specific boundaries that are often associated with such networks. Also, attempts to implant and catalyse inter-firm networks through public policy intervention are examined. Principally, it is economic geography (and to a lesser extent the disciplines of small business development/economics and entrepreneurship) that has led the way in producing empirical support for the theoretical arguments, particularly as many of the identified networks have been of a spatially restricted nature. The first part of this chapter gives an overview of some of the methods by which networks have been researched, before a more detailed account of the most pertinent issues arising from the research.

The work of economic geographers, in particular, is usually grounded in the socio-economic approach, drawing on the notion of the 'embeddeness' of non-economic factors developed by Granovetter (1985) and others, as well as discourses concerning networks of learning, knowledge and innovation. The debate on the spatiality of networks has become closely linked to new theories of economic development that are primarily advocated as being best implemented as the 'local' or 'regional' level, i.e. sub-national strategies. Typically, it is argued that the existence of established inter-firm networks is one of the key reasons why a number of the most successful localities and regions throughout the world have become or remained more industrially competitive than those that have not adopted a networked approach. In particular, it was studies of the 'industrial districts' of the northern Italian region of Emilia-Romagna that highlighted the potential for specific localities to contribute to economic development, and most noticeably entered the literature through the work of Piore and Sabel (1984). As Grabher and Stark (1997) outline, accounts of regional production systems have typically been written as success stories of a coherent system of economic institutions, whereby the compatibility of these institutions acts as the catalyst for transaction-cost efficient regional co-operative networks. Therefore, whereas it has already been suggested that inter-firm networks function in what Sayer and Walker (1992) label the 'new social economy', in which there is a web of economic and social forces at play, there is also a parallel spatial function through exposure to an array of more or less local and global forces (Cho, 1997).

**Table 3.1    Survey Based and Other Quantitative Studies Relating to Inter-firm Networks**

| Study | Research Context | Key Finding |
|---|---|---|
| Appold (1995) | Agglomeration and networks as an influence on firm performance within the US metalworking sector | Firms located in agglomerations were not competitively advantaged |
| Brown and Butler (1993) | The influence of 'borders' on network development among wine companies in California | Social and cultural factors embedded in national and/or regional borders inhibit the freer flow of information |
| Donckels and Lambrecht (1995) | Impact of networks on small business growth in the three Flemish regions of Belgium | Networks have an influence on the growth of a small business, especially through contacts with national and international entrepreneurs |
| Gelsing and Knop (1991) | Evaluation of the Danish 'network programme' | Participation had a positive effect on the 'competitiveness' of the majority of firms |
| Greve (1995) | The relevance of social networks to new entrepreneurs in Norway | New entrepreneurs have smaller networks and spend less time interacting than more established entrepreneurs |
| Lincoln et al. (1992) | Use of secondary sources to analyse Keiretsu networks in Japan | Shareholding ties form 'true' networks with high connectivity and long chains |

| | | |
|---|---|---|
| Lipparini and Sobrero (1994) | The role of the entrepreneur in promoting and managing external ties among small firms in Italy | Inter-firm ties are a key vehicle for transferring and combining embedded learning capabilities |
| Mason and Harrison (1997) | Policy-driven and private sector business angel networks (BANs in the UK | Emergence of private sector BANs has not eliminated the need for public sector support of locally-oriented networks |
| Mowery et al. (1996) | Use of existing commercial databases of patent patterns to assess inter-firm knowledge transfer in the US | Alliance activity can promote increased specialisation |
| Ostgaard and Birley (1996) | Effectiveness of personal networks for new venture owner-managed firms in England | Personal networks are an important influence on performance and development |
| Powell et al. (1996) | Use of commercial database to assess the influence of networks on the knowledge-base of the US biotechnology industry | Networks sustain a fluid and evolving community |
| Staber and Aldrich (1995) | Social embeddedness of entrepreneurs and small business owners in North Carolina and Canada | Friends and family are at the centre of owners' networks, owners make moderate use of brokers in assembling networks |
| Strambach (1994) | Importance of networks for knowledge-intensive service firms in the Rhine-Neckar region of Germany | Networks provide flexibility to meet the needs of a range of individual client demands |
| Welch et al. (1997) | Assessment of a policy-driven set of manufacturing business networks and the impact on member companies in the US | Positive effects of network initiatives increases as the level of network formality increases |
| Zhou (1996) | Social embeddedness of linkages among Chinese-owned computer wholesale firms in Los Angeles | The presence of ethnic identity plays a significant role in the internal operation and external transactions of Chinese firms |

**Table 3.2    Interview Based and Other Qualitative Studies Relating to Inter-firm Networks**

| Study | Context | Key Finding |
|---|---|---|
| Bryson et al. (1993) | Small business service firms in the UK | Networks of informal contacts are an inherent and vital component of the relationship firms have with clients and other business service firms |
| Cromie et al. (1993) | The role of community brokers as generators of inter-firm networking in the UK | Community brokers, and the social networks they are able to access, are linchpins in the process of business creation and development |
| Curran and Blackburn (1994) | The relationship of the owner-managers of small firms with their locality, large firms, and the prevalence of local economic networks in the UK | Small business owners contribute little to the development of local embedded ties |
| de Toni and Nassimbeni (1995) | Supply networks in Italian clothing and glass districts | Networks were formed as a result of the inadequacies of traditional governance structures |
| Grotz and Braun (1993) | The relevance of networks to an innovative SME environment in the Neckar-Alb region of Germany | Networks were not a dominant feature of company strategies |
| Hakansson (1989) | the role of networks for the technological strategies of firms | Managers can improve technological research by exploiting networks efficiently |
| Hallen et al. (1991) | Inter-firm adaptations among industrial suppliers in Germany, Sweden and the UK | Inter-firm adaptations are closely related to processes of social exchange |
| Hara and Kanai (1994) | Entrepreneurial networks as a mode for promoting international strategic alliances for small businesses in Osaka and Silicon Valley | The key to success was the involvement of a 'networker of networks' - a person or company whose role is to create a global network of local networks |

| | | |
|---|---|---|
| Izushi (1997) | Changing inter-firm relations in the Japanese ceramics industry | The growth of external ties in the ceramics district endangered the existence of local innovative ties |
| Joyce et al. (1995) | The link between co-operation and competitive conditions among small firms in London | Firms constrained by market demand and/or increased demand are more likely to join networks |
| Larson (1992) | Social control in networks of high-growth entrepreneurial firms | Reputation, trust, reciprocity, and mutual dependence are key factors in network formation |
| Malecki and Tootle (1997) | Policy-driven and 'organic' networks in the US | Some public-policy support was necessary to foster networks at the local level |
| Malecki and Veldhoen (1993) | Informal network activities among small firms in Florida | Firms were best integrated into international networks both for customers and suppliers |
| New and Mitropoulos (1995) | The application of 'academic frameworks' to the 'reality' of networks used by business managers in the north west of England | Firms may require tools which enhance their ability to manage information about their commercial relationships |
| Robertson et al. (1996) | The influence of networks on the diffusion of technological innovation in the UK manufacturing sector | Companies involved in networks of 'weak ties' best promoted the diffusion of certain technologies |
| Sweeting (1995) | The role of agencies in offering innovation support to manufacturing firms in the north west of England | Strong and effective networks were being developed with extensive management socialising taking place |
| Uzzi (1996) | Ethnographic research on the sources and consequences of embeddedness in the New York apparel sector | Networked-firms' have a higher chance of survival; the positive effect of embeddedness reaches a threshold after which the effect reverses itself |
| von Hippel (1988) | Informal know-how trading and co-operation between rivals in US steel mini-mills | Firms routinely traded proprietary process know-how |

**Table 3.3    Combined Method Studies Relating to Inter-firm Networks**

| Study | Context | Key Finding |
|---|---|---|
| Kingsley and Klein (1998) | Application of a survey questionnaire to a collection of policy-driven case studies in the US | Factors that produce successful networks vary with the networking objective |
| Chaston (1996a) | Review of secondary data and the undertaking of interviews for an early assessment of the application of the 'Danish network model' in the UK | Changes were necessary in the model as it was currently being applied |
| Saxenian (1990) | Review of secondary data and undertaking interviews to assess the influence of networks on growth in Silicon Valley | Silicon Valley's resilience owes much to its rich networks of social, professional and commercial relationships |
| Rosenfeld (1996) | Survey and interviews of participating firms and facilitators to assess the impact of network development initiatives in the north west of the US | Businesses are more open to co-operation than sceptics suggest |
| Penn (1992) | Case study and postal survey of the changing relationships between firms in Rochdale | Firms in the locality were becoming less integrated |

## Researching Inter-firm Networks

A review of recent empirical inter-firm studies, based around the network concept, indicates that methodological approaches have incorporated a range of both quantitative and/or qualitative methods. Tables 3.1, 3.2 and 3.3 illustrate that researchers have employed a range of primarily survey and interview/case-study methods in an attempt to explore and explain a whole host of issues relating to inter-firm networks (the 'Key Finding' column in the tables is this author's personal assessment of the most notable feature of a particular study with regard to inter-firm network theory). As Monsted (1991) argues, the lack of a general and standardised methodology is partly due to the heterogeneity of inter-firm networks, with their study covering a range of disciplines including sociology, management, industrial relations and regional development. In general, quantitative methods have become associated with attempts to 'measure' networking activity, in terms of the size/density of networks and frequency of contact. Quantitative measures are, perhaps, most useful where the objective is to compare network development between different groups of businesses and/or in different socio-economic or cultural settings (Perry and Goldfinch 1996). Indeed, as indicated in Table 3.1, survey methods (most commonly through the postal distribution of questionnaires) and other quantitative techniques (such as the numerical analysis of existing databases) have predominantly been used to assess the importance and relevance of inter-firm networks in an array of environments, with the findings often relating to the influence of network arrangements on the business capabilities of firms, in particular SMEs.

Methodological approaches to the study of inter-firm networks that are purely quantitative have been criticised on the grounds that they explain little about the actual content of firm relations and connections. For example, Blackburn et al. (1990) argue that 'counting research strategies' yields results that are often difficult to interpret and offers limited insight into the nature of 'networking behaviour'. They further suggest that quantitative approaches should not be ruled out, as they are a key measuring tool, but that it is qualitative approaches that are best suited to exploring the processes and motivations to network (Blackburn et al. 1990). Similarly, Borch and Arthur (1995) argue that there is a need for a more in-depth knowledge of the cultural contexts and socio-economic relations of actors within networks, and suggest the applicability of the qualitative methodological tools associated with disciplines more experienced with human interaction research, such as social anthropology. Despite this criticism, Table 3.2 indicates that a number of qualitative studies, usually of an interview-based nature, have been carried out into the study of inter-firm networks in recent years.

As Table 3.2 shows, these studies are most often concerned with trying to explain the types of relationships and contact, and the reasoning behind the development of networks. An example of a qualitative interview-based approach is the so-called 'critical incidents' technique, which attempts to explain the motivation for individuals to act in a certain fashion in light of some 'non-routine event' occurring (Curran et al. 1993, Ring and Van de Ven 1994). Curran and Blackburn (1994) and Joyce et al. (1995) both use a critical incidents approach to explore the motivations of owner-managers of small firms to join networks due to occurrences that may potentially destabilise their business. A criticism of this approach is that it appears to assume that decision-making processes associated with network participation occur only during periods of crisis. Nevertheless, the use of critical incidents and other qualitative methods are an important recognition of the need to understand and interpret the characteristics and organisation of networks. A feature of critical incidents and other qualitative research is that it has often focused on dyadic, rather than multi-actor, inter-firm network relationships. For instance, Larson's (1992) detailed ethnographic study of the importance of social control between entrepreneurial firms is an excellent analysis of the level of formality in 'one-to-one' network exchanges. However, the nature of policy implanted networks is such that they require an exploration of the emergence of multi-actor structures. Also, previous network research has taken little account of the role of negotiators in organising network relationships, who, as Ring and Van de Ven (1994) have highlighted, often take a key role in nurturing the 'psychological contract' that binds together network actors. Within the network initiatives covered by the empirical research in this book, the role of negotiators - in the form of TECs, as institutional policy agents, and their 'network brokers' - is paramount.

Although the majority of inter-firm network studies have utilised either a predominantly survey or interview-based approach, a smaller number, as shown in Table 3.3, have genuinely triangulated combined methods. The use of combined methods has increasingly been applied to studies that have attempted to evaluate inter-firm networks developed through public policy initiatives, for example: Chaston (1996a); Rosenfeld (1996); Kingsley and Klein (1998). These studies indicate that there is a requirement to try to both measure network development and also understand the processes leading to the success or failure of a particular network initiative. In this sense, as Monsted (1995) states, it is important to determine what aspect of networks and their development processes the research is concerned with and then apply a relevant methodology. Another consideration, as Johannisson (1995) suggests, are limitations in terms of research time and resources; for instance large-scale qualitative research is often laborious and highly time-intensive. In these circumstances quantitative analysis can be used to collect data that subsequently acts as a framework for more focused in-depth qualitative research (Johannisson, 1995).

## Post-Fordism, Flexible Specialisation and Industrial Districts

The catalytic force behind the revival of interest in 'space', and the notion of 'industrial districts' resembling those districts first identified by Alfred Marshall in the north of England and south Wales in the late nineteenth century, was Piore and Sabel's (1984) work on economic restructuring and the emergence of a model of 'new industrial spaces' based on processes of 'flexible specialisation' (Scott, 1988). Piore and Sabel's (1984) thesis rests on emphasising the differentiation, and the shift from, a so-called 'Fordist' mode of production to one of 'post-Fordism'. Essentially, the post-Fordism argument contends that small firms have risen in importance as a response to the crisis of mass modes of production and consumption. It is argued that locally agglomerated production systems have risen out of the demise of Fordist modes and triggered the re-emergence of industrial districts, often specialising in niche market goods, that are able to learn, change and adapt, rather than rely on their allocative efficiency, to boost their long-run performance (Maskell and Malmberg, 1995). The model suggests that small firms have a much more central role to play within economies, and due to the adoption of 'flexible specialisation' have a higher probability of securing stable futures.

The key feature of Piore and Sabel's (1984) flexible specialisation model are: (1) the introduction of new and flexible manufacturing technology that aids the reduction of costs; (2) a renewed 'craft' tradition, providing workers with a degree of autonomy over decisions-making processes; (3) the break-up of mass markets into niche markets; (4) the resurgence of local and regional economies; (5) new market opportunities and market independence for small firms (Curran and Blackburn, 1994). In other words, as Amin (1992) summarises:

> 'The key argument is that the irreversible growth in recent decades of consumer sovereignty, market volatility and shortened product life cycles requires extremely flexible production organisation.........Such a transformation, it is argued, implies a return to place: a dependence on locational proximity between the different agents involved.' (p. 129).

The flexible specialisation discourse draws specifically on the 'markets versus hierarchy', 'social versus economic', and 'embeddedness' debates outlined earlier, whereby within economies based on flexible specialisation it is difficult to tell where economic organisation begins and where society ends. Piore and Sabel's (1984) analysis of the importance of a post-Fordist mode of production, based on small-scale craft production, highlights a key feature of this system to be networks of SMEs that successfully compete with large enterprises. These co-operation networks of SMEs are seen to be superior in adapting to changing economic and technological frameworks that are characterised by increasing competition, an increasingly differentiated demand and a decreasing stability of markets (Grotz and Braun, 1993).

Piore and Sabel's (1984) analysis is primarily based on examples of networks from the craft-industries in north-central Italy (the so-called

'Third Italy') - in particular high-fashion textile firms around Prato; the Brescia mini-mill steel producers; the motorcycle industry of Bologna; the ceramic tile makers of Sassuolo - in which networks of small firms combine low vertical integration and high horizontal integration, through the use of extensive sub-contracting and the 'putting-out' of extra business to temporarily under-employed local competitors (Putnam, 1993). These small firm networks have become typified by the readiness of firms to co-operate, to engage in the collective organisation of services and the promotion of the industry, and to pass on information amongst individuals and firms (Brusco, 1992; Pyke, 1994). Although Piore and Sabel (1984) argue that these localised networks have emerged as a reaction to new market conditions and changing technological frameworks, it is also suggested that there are other important factors that have acted as the catalysts for the development of these networks, in particular: (1) the existence of small-scale communities anchored by well-developed social networks; (2) national tax policies and efforts that stifled the development of the large-firm sector and favoured the development of non-unionised small firms; (3) a range of local public-private partnerships that followed the decentralisation policies of the national government (Ettlinger, 1997).

The influence of Piore and Sabel's (1984) work was such that it stimulated a flurry of studies on the endogenous development potential of localised and collaborative production complexes that came to be referred to as 'industrial districts' or 'neo-Marshallian districts' (Staber, 1996b). In particular, the analysis of the spatial 'closeness' of firms came to prominence in debates concerning the economic progress of high-technology firms and the successful implementation of advanced technologies, it being argued that an important component of the economic restructuring occurring in Western Europe, North America, and Japan is the emergence of powerful networks of mainly small enterprises (Curran and Blackburn, 1994; Gertler, 1995).

As Amin (1992) observes, the examples cited have become only too familiar, and in addition to studies of the Third Italy include: Baden-Wurttemberg in Germany; Quebec; lower Austria; southern France (Grenoble); as well as the much documented Japanese agglomerations, and the Silicon Valley and Route 128 technopoles in the United States (for example: Hassink, 1992; Pyke and Sengenberger, 1992; Semlinger, 1993; Cooke and Morgan, 1994b; 1998; Castells and Hall, 1994; Staber, 1996c). The advantage to firms situated in these agglomerations are seen to include a reduction in the cost of transactions between firms through co-operation, resulting from dense social interaction and trust relations, as well as: reduced transport costs; a build-up of a local pool of expertise and know-how; a culture of labour flexibility; and the provision of an infrastructure of specialised services, distribution networks and supply structures (Amin, 1992). It is argued that inter-firm networks of production have become prominent features of industrial organisation as firms choose to reduce linkage costs and take advantage of specialised labour pools and information sources through agglomeration. Firms, therefore, integrate their operations through malleable external linkages and labour market relations in relatively durable relationships through an organised market involving both competition and co-operation (Scott, 1988; Storper, 1995).

One of the attractions, for theorists, of the network model associated with flexible specialisation and industrial districts is that economic co-ordination appears to take place neither principally in the markets nor hierarchies characterised by Fordism. Also, the 'power frameworks', constituting the relationships between large corporations and the pool of small firms, are seen to be largely absent due to the trustworthy as opposed to exploitative nature of the interaction. That is, a shift occurs from so-called 'arm's-length' relations, in which 'price' is dominant, to more long-term stable and collaborative relations. In other words, it is suggested that in effect these districts operate within a structure of equal exchange relations in a modern version of an embedded society and economy.

Although it is the facilitation of information exchange through well-functioning relations that is often highlighted as the most common content of this geographically defined interaction (Vatne, 1995), it is the ability of organisations to 'learn' that has come to the fore as being a key feature of effective relationships in local and regional SME networks. For example, Gibb (1997) discusses SMEs turning intermittent or transactional relationships into social and ongoing interaction in order to access a 'how to' and 'who with' learning need. These networks, therefore, stress the interactive nature of learning, and Asheim (1996a), who builds primarily on Perroux's (1970) work on 'growth pole' theory as well as Porter's (1990) theories of 'the competitive advantage of clusters' (discussed later), argues that these processes can be intensified through localised territorial agglomeration. Similarly, Sweeney (1996) suggests that a learning capacity is closely correlated with the maintenance and generation of new economic activity, and is most efficiently enhanced through localised networks. Drawing on the work of the North Italian districts, Sweeney (1996) argues that:

> 'Learning efficiency and the generation of new economic activity and maintenance of economic prosperity which stem from it, are local phenomena and result from the transaction-intensive information sharing of communities with distinctive cultures and a spirit of communitarianism, and the technological orientation of the education system. The networks

integrate each actor in a geographic area in an intensive melange of social, business, technological and civic information and work sharing.' (p. 5).

'Solutions to problems are found more efficiently; they are more creative, and innovative ideas are more frequently generated. New ideas are more quickly converted to products on the market. Creativity and efficiency rise sharply as the average frequency of personal information intensive contacts increases' (p. 8-9).

Although bordering on the utopian, Sweeney's (1996) scenario of industrial districts does, nevertheless, resonate with evolutionary thinking of 'learning-by-interacting', whilst reinforcing the importance of 'bounded space'. However, while the work of Piore and Sabel (1984) was based on concrete qualitative research, an 'academic cottage industry' has formed, using their examples in a secondary fashion, that has diluted the link between the empirical and the theoretical, and led to a wave of criticism. Murdoch (1995) has categorised these criticisms into two broad areas: (1) those that argue that the categories of mass production (Fordism) and flexible specialisation (post-Fordism) dichotomy are over-generalised; (2) those that ask how or when is an 'industrial district' recognisable, due to the given examples appearing to 'stuff too much into the same bag'; thus making it sceptical as to whether any overarching structure of the transformation of economies towards the notion of post-Fordist industrial spaces actually exists. This apparent vagueness has led Curran and Blackburn (1994) to criticise accounts of industrial districts as 'approaching the literary', rather than being based on rigorously argued and well supported theoretical formulation, and whereby the assertions offered are mainly arguments by illustration 'which have melted away under serious scrutiny'.

Other informed criticism includes Markusen (1996), whose analysis of the conditions of industrial districts, concerning what she refers to as 'sticky places in slippery spaces', leads to her rejecting the concepts of industrial districts as being a 'dominant paradigmatic solution' due to their generally endogenous 'in-look'. Furthermore, Staber (1996c) has recently argued that there is little evidence to suggest that business relations in Baden-Wurttemberg, Germany are embedded in local social structures or that firms make substantial use of the institutional arrangements that might support co-operation. Despite these criticisms there has been growing recognition from outside the spatial sciences of geographic perspectives, in particular how SME-based localities and regions facilitate growth and prosperity.

**Localities, Regions and Globalisation**

The interest in industrial districts and network forms of organisation reflects a more general concern in economic geography with the ways in which economic activities are embedded and made possible by social and cultural conditions (i.e. the application of socio-economics), being applied with particular force to studies of high-technology districts such as Silicon Valley and Route 128 in the United States (Martin and Sunley, 1996). Although a local and regional focus has been advocated from the viewpoint of locational efficiency, induced by a reduction in transaction costs and the presence of external economies, the focus on high-tech complexes has added an increasing recognition of the ability of innovative regions and localities to quickly respond to changing economic conditions. Nijkamp et al. (1994) summarise these potential benefits as being those of collective learning process that stimulate local creativity and techno-genesis through local synergies, creating a decline in the dynamic uncertainty intrinsic in technological developments and innovative processes.

It is the work of Scott and Storper (for example: Scott, 1988; 1994; 1998; Scott and Storper, 1992; Storper, 1992; 1993; 1994; 1995; 1997; Storper and Scott, 1995) and Saxenian (1990; 1994) that has most closely analysed the transition to vertically-disintegrated firm networks and locally-agglomerated production complexes within high technology-based sectors, specifically in the United States. Storper's work has refined efforts to explain relationships between technological change and geography, and draws essentially on evolutionary thinking regarding the 'path-ways' through which innovation takes place and the so-called 'spill-overs' that are produced by key technologies. Storper (1993; 1994; 1995; 1997) argues that learning and innovation are facilitated through 'untraded interdependencies' generated by 'intelligence' spill-overs involving networks of locally agglomerated firms and institutions. Therefore, these untraded interdependencies are, in this case, mainly technological externalities that form a collective asset via forms of social exchange.

Despite agglomerative forces, Storper (1995) acknowledges that evolutionary pathways of technology go well beyond localised effects. Saxenian (1990; 1994) has further drawn on arguments concerning the geography of untraded interdependencies to explain the diverging economic prosperity of the Silicon Valley and Route 128 regions, that had previously been seen as complementary (for example: Scott, 1988). According to Saxenian (1994), the continued success of Silicon Valley, compared to the relative demise of the Route 128 region of Boston, is due to the differing forms of social organisation. Saxenian (1994) argues that while Silicon Valley has continued to develop a trust-based, information sharing and high mobility character, Route 128 has increasingly become secretive, more vertically integrated and less mobile. This has resulted in Silicon Valley creating dense social networks, and by which untraded interdependencies are formed not only within the locality but beyond to global structures.

The differences in nature of districts that were previously argued to have complementary features has added fuel to those whose have suggested that industrial district and agglomeration discourse tries to stuff to much into the same bag. For example, Amin (1994) argues that the dynamics of growth in craft-based industrial districts associated with the Third Italy are quite different from those examples of local agglomeration in high-tech complexes. Furthermore, commentators such as Hobday (1991) have remained sceptical about the sustainable competitive efficiency of network organisations, compared with large firm organisation, arguing that individual firms within local networks suffer from: (1) limited growth imposed by a shortage of finance and assets; (2) limited access to global marketing outlets; (3) confinement to locally generated and regional niche markets; (4) an inward-looking approach; (5) an inability to adequately address international market and technological needs. Indeed, Hobday (1994) has further suggested that even the small firm network culture of Silicon Valley has proved incapable of realising many of the rewards of its innovation, due to a lack of the complementary assets that are produced through vertical integration and large firms.

Criticisms concerning the importance to economic prosperity of small versus large firms has been further discussed by Harrison (1994) and Krugman (1995), who both argue that it is larger vertically integrated organisations that are still the dominant and powerful force within economies. To an extent, some validity has been given to this argument through the relative demise of Route 128, and also due to the economic crisis that occurred in the late 1980s and early 1990s within the Italian industrial districts. Much discussion has recently taken place as to whether or not the districts will survive. Interestingly, Varaldo and Ferrucci (1996) have recently suggested that the flexibility inherent in the district model will sustain those firms that link to global networks.

It is this local-global relationship that has been used to counter arguments concerning the inwardness and constraints of agglomerative behaviour, in particular highlighting the role of both local and global networks. It is often argued that the global economy, and its global markets, are increasingly becoming the exclusive domain of power-hungry multinational corporations. However, there is a growing counter-argument that globalisation is actually reinforcing the role that geographic clusters of production play in the competitive international arena (Porter, 1990; de

Vet, 1993; Cooke, 1994). For example, Scott and Storper (1992) view the global economy as a mosaic of regional production systems, each with its own intra-regional markets and activities, and also a global web of inter-regional linkages. Therefore, there appears to exist a paradox, highlighted by Castells and Hall (1994), that although the technological revolution has provided the infrastructure for the increasing  globalisation of economic structures, both cities and regions are becoming increasingly crucial agents of economic development. De Vet (1993) argues that regions, in particular, are becoming stronger economic entities through the fostering of growth via the mobilisation of their asset base, including the specialised competences of their local firms.

As innovation is highly dependent on information and knowledge, these elements are becoming the critical success factors for new models of regional development in a global environment (Nijkamp et al., 1994). A capacity to innovate appears prefiguratively to imply the necessity to access such 'invisible factors' through a networking capacity. This reinforces the argument that globalisation intensifies regionalisation, as information and knowledge is often of a global nature but needs to be delivered locally (Kogut et al., 1993; Nielsen, 1994). Therefore, network characteristics are seen to be of particular importance for innovation and technological change, and the growth prospects of spatially defined regions (Bergman et al., 1991).  Although such regional networks enable firms to tap into local expertise and knowledge, their true strength comes from their ability to inter-link with other networks on a wider spatial basis. Camagni (1991) views such links as imperative, pointing to the fact that the region, or what is sometimes referred to as the 'local milieu' (see for example: Maillat, 1998), needs to be linked to international and global networks in order to stay innovative in the long term and avoid 'entropic death'. Also as Christensen et al. (1990) argue, 'tight' networks in a regional frame can be seen as a preconditioning factor underlying the gain of competitive advantage in a global frame.

These global-regional networks clearly have a different relevance for different actors, and it is argued that it is primarily SMEs that have the most to gain (Tödtling, 1994). In effect, tight local and weaker global networks resembles Granovetter's (1973) argument of the strength of weak ties as well as Burt's (1992) thesis concerning the power of 'plugging' structural holes. In this case it is strong local ties that are of importance for facilitating access to weaker, although often more powerful, global networks of production and innovation. Murdoch (1997) has further drawn on actor-network theory to argue that the duality in the socio-spatial analysis of the localised and globalised can be overcome by configuring the non-human entities, for example telecommunications, that permit human actors to act at distance. As well as breaking down the barriers of the local and the global, Murdoch (1997) argues that as these geometries are drawn patterns of power, centrality and marginality emerge. Consequently, it appears that global networks may have more in common with power-dependence theories than the more local reciprocal models.

Grotz and Braun (1993) suggest that the relevance of strong local and weak global ties is that the local milieu often appears to be more important for gathering information about management and distribution strategies, whereas with respect to innovation and technology-oriented information, inter-regional and global linkages are more common. Thus, as de Vet (1993) has argued, it seems that:

'....a combination of both approaches, linking global to local interests, has the best chance of success. The blurring of global and local interests is reciprocal. Even when using their own resource potential to its full, local industries still face the task of acquiring some of the necessary ingredients for success from the international scene. A successful integration of geographically-restricted and global networks of production and innovation is likely to be the key to the achievement of local and regional competitiveness in the 1990s.' (p. 118-119).

The dynamics of local and regionally-based networks are, therefore, providing an entry route for local innovative SMEs to global networks of information and knowledge. As the prevalence of mobile capital has increased the presence of large global companies, so networking capacity has facilitated the creation of learning regions (Storper, 1994; Florida, 1995; Asheim, 1996b), or global regions (Huggins, 1997), that are able to integrate geographically-restricted economies into the global web of industry and commerce. Florida (1995) argues that these learning regions are becoming focal points for knowledge creation and learning in the new age of global and knowledge-intensive capitalism. However, as Tödtling (1994) reminds us, it should be borne in mind that empirical evidence concerning the local embedding of firms, and its role in the innovation process, is still very limited; and in contrast to some of the 'findings' of what he refers to as the more 'euphoric' literature, there seems to be relatively few substantiated cases of 'milieu-driven' innovative regions.

Probably the most rigorously argued empirical study of the relationship between more localised and globalised factors and economic prosperity has come not from economic geography but the discipline of business and strategic management. Porter's (1990) study of firms in ten nations argues that the most successful companies are increasingly interacting with the external environment and gaining competitive advantage through innovation, which he sees as improvements manifested in product and process changes, new approaches to marketing and distribution, and new conceptions of scope. Within his framework, Porter (1990) defines four locational determinants of competitive advantage: (1) factor conditions (for example: skills; infrastructure; R&D; capital); (2) demand conditions; (3) related and supporting industries; and (4) strategy structure and rivalry.

Porter's (1990) model is based around national systems of competitive advantage, however, he argues that proximity is important and that localities and regions are in many ways more important than the nation as a locus of competitive advantage. Furthermore, in a period of heightened global competition, a competitive home base becomes more important to companies than ever before (Porter, 1990; Harrison, 1994; Rosenfeld, 1997a). Although Porter (1990) advocates that to be successful in international markets, firms must first develop the knack of competing domestically (Robertson and Langlois, 1995), his focus on key factor conditions and the availability of related and support industries points to the importance of a significant degree of linkage and interchange. Indeed, Porter (1990) further argues that the most successful industries within a nation will usually be linked through vertical - buyer/supplier - or horizontal - common customers, technology channels, etc. - relationships that operate most efficiently when industries are geographically agglomerated in what he terms 'clusters'.

Porter's (1990) notion of industrial or sector specific clusters of concentrated economic activity has proved to be a highly popular concept, particularly within economic geography, with their dynamics often being overlapped with the discourse of industrial districts. For example, Rosenfeld (1997a) indicates the importance of social capital within clusters, and the ability for people to work together for common purpose via a 'social glue'. This social glue enables firms to operate in a local production system and simultaneously be part of a global economy, which results in clusters, like products, having life cycles. In his study of regional clusters, Enright (1996) argues that recent literature on clusters and localised industries has virtually ignored the fact that many clusters of firms and industries that do succeed for a time will eventually fail. Enright (1996) further contends that much of the recent work in economic geography has become overly concerned with factors such as trust, social capital, cultural similarities, and community cohesiveness, to the point where any economic explanations are given increasingly short shrift. In particular, Enright (1996) suggests that transaction frameworks integrating the type of instrumental trust highlighted by game theorists, whereby reputational effects and the potential for sanctions are invoked to explain the limits to opportunistic behaviour, have been overlooked to the detriment of Porter's (1990) original model.

## Entrepreneurship

Clusters are seen to serve as a spawning ground for new entrepreneurs, who are linked by a strong 'professional culture' and are likely to depend on a local network of colleagues, suppliers, clients, servicing firms, and financial organisations (de Vet, 1993; Storper, 1993). In recent years, the study of entrepreneurship has increasingly reflected the general agreement that entrepreneurs and new companies must engage in networks to survive. Also, it is accepted that the socio-economic climate in which entrepreneurs operate will vary their ability 'to capture the benefits of economic efficiency' that networks facilitate (Szarka, 1990). Johannisson (1995), for instance, found evidence that entrepreneurs situated in innovative settings are more successful at building networks that blend business and social concerns through both individual dyadic ties, and larger socio-centric contextual networks at large. In particular, research on the networking behaviour of entrepreneurs has tended to focus on personal-social and professional networks as contributing to the success potential of a venture (Birley, 1985; Aldrich and Zimmer, 1986). Entrepreneurship models of networking have mainly incorporated social network and resource-dependence theories, as well as a 'resource-based view' of the entrepreneur. For example, as Ostgaard and Birley (1996) have recently contended:

> '...entrepreneurs of a new venture gather access to critical resources which, for a variety of reasons, the new firm does not possess internally. Consequently, this research has argued that this resource base cannot be ignored when attempting to understand the relationship between the resources a new firm has at its disposal and the subsequent growth of the firm.' (p. 45).

Network perspectives are, therefore, seen as contributing to explaining patterns of entrepreneurship, by which it is the social role and embedded social context that facilitate or inhibit the activities of entrepreneurs (Aldrich and Zimmer, 1986). The action oriented nature of this networking, entailing making contact and building relationships with other individuals, is necessarily dynamic, focusing on new venture development that shifts network building from the 'start-up network', consisting mainly of social relationships, to the growing network where professional networks predominate (Aldrich and Zimmer, 1986; Birley and Cromie, 1988; Ostgaard and Birley, 1996). According to Birley (1985), this is typified by gradual transformation from the use of informal networks - of family, friends, previous colleagues and employers, etc. - to more formal networks - of banks, accountants, lawyers, the local chamber of commerce, etc. Ostgaard and Birley (1996) further suggest that the most successful entrepreneurs tend to have denser networks in terms of the 'percentage of strangers' involved, i.e. highlighting the importance of weak ties to entrepreneurs. Therefore, as Schneider and Teske (1995) argue, networks appear to matter to entrepreneurs because they create efficiencies in assembling the resources necessary in the entrepreneurial process.

In a sense, entrepreneurial activities are one of the most visible examples of economic transactions occurring neither through discrete market exchanges or vertical administration, but via repeated interaction and mutually supportive action. Trust undoubtedly plays an important role in this process, particularly as entrepreneurs often need to assemble teams in an efficient manner, establishing good communication flows and high levels of commitment during short time periods, due to the uncertainty inherent to the tasks at hand (Schneider and Teske, 1995). Successful entrepreneurs, therefore, appear to possess and engender the type of 'swift trust' discussed by Meyerson et al. (1996).

In general, there are still few empirical studies of the impact of network formation on the success of entrepreneurship and the growth of a small businesses. Examples of those studies that have been undertaken include Donckels and Lambrecht's (1995) work on small firms and their communication with the external environment. They conclude that network development is necessarily related to economic growth, particularly networks involving the gathering and dissemination of information (Donckels and Lambrecht, 1995). Bryson et al. (1993) have shown that in order to survive and compete successfully with large companies, small business service firms must occupy a web of well-developed demand- and supply-related networks. They further found that the nurturing of these networks was an important element in the recent growth within the business services sector (Bryson et al., 1993). Also, Greve's (1995) empirical study of entrepreneurs confirms the importance of social networks, whereby entrepreneurs use their non-business specific relationships for mobilising resources, getting support and help, and establishing viable business relations. As Gibb (1993) highlights, these factors indicate that entrepreneurs are often more tied to their 'local organising context' than business actors within larger corporations. In this respect, it can be argued that the 'logic of collective action' developed by Olson (1965) has a particular relevance for entrepreneurs, particularly as evolutionary thinking on innovation indicates that it is most successfully undertaken through collective rather than individual action. However, as Olson (1965) indicates the 'problem' of collective action is that:

> ....unless the number of individuals is quite small, or unless there is coercion or some other special device to make individuals act in their common interest, rational, self-interested individuals will not act to achieve their common or group interests' (p. 2).

Olson's (1965) dilemma brings us almost full circle back to debates concerning neo-classical versus socially embedded theories of economic behaviour. However, undoubtedly one of the key prosaic factors hindering collective economic action, through networks, is that such networks do not emerge overnight. It can often be a daunting task to make the necessary contacts, with the setting-up of an efficient network requiring considerable resources in terms of effort, time and money. In other words, as Sako (1992) has recognised, the high set-up costs of 'investing in trust' may initially be detrimental to efficiency, with transaction costs possibly increasing in the short-term, acting as a deterrent to firms pursuing more lucrative and common interests. These factors have been a source of perplexity for those public policy makers and institutions that have attempted to launch initiatives to strengthen the position and growth potential of individual entrepreneurs and firms through the development of networks that focus, primarily, on learning and the exchange of experience and knowledge at both a local level and beyond.

## Public Policy Intervention

As academics have sought to study inter-firm network structures, policy makers have become increasingly concerned with the role that institutional infrastructure can play in the facilitation of networks as a tool for stimulating economic development. Networks of this type are by no means a new phenomenon, and the idea of networking itself is not new, with businesses having always practised some form of networking, such as in bidding consortia, buying clubs, business forums, trade associations and other private sector clubs that have existed for hundreds of years. However, it is argued that despite the existence of such groups, there is a general absence of a supportive inter-firm culture in many states at either the national, regional or local level (Hirst and Zeitlin, 1989; Fukuyama, 1995). It is, therefore, only recently that public policy makers have begun to consider systematically and positively the potential of inter-firm network generation as an agent for economic development. In many respects, inter-firm networks have been offered as a possible 'blueprint' for economic success, if adopted in a context that balances both co-operation and competition (Staber, 1996a).

## The Context of Network Policy

The popularisation of inter-firm networks as a specific response to economic development issues is highlighted by the growing public policy interest in stimulating business co-operation in a number of states and regions in Europe, the United Sates and beyond. Governments have used a variety of methods to encourage networking, with the common thread being a concern for an institutional infrastructure that facilitates information and knowledge exchange and limits opportunistic behaviour. In particular, as Lundvall and Johnson (1994) emphasise, there has been a focus on the ways that public policy can strengthen the means, incentives and capability to learn. As well as the more obvious policies of increasing investment in education and training, Lundvall and Johnson (1994) further point to public sector support for projects concerning networks and co-operation as being a systematic way of increasing the capability to learn; in particular, programmes relating to 'best practice' and 'benchmarking' that attempt to diffuse the experience of 'lead' to 'laggard' firms. Also, it is SMEs that have increasingly become the focus of attention from public policy makers, as it has become recognised that it is these firms that suffer most from a lack of interaction, at both a formal and informal level, with sources of knowledge and innovation (Giaoutzi et al., 1988).

Essentially, the policy concept has been that SMEs should form networks, based around processes of group formation and institution building that stimulate experience exchange, in particular the promotion of collaboration in areas of management and production know-how, facilitating increased competitiveness (Indergaard, 1996). In general, it is local, community and regional development agencies and corporations that have taken the key role in mediating these new networks supporting both existing indigenous businesses and stimulating new entrepreneurship. The participating agencies, and their personnel, have come to be viewed as brokers of networks, adopting either a non-direct and/or prescriptive approach to developing the personal contacts that are manifold to the needs of businesses (Cromie et al., 1993).

The context of the policy interest in inter-firm networks can be traced to firstly, the influence and inspiration of the craft-based industrial districts of the Third Italy, or what has been termed the 'epicentre of the network system' (Harrison, 1994; Pyke, 1994). Secondly, it is rooted in the widespread popularisation of the work of Porter (1990) on 'The

Competitive Advantage of Nations', which stressed that the most economically successful nations have firms embedded in clustered and innovative networks (Fahrenkrog, 1994). The emphasis on localised inter-firm networks and clusters has, according to Humphries (1996), led to the territorialisation of economic development policy. Wilson (1995) has further suggested that a shift in policy has occurred from the logic of exogenous business development to an endogenous approach, moving from regional and national planning policies that emphasise factor costs, to a more finely tuned attention to territory as the clustering ground of social relations. However, while Fahrenkrog (1994) agrees that policy approaches should be an organic process of fine tuning relations, he argues that in effect initiatives have usually consisted of a very ad-hoc combination of many types of policy instruments, with a tendency towards a preoccupation with establishing clusters and networks of high technology firms.

These cluster initiatives have often been termed 'technopole' developments, after the French dirigiste science park tradition (Cooke and Morgan, 1994a). They have generally been associated with attempts to implant innovative clusters, that replicate technology and knowledge centres such as Silicon Valley, Route 128 and the successful science parks of Japan, in under-performing regions (Cooke et al., 1995). These attempts have failed more often than not, usually as a result of the nodes of the potential technopole - universities, research institutes, training and technology transfer agencies, banks, firms, etc. - remaining strategically isolated, or non-networked, despite being in the same geographical vicinity. As Castells and Hall (1994) have concluded, technopoles initiatives have usually consisted of:

> 'A hasty, hurried study by an opportunistic consultant......to provide the magic formula: a small dose of venture capital, a University (invariably termed a 'technology Institute'), fiscal and institutional incentives to attract high-technology firms, and a degree of support for small business. All this, wrapped within the covers of a glossy brochure, and illustrated by a sylvan landscape with a futuristic name, would create the right conditions to out-perform the neighbours, to become the locus of the new major global industrial centre. The world is now littered with the ruins of all too many such dreams that have failed, or have yielded meagre results at far too high a cost.' (p. 8).

## The Danish Network Programme

Despite this gloomy conclusion to high-tech related developments, in which it appears that policy makers have attempted to imitate without innovating, other network and cluster initiatives, based around the more traditional Emilia-Romagna model, have continued to be implemented in countries that include Denmark, Spain, Portugal, Norway, United States, Canada, New Zealand, Australia, as well as the United Kingdom. Undoubtedly, the most well known example to date is that of Denmark. Through the intervention of the Danish Government a programme was introduced in 1989 that attempted to replicate the organisational order of firms that had emerged organically in the Third Italy. The initiative consisted of the introduction of a brokerage system to act as the key node in facilitating company co-operation. Evaluation of this programme has generally been positive, and has stressed the success of raising awareness of 'networking philosophies' as well as the growth of many participating firms (Pyke, 1994; Huggins, 1996). However, the actual number of firms actively involved in networks has been disputed, and the programme has developed not without its problems and critics (Pyke, 1992). Some of the problems with regard to evaluation have included difficulties in undertaking meaningful analysis due to a lack of rigorous methodological procedures, in particular concerning the constitution of success or failure and the time periods that should pass before significant results could be expected.

The key element of the Danish network programme consisted of a three-year £15 million government subsidy to encourage network co-operation among SMEs, designed to have a maximum short-term effect on awareness, and to promote networks by providing 'seed money' incentives to firms that participated in a number of phases of network formation from 'feasibility' to 'implementation'. Essential to the formation and success of networks was seen to be the 'network brokers' who: (1) identified network opportunities; (2) brought potential partners together; (3) administered new co-operation areas, new network participants, new market opportunities; and (4) mediated co-operation through the critical planning and agreement phases.

In total, the recruitment and training of 40 industry advisers was undertaken - from banks, accountants, lawyers, private consultants - who subsequently undertook the role of network brokers and were crucial in gaining a positive initial response to the programme. It is estimated that approximately 3,000 Danish companies were involved in submitting proposals to the programme, and that in the period 1989-1992 approximately 150 networks were funded through an implementation phase, with more than 80 reaching the 'production' phase (Gelsing, 1992). The nature of the networks created by the programme varied considerably, characterised by a mix of: (1) information exchange or knowledge networks with a low degree of interaction between the firms; (2) networks involving companies that wished to take advantage of marketing economies of scope, whereby firms try to reduce their transaction costs to reach end markets; (3) more ambitious innovation-led networks with projects aimed at the joint development of new products (Pyke, 1994; Huggins, 1996).

Evaluation of the Danish programme indicate that 42 per cent of participating firms had increased turnover by 4 per cent or more per year, and one in five by 10 per cent or more since joining a network (Gelsing and Knop, 1991; Cooke, 1994). However, this evaluation appears to have taken little account of dead-weight factors and other potential externalities. Beyond the three year subsidy stage, Gelsing (1992) has estimated an annual death-rate of 10 per cent in the total number of networks. However, another unsubstantiated, and debatable, figure has suggested that an estimated 1,000 companies have subsequently entered networks without applying for grants from the programme (Jakobsen and Martinussen, 1991). Perhaps, one of the most important and telling institutional evaluative insights into the programme is the fact that the Danish Government has since shifted its network policy from a system based on localised brokers and formal network development to one in which government agencies, in particular the Danish Technological Institute, themselves act as brokers in facilitating less formal linkages. These linkages involve 'open forums' of indigenous firms and relevant partners, primarily in the area of technology development and administered at a more global level (for example involving companies and organisations in the United States), from which it is hoped that more formalised networks will eventually evolve (Huggins, 1996).

The Emilia-Romagna model has further acted as the inspiration for policy developments in Portugal and Valencia (Spain) where local technical institutes and service centres, affiliated to employers associations, have become catalysts of collaborative relationships between mainly small firms (Pyke, 1994). In other European regions networking has become an implicit feature of economic regeneration policies. For example, in North-Rhine-Westphalia (Germany) there has been a focus on technology policy creating a strategy of innovating through networking, with both private and public sector technology centres acting as gateways to 'dense knowledge networks' (Huggins and Thomalla, 1995). Also, in Baden-Wurttemberg (Germany) chambers of commerce, that act as strong employer associations with significant assets, have become as a key mechanism through which firms are brought into collaborative relationships (Hassink, 1992; Cooke and Morgan, 1994b). As Pyke (1994) notes, within Europe new developments in the field of inter-firm co-operation have been a mix of both formal programmes, such as in Denmark, and those initiatives that have been introduced on an ad hoc basis and have not been integrated with other development policies. It has been suggested that network policy aimed at the regeneration of the less-favoured regions of Europe, whether stand-alone or part of integrated economic development strategy, may prove to be an exercise that is ultimately both too costly and time-consuming for all involved (Amin, 1993). However, as Bennett (1996) has found, even the relatively 'weak' chambers of commerce in the United Kingdom offer significant transaction cost gains for firms participating in their activities, which if built upon could become an important economic development tool.

*The USNet Initiative*

In the US, the Danish model became the pathfinder for a programme to create networks in 15 states, organised around a top-down model of broker training - prospective brokers being identified by state economic development agencies (Malecki and Tootle, 1997). The 'USNet' initiative began operation in 1995 as a national consortium of state-based manufacturing assistance organisations and the US National Institute of Standards and Technology's (NIST) Manufacturing Extension Partnership (MEP). The desired aim of USNet is to build the capacity of its partners to promote inter-firm collaboration that strengthens the competitiveness of SMEs. The initiative has operated on fairly modest resources, with a mix of state and federal matched funding, and in a fashion similar to the Danish programme has focused on developing formal and organised networks, with a defined membership and internal structure, among a relatively small group of firms that share specific interests and objectives (Bosworth, 1997; Rosenfeld, 1997b). Outside of USNet there has also been growing momentum towards networking and collaborative policies, that stimulate entrepreneurship among embryonic technology-based firms, through the increasing prevalence of small business incubators (Carlisle, 1993). Studies of incubators in the US have found that networking positively contributes to increased technical and managerial capabilities, as well as widening market scope and reducing operation costs through: (1) resource exchanges involving products, commodities and labour; (2) competence exchanges involving the sharing of skills and knowledge; (3) exchanges involving mutual support through encouragement, or simply the proximity of individuals with similar interests and problems (Carlisle, 1993). According to Malecki and Tootle (1997), it is the state of Oregon that has taken the largest overall step towards the development of networks, particularly through its Key Industries Programme designed to increase international competitiveness in 27 clustered sectors.

Returning to USNet, it has proved difficult to estimate the total number of networks generated, although Shapira (1997) suggests that it has fallen short of an implied 3-year goal of approximately 300 networks. The most detailed evaluation of USNet, and perhaps of inter-firm network initiatives in general, is that of Welch et al. (1997) who found the typical net benefit of network participation to be a meagre $10,000 per firm over a 2-3 year period. Although network member companies reported an average net increase of 4.7 jobs as a result of network participation, the bulk of employment changes occurred at a very small number of firms, with the majority experiencing no net change. Information sharing was seen by firms as the primary network objective, with less than a third of firms stating that network participation had a 'strong positive effect' on economic performance (Welch et al., 1997). Nevertheless, 51 per cent and 38 per cent of respondents, respectively, attributed improved skills on the part of their management staff and employees to network participation (Welch et al., 1997). Welch et al. (1997) suggest that positive experiences with informal discussions, and seminars and other soft network activities, are for many firms a necessary antecedent to 'harder' higher-commitment relationships that have the potential to generate the most significant impacts. In 68 per cent of cases, network members were located within a 50 mile radius of one another. Those companies that undertook on-site visits and shared special technical capacities with other firms were approximately three times more likely, than firms that had not engaged in such activities, to report 'strong positive' impacts (Kingsley and Klein, 1998; Welch et al., 1997).

Reflecting on these results, Rosenfeld (1997b) suggests that USNet has suffered from a lack of groundswell support or long-term funding streams due to too little attention being paid to educating policy makers and key potential private sector supporters. He also contends that any new initiatives should turn their attention from the facilitation of formal and organised networks, to more soft networks that can be nurtured as 'wellsprings for hard networks' (Rosenfeld, 1997b). Malecki and Tootle (1997) contend that the most successful US generated networks are those that have community entrepreneurs as their brokers, who have taken on roles outside and larger than the network itself, and who view inter-firm networking as just one of several mechanisms for generating and maintaining economic development. Gittell and Kaufman (1996) have further found that the promotion of manufacturing services in the US is best facilitated by political entrepreneurs that can foster social learning and the creation of social capital.

Outside of Europe and the US, Perry (1995) has reported the promotion of joint action groups (JAGS) in New Zealand as the basis for co-operation in overseas market development for more than twenty indigenous sectors. However, Perry (1995) states that the JAG experiment has been frustrated in many sectors by 'historic mistrust' among firms and 'uncommitted fringe membership'. Perry (1995) suggests that it would be sensible to encourage the evolution of JAGs into broader industry development initiatives, enabling the capture of linkages between exporters and supporting industry services, and allowing groups to diversify their activities. Furthermore, Perry and Goldfinch's (1996) study of a regional development agency in New Zealand found that it had not had any great effect in directly assisting network formation, primarily due to a lack of targeted support and education about networks. In Australia a formal business network programme has been operated by the Department of Industry, Science, and Tourism since 1995, claiming to be currently facilitating more than 250 network projects (Dean and Frost, 1997).

## Building Networks

As Rosenfeld (1996) makes clear, efforts to evaluate and assess network policies are still in their infancy, and although there are a growing number of local, regional and national efforts to encourage and accelerate inter-firm collaboration there have been few systematic studies of their impact, thus:

> '.......in the absence of hard data, policy makers rely on claims of effects and outcomes based on anecdotal evidence. Some of this undoubtedly has been exaggerated to influence policy and grant makers but some also is understated because network members do not report (or may not even realise) all of the ways in which working more closely with peers affects their operations.' (Rosenfeld, 1996, p. 247-248).

Indeed, what actually constitutes the success of networks is still open to debate. For example, Staber (1996a) has suggested that economic growth is only one of several indicators of success, and that from a sociological-institutional perspective the performance of a business network is only indirectly linked to economic efficiency, more immediately including indicators such as conformity, trust, flexibility and reciprocity, and co-operation. Staber (1996a) rightly questions whether or not such variables should be treated as measures of network performance or as factors explaining relative effectiveness. Within a business environment it appears that although network participants may have 'multiple goals and constituencies', bottom-line performance will in most circumstances be necessarily economically-related. Nevertheless, the possibility does exist that involvement may purely concern factors relating to social capital building, without 'economic forethought', such as overcoming isolation, seeking acceptance or improving ones position in the business and/or social community. However, social capital building can also be used as an economic tool, and is, according to Rosenfeld (1996), perhaps the least visible but most undervalued contributor to local economic development. Rosenfeld (1996) adds, that policy intervention should directly provide incentives to activate local business and civic associations as a means of increasing the stock of social capital. Wilson (1996; 1997) describes the 'nuts and bolts' of social capital as being communication and relationship skills, involving attributes such as listening, understanding, respecting, empathy and honesty. Interestingly, Putnam (1995) has shown that some public policy measures actually impinge on social capital formation, and he highlights the example of the American slum-clearance policy of the 1950s and 1960s which renovated physical capital, but at a very high cost to existing social capital.

As has already been suggested, the most effective way to develop social capital, in a network policy sense, may be via empowering a broker or local development animateur who also acts a community or civic entrepreneur, seeking to build partnerships, find resources and link personal networks (Gibb, 1993). So far, the most stable policy-induced networks have been those that have pursued relatively modest and limited initial goals, beginning with activities around which inter-firm co-operation is relatively easy to induce (for example: an export and international market focus). The hope being that some early success from relatively short-term and superficial activities will build up commitment to co-operation (Gertler and Rutherford, 1996). Rosenfeld (1996) summarises some of the practical barriers that have been encountered in establishing both informal and more formal structures as: (1) the high start-up investment in terms of both time and resources that is often necessary; (2) defining projects that appeal to the self-interest of all involved; (3) an inherent distrust on the part of firms of government policy; (4) a lack of vision by both public and private sector participants; (5) ensuring a critical mass of the 'right' people. As Kingsley and Klein (1998) indicate, the 'right' people partly concerns the involvement of sufficiently empowered employees, i.e. those that are able to make decisions on behalf of their company. Brusco (1996) suggests that although it is undoubtedly impossible to simply copy the Italian districts model, lessons can be learnt and that projects involving firms in benchmarking, best practice and the like can foster the type of trust generated in these districts through processes of peer review and sanction.

It is recognised that to emulate the Italian model in total involves far more than generating networks of small companies, but also the whole well-oiled social and cultural infrastructure and communal support system (OECD, 1992; Rosenfeld, 1997b). Commentators such as Amin (1993) remain sceptical as to the merits of network policies as a 'growth model', arguing that such policies will be unable to sweep aside local traditions that resist change, highlighted by the 'dismal failure' of strategies to promote technopoles in the less favoured regions in Europe. Amin (1993) concludes that the development prospects of the majority of localities will become increasingly tied to their position in relation to different international corporate networks, and that as such local business networks will remain a privilege enjoyed by only a small number of regional economies. To an extent the network theory literature confirms Amin's (1993) assertion, as it has been shown that it is utopian to view networks as a 'harmonious collaboration and concord' (Grabher, 1993), with the concept of power, in particular, often playing an important and significant role in exchanges patterns within international corporate networks.

Gertler and Rutherford (1996) argue that public policy intervention will encounter difficulties in many localities and regions due to strongly ingrained competitive instincts, fostered by tight local markets. Indeed, it is now generally accepted that there will undoubtedly be problems concerning the 'transferability' of growth models, due to specific regional and national cultures and social structures, with the result being that they cannot 'mechanistically' be transferred to other locations (Hudson et al., 1997). Most critically, perhaps, Appold (1995) has argued that policy prescription concerning spatial agglomeration and inter-firm networks is premature, misguided and lacking in empirical support. However, it appears that some commentators have 'lumped' agglomeration policies and network policies into one concept. Therefore, while a mix of agglomeration and networks may turn into what Powell and Smith-Doerr (1994) refers to as the 'ties that blind' - essentially 'lock-in' leading to parochialism - policy intervention that also incorporates the development of wider global networks may alleviate the possibility of entropy. For example, Forsgren et al. (1995) suggest that policies must be designed to create the conditions allowing domestic firms, and firms within domestic networks, to link with international networks. In general, however, there is still very little is known about the role that network policy can play in economies.

## Conclusions

Debates concerning the socialisation of the economy have been vociferously joined by economic geographers, many of whom have contended that space and place, in particular agglomerative forces, are important factors not only for network development but also as wider factors concerning economic prosperity. It is argued that concepts such as untraded interdependencies have been crucial in aiding certain localities and regions to attain or maintain competitive advantage in an era of so-called post-Fordist production, characterised by a shift away from the dominance of large hierarchical organisations to smaller more efficient organisations operating in a networked fashion.

Although the importance of both small firms and locally or regionally focused networks has been disputed, in part due to an over-reliance on a small number of case study areas that have been 'outpaced' by conceptual theorising, it has been empirically shown that networks and networking positively contribute to patterns of entrepreneurship. Furthermore, to counter-arguments concerning the possible 'entropic' and 'locked-in' nature of spatially defined networks, the importance of global linkages and networks, in particular relationships between the local and the global, have grown in prominence. Nevertheless, the majority of network developments resulting from public policy intervention have been designed to support locally focused initiatives.

In general, many of the networks implanted through policy intervention have had difficulty sustaining operations. This is partly related to the fact that many of the participating firms cannot afford the high-degree of 'trust' resources identified by Sako (1992). The literature is still unclear whether proximity reduces or increases the cost of these resources. In effect, the management and operation of successful inter-firm networks requires both co-operation and competition, that can provide simultaneous routes to competitive advantage. Baker (1994) describes this successful management and operation as 'networking smart', involving intelligence, resourcefulness and ethical means.

Finally, it seems that publicly induced or implanted networks cannot implicitly be said to reduce transaction costs in the short-term, as the activities of firms in such networks are usually additional and new to their normal operations, i.e. the firms would not necessarily buy, sell or produce the outputs of their network activities. However, if the activities of these networks are continued over a significant period their cessation may result in increased transaction costs for participants, as they attempt to substitute the outputs of the networks via a non-networked market or hierarchical approach. The following chapter examines the relevant literature in order to assess how TECs, as institutional policy agents in the UK, have attempted to instil such a networked approach, at both an inter-firm and a more general level, within their framework of local economic development activity.

# 4 TECs and their Network Policies - The Early Years

## Introduction

The almost eclectic agenda and nature of the responsibilities of TECs resulted in their study quickly becoming 'salami-sliced' by academic researchers and other commentators into numerous interrelated sub-disciplines of economics, politics, geography and social policy. However, TECs were first and foremost introduced to assist the regeneration of local economies through an emphasis on training and enterprise development, and a core of relevant literature was generated in relation to this issue. This chapter reviews this literature in order to assess the emergence of TECs during the early 1990s as facilitators of local economic development, and how this was approached through the creation of local networks. Facilitating involved encouraging other institutions, from both the private and public sector, to participate and undertake activities, thus producing a multiplier effect. Therefore, the capacity of a TEC to lever change, through its role as a facilitator, was to a large extent dependent on the commitment to such changes by other local organisations (Bennett et al., 1994).

An important feature of the emergent system of local governance in the UK was the focus on new mechanisms for development that were to be undertaken by a wide range of individuals and organisations (Hart et al., 1996). Within this system the local economic development role of TECs was primarily to create enabling and stimulating infrastructure for regeneration. According to the Department for Education and Employment (DFEE, 1995a) the role of TECs in economic development was essentially two-fold. First, to act as strategic partners with responsibility for generating and implementing a shared framework for development; and second, to act as developers, deliverers, funders and influencers, responsible for ensuring the effective provision of specific initiatives within this framework. Both of these factors emphasise TECs as both players within, and catalysts of, networks. It is of interest to note that the dual role allocated to TECs is to be continued under the Labour Government within the structure of the Learning and Skills Councils, the Small Business Service and the regional development agencies throughout England. In the context of this chapter the network, or networking, forms examined consist of both the inter-firm types, already outlined, and the linkages with and between public sector bodies and intermediary organisations, predominantly at a local or regional level, that may pool specific resources.

## Emergence, Structure and Change

The system of TECs was announced by the then Conservative Government in the 1988 White Paper 'Employment for the 1990s' (Employment Department, 1988), with a phased introduction of 82 TECs in England and Wales (subsequently reduced to 76 with the bankruptcy of South Thames TEC, and the merger of TECs in both Wales and London) between April 1990 and October 1991 (Bennett et al., 1994). In Scotland, a system of 22 Local Enterprise Companies (LECs) was also launched, essentially similar in nature to TECs but vested with additional responsibilities and funding for economic development activities. Charged with contracting with the Government 'to plan and deliver training and to promote and support the development of small businesses and self-employment in their area' (Employment Department, 1988, p. 40), TECs were marketed by the Government as institutions of a hybrid nature operating as private companies with a public role (Employment Committee, 1996). In many respects, the introduction of TECs was an encapsulation of the Thatcherite market-led approach to economic policy, with the intention of ownership, control and responsibility for the system of training and enterprise support in the UK being placed with employers at a local level. Thus, they claimed to remove bureaucratic red tape and stimulate innovation (Peck, 1993; Peck and Jones, 1995). The representation of TECs as the epitome of the 'radical Thatcherite' reforms of the late 1980s (Jessop, 1991) was coupled with accusations of a lack of accountability similar to that directed at the emergence of non-elected QUANGOs (quasi-autonomous non-governmental organisations) that have been given responsibility for activities that were previously regarded as the Government's domain (Hart et al., 1996; Peck and Jones, 1995).

The TEC model was partly based on the experience of Private Industry Councils (PICs) in the United States, with an emphasis on developing supply-side factors on labour market constraints and on endogenous growth within localities (Bennett and Krebs, 1991; Bennett et al., 1994). However, the validity of the structure and operation of PICs was quickly called to question through evidence suggesting that in the United States these organisations have become marginalised, only operating low budget programmes with little prominence given to a wider economic development role (Employment Committee, 1991). Indeed, this had a particular resonance for TECs, which the Conservative Government anticipated would act as catalysts for levering in private sector funds (Peck and Emmerich, 1993). The reality is that more than 95 per cent of TECs' income continued to come from Government sources. The rest sourced mainly through European-financed programmes (i.e. the European Regional Development Fund and the European Social Fund), with only the very small remaining proportion actually coming from employers and individuals (Employment Committee, 1996). As Hart et al. (1996) argue, this reliance on the national funding model meant that TECs' power lay predominantly in 'their ability to spend central government monies largely to a central government agenda, but with some areas of local discretion' (p. 430), thus weakening their ability to engage in local functions. Despite the obvious gulf between the rhetoric and practices of TECs, they were cast as institutions 'emblematic' of a post-Fordist approach to state policy (Peck and Jones, 1995). This approach was exemplified by a change in decision making processes from hierarchical and top-down (i.e. typical of former central-local government relations) to networks and alliances of organisations incorporated into an emerging system of local governance, with TECs occupying a relatively privileged position (Hart et al., 1996).

TECs were envisaged by the Conservative Government as contributing to employer investment in skills, fostering economic growth and the regeneration of communities, through a focus on five key principles governing organisation and management: employer-led; locally based; focus upon community revitalisation; an accent on performance; and enterprise driven (Bazalgette et al., 1994). In practice these principles were implemented through an institutional framework consisting of a board of directors (two-thirds of whom must be local business leaders), with spatial demarcation relating mainly to counties and metropolitan district boundaries, staffed primarily by seconded civil service personnel and operating as private companies limited by guarantee. The initial operating portfolio was mainly concerned with adapting former government programmes, many of which had previously been administered by the Training Agency (formerly the Manpower Services Commission). Programmes such as Youth Training and Employment Training (these two accounting for by far the largest share of TEC budgets), Business Growth Training, Enterprise Allowance Scheme, Small Firms Service, Training Access Points and Work-Related Further Education formed the backbone of TEC services, with the majority being sub-contracted to local providers.

The Scottish LECs were given a wider remit and as well as administering similar programmes to TECs they have additional responsibilities for physical development and infrastructures programmes transferred from the former Scottish Development Agency (SDA) and the former Highlands and Islands Development Board (HIDB). These responsibilities consist of the provision of business sites and premises; environmental renewal and derelict land; advice and information including inward investment; and business development finance for use as working capital, management buy-outs and other business development (Bennett et al., 1994).

The expectations and ambitious objectives for TECs to become more sensitive and business-oriented than predecessor bodies led to the specification of a management structure that was not only highly prescribed but also a key factor in empowering business into government programmes (Bennett et al., 1994; Hart et al., 1996). This structure was undoubtedly more employer-led than former incarnations with the board, sub-boards and membership schemes of TECs providing a communication link with local firms. The role of a TEC board involved: providing strategy and ideas; heading up sector groups/area boards; acting as 'ambassadors' for the TEC; sponsoring TEC events; acting as examples of good practice; passing on expertise to TEC staff; and providing contacts from their respective industries and networks (Crowley-Bainton, 1993). Although the Government did not have any role in the appointment of TEC board directors it maintained a right of veto over the appointment of TEC Chairmen (Employment Committee, 1996). A TEC board consisted of 15 members, 10 of whom must be from the private sector. Vaughan (1993) found that on average TEC boards consisted of 1 member from a company with less than 10 employees, 1 from a company with 10-24 employees, 3 from companies with 25-199 employees, and 5 from companies with more than 200 employees. Sub-board structures and memberships schemes were a further and broader means of involving community 'stakeholders', from the private and voluntary sectors, in the activities of particular TECs (Hart et al., 1996). Haughton et al. (1995a) criticised those TECs whose sub-boards and membership schemes privileged business interests over non-economic interests, contending that such TECs were unlikely to establish a base within the locality necessary for accountability and openness to develop.

Although business leaders were brought on to TEC boards amidst the rhetoric of local business people 'knowing' the needs and aspiration of local businesses, a number of commentators pointed to an under-representation of local small firms, with the majority of private sector members coming from large or medium sized companies (Curran, 1993; Vaughan, 1993; Bennett et al., 1994; Haughton et al., 1995a; Adam-Smith and McGeever, 1995; Employment Committee, 1996). Vaughan's (1993) analysis indicated that 11 per cent of TECs actually had no board members from small companies, whilst Bennett et al. (1994) reported that only 15 per cent of directors came from companies with under 50 employees. Adam-Smith and McGeever (1995) argue, that although this lack of small firm representation was partly due to owner-managers lacking the time to become involved in such activities, it is nevertheless of concern in light of the fact that firms with less than 20 employees constitute 95 per cent of the total number of companies in the UK and account for more than a third of private sector employment.

Haughton et al. (1995a) found that the role of TEC boards changed very early on to incorporate a growing interest in the enterprise and local economic development aspects of TECs' remit, and as trust between TECs and other local partners and agencies, in particular local authorities, increased so did the institutional capacity of TECs (however, the actual evidence of this will be further discussed in chapter 6). A survey of TEC directors undertaken by Haughton et al. (1995a; 1995b) revealed that most directors found such 'external' roles far more rewarding than the operation of internal run-of-the-mill activities, with directors actively increasing their role in networking with other local partnership organisations in the economic development arena. Furthermore, a survey undertaken by the Financial Times (Financial Times, 10 May 1993, cited in Peck, 1993) indicated that 63 per cent of TEC directors saw local economic development as their top priority. Crowley-Bainton and Wolf (1994) argue that this led to a continuing tension between training promotion and economic/business development activities.

As the pressure to take economic development as the overarching framework for their activities became more and more explicit (Haughton et al., 1995b), these advances were recognised by the Conservative Government in its 1994 strategic guidance document to TECs, 'TECs: Towards 2000' (HM Government, 1994a). This document set an agenda for TECs to become actively involved in increasing the competitiveness of local economies through sustainable economic development and regeneration. The guidance was a clear indication that the Government saw TECs emerging as agencies with a similar scope to that of the Scottish LECs, or what may be better termed 'mini-development agencies'. The emphasis throughout the guidance was that TECs should form networks and partnerships with local institutions, from both the public and private sector, to 'broker' innovation and best practice activities for growth into local firms, primarily SMEs. In order to fund their local economic development role TECs used the money they received from the Department of Trade and Industry (DTI) for business support services and also what they receive through the Single Regeneration Budget (in Wales such funds are distributed through the Welsh Office). Originally, TECs had a small

Local Initiative Fund used to undertake projects for which they received no Government funding, however, in 1995 this fund was diverted to the Single Regeneration Budget (in Wales similar funds came through the Welsh Office and the continuance of the Local Initiative Fund) (Employment Committee, 1996)

## TECs as Institutions of Local Support

TECs differed from previous institutional mechanisms for enterprise and training development in that they were geographically rather than industry or sector based (Vickerstaff and Parker, 1995), with the Conservative Government contending that such an approach would result in a far more even pattern of the provision of business services (Bennett, 1995a). This focus on 'local empowerment' or 'local capacity building' (Bennett and McCoshan, 1993; Bennett et al., 1994) positioned TECs so that they had a potentially very powerful role, due to what Hart et al. (1996) state was 'their insertion into a highly politicised system of edge-of-state bodies which has emerged at the local and regional level in Britain' (p. 430). However, the ability of TECs to embed themselves locally, particularly during their early years, was the focus of much debate. Peck (1993) argued that, being government imposed, TECs were far from being institutions born of their local communities, and faced major difficulties in becoming integrated into the local economy and society. According to Bennett et al. (1994), TECs experienced major difficulties in founding themselves because of the actual concept and reality of local business communities in the UK being weakly developed. They further argue that the existence of such weaknesses, apart from a few major cities, are:

> 'in marked contrast to many other countries, notably the USA, Germany, France and Japan, where strong local business communities exist. These local business communities have been stimulated in the USA, and to a lesser extent in Germany, by the existence of a strong State/Länder level of government. Business has organised itself to address this level of government, and this has also stimulated local business commitment and community identity' (Bennett et al., 1994, p. 91).

There are obviously many difficulties in satisfactorily defining a local economy, and it can be questioned as to whether or not many of the geographical TEC boundaries coincide with the conception of a locality. Curran (1993) and Curran and Blackburn (1994) argued that in a business sense it is the perception of the owners and managers of indigenous firms, which are predominately small in size, that has the most meaningful sense as to the existence of local economies. According to their research findings, Curran and Blackburn (1994) claim that most small firms place little significance on the existence of the local economy as a focus of small firm business activities, particularly in relation to business-to-business networks. More generally, they point to an under-development of local economic networks in most areas, arguing that TECs substantially failed to meet one of their key objectives i.e. the business needs of local small firms. These arguments were taken further by Adam-Smith and McGeever (1995) whose study of one TEC in southern England led them to conclude that TECs were having a limited impact on the small business sector.

Writing particularly on the issue of TECs and small firm development, Vickerstaff and Parker (1995; Parker and Vickerstaff 1996) argue that small firms have traditionally not been the most receptive to support schemes designed to help them. They summarise the difficulties in 'reaching' small firms as: (1) the scepticism of small firms towards government initiatives; (2) the lack of resources in small businesses; (3) the fragmented and diverse needs of different small enterprises; (4) the fact that many small firms are not part of business community networks (5) the fragmented system of business support activities (Vickerstaff and Parker, 1995). Vickerstaff and Parker (1995) suggested that one of the key reasons for a 'knowledge gap' existing between TECs and small firms, is that the majority of firms are not part of established business networks and therefore have a high level of insularity. Such a barrier necessarily presents access problems to support organisations and varies so that 'those TECs which are the best networked, that is, have formal or regular links with a range of existing business and trade organisations, are most likely to be able to attract small-business interest' (Parker and Vickerstaff, 1996: p. 254).

It should be recognised that the problems TECs faced during their early years was exacerbated by the effects and after-effects of a period of economic recession. This period of economic instability meant that TECs did not capture what Haughton et al. (1995a) saw as their enormous scope for innovation, with the potential capacity to facilitate the emergence of the key characteristics of competitive economies, i.e. the ability of individuals and businesses to be flexible, to anticipate and adapt to change, and to innovate through increased application to the tasks of accessing information and assessing situations and opportunities (Field et al., 1995). During the mid-1990s a report by PA Cambridge Economic Consultants (PACEC, 1995) to the DTI implied that this potential could only be fulfilled by a period of stability, where TECs were able to consolidate their activities and develop their services. PACEC (1995) further argued that it would be counter-productive to undertake any widespread alteration of

TEC boundaries, as any administrative gains would be offset by the losses from a weakened local presence. Instead of altering TEC boundaries a more positive policy was seen to be the introduction of more 'satellite offices', particularly for those TECs which covered a large geographical area, making the 'local element' of support even more prominent.

## TEC Mechanisms for Economic Development

Although a key part of the original TEC mission was for them to act as catalysts and stimulators of local economic change (Bennett et al., 1994), a major reason behind their lack of stability was that their actual role rapidly spread beyond the policy areas for which they were initially given responsibility by the Conservative Government, without significant additional funding being made available to support this policy expansion. The Government confirmed this policy expansion in its document 'TECs: Towards 2000', which described the 'new' role of TECs as to:

> 'ensure effective private sector leadership within economic partnerships to contribute to the development of local strategies and growth targets, and lever in all forms of private resource ... [and also to] ... develop and implement local strategies for enhancing the competitiveness of people and business as central components of the overall vision for economic growth.' (HM Government, 1994a, p. 10).

A study undertaken by Rajan (1993) showed that the economic development activities that TECs were undertaking included business support, technology transfer, local sourcing, export promotion, inward investment and finance support, with TECs forging partnerships with local authorities, firms and other bodies that led to the formation of local economic forums and collaborative ventures. However, the prevalence and effectiveness of such initiatives was still unknown.

Cay Stratton, one of the chief government advisors in the implementation stage of TECs, recognised at the outset that if the TEC movement:

> '...... is to be a catalyst for change, if it is to influence people and institutions beyond its immediate control, the TEC must be broadly perceived as an objective intermediary organisation. It must be convenor, facilitator, broker, the builder of coalitions and networks' (cited in Bennett et al., 1994, p. 299).

Bennett et al. (1994) indeed provided evidence that this view of TECs as primarily agents to improve linkage and networking was consistent with how other local bodies generally view the enterprise role of TECs. In more recent years few empirical studies of the local economic development activities of TECs have appeared (with research fashion switching to the study of Business Links as discussed later in this chapter and in chapter 6). However, the PACEC study published in 1995 found the development of new services to be an ongoing activity for TECs, gaining in importance as economic development increasingly came to the fore as the TECs' overriding policy concern. The main services introduced related to (in order of importance): technology and innovation; exporting; diagnostic health checks; quality/standards; information technology; management workshops; manufacturing competitiveness initiatives (including purchasing and sourcing); and business angels/financing (seed-corn and venture capital) (PACEC, 1995). In terms of the performance and output of TEC services, PACEC estimated that allowing for displacement, a local level expenditure on services of £4,380 generated one net additional job, and every £1 of expenditure generated £16.5 of additional turnover. However, it should be borne in mind that these figures are undoubtedly subject to a wide margin of error.

As well as the services funded by the DTI, TECs provide other services support to local firms. The most important of these initiatives was Investors in People (IiP), which was undertaken by all TECs and is a system of accreditation and quality control for employer-based training, leading to an award to the employer similar in nature to that of a 'kitemark'. IiP has gradually gained momentum in recent years and was the key TEC mechanism for spreading the training culture to smaller firms. Other business support services in existence included: management development; business start-up schemes; grants/loans; National Vocational Qualification training awareness; and specific business network programmes. In many cases these business support services were devised, steered and overseen by particular TEC company groups. These groups usually took one of three generic forms: advisory groups; sector groups; and area groups. The intention of advisory groups was to focus on particular cross-sector issues such as small firms or IiP, whereas sector groups acted as a forum for employers from one particular industry to make their needs known or to share experience and generate ideas.

## TEC-Facilitated Network Forms

Bennett and McCoshan (1993) argue that the common factor differentiating innovative and entrepreneurial localities in the UK from those with low levels of innovation (e.g. parts of south-east England compared to Wales,

Scotland and north-east England), is the operation of effective networks. If this argument is accepted, it follows that the enhancement of networks, and in particular networks of local economic actors, has the potential to be a key policy instrument in stimulating innovation and economic development. Such networks must, to some extent, resemble those which have developed spontaneously in successful localities. The most important characteristics are a coherence and pro-activity among local institutions (e.g. trade organisations, local government, universities, technology transfer agencies, chambers of commerce, etc.) coupled with an environment of collaboration between local businesses. The form of these networks, as described in chapters 2 and 3, includes formal and informal agreements concerning purchasing and subcontracting; marketing, sales and distribution; research and development; and corporate venturing through equity stakes (Bennett and Krebs, 1991).

In the UK, Conservative Government policy by the mid-1990s had become more aware of the importance of local networks, with numerous White Papers (e.g. HM Government, 1994b; 1995) seeking to encourage partnership among local firms and institutions, with TECs being the key policy node in an effort to implant a culture of competitiveness through co-operation. This profile-raising exercise by the Government was accompanied by the claim that inter-firm networks are developing throughout all UK regions (HM Government, 1995). Although the Government appeared to have little evidence to support this claim, it is nonetheless apparent that the introduction of TEC employer groups, at both a sector and cross-sector level, consisted of relatively formal networking mechanisms for information exchange between firms and their involvement in processes of local economic regeneration. Furthermore an increasing number of TECs were supporting programmes specifically aimed at creating business networks, and were also putting in place a framework to enhance their own participation in regional networks, in particular their relationships with their respective local authorities (TEC National Council, 1995). The main objective of these regional networks was to establish effective joint and co-operative relationships, to produce a coherent approach to accessing the increasing amount of resources for economic development which the European Commission/Union distributed at a regional level. TECs, therefore, were increasingly looking to a regional presence and were further establishing collaborative fora at this level to develop common strategies (Mawson, 1995).

In general, TECs established a dual, but overlapping, capacity in their networked approach to economic development. First, to act as a catalyst for the generation of new networks, predominantly of an inter-firm nature; and second, to create partnerships and communication networks between themselves and other local institutions and businesses. A baseline evaluation of six TECs undertaken by Coopers and Lybrand (1994) highlighted that TECs had produced what they termed a 'minor' success in networking generation, with all case-study TECs creating and/or encouraging company networking both sectorally and non-sectorally. Coopers and Lybrand (1994) found the networks to be a mixture of both formal and informal structures, with sector networks often being the most formal and, in most cases, well regarded by their participants. However, although the study involved more than 200 interviews no substantive evidence of these networks was provided in the final report. A number of examples of TECs taking the lead in network development were illustrated in a Department for Education and Employment (DFEE, 1995b) publication. These examples included: a manufacturing network established by Birmingham TEC; a rural business network created by Cumbria TEC; a regional policy network involving Western TEC; as well as other examples from Cardiff, Gloucestershire, Hertfordshire, Milton Keynes and Wigan.

Despite the upbeat message promoted by the DFEE, other early evidence of the effectiveness of TEC network policies suggested that they faced a number of constraints in reaching their key target market - small firms. Vickerstaff and Parker (1995; Parker and Vickerstaff, 1996) found evidence of a number of barriers to small firm involvement in TEC networks, including such firms being circumspect about public sector schemes, a lack of resources and managerial time, thus putting participation at a premium. Furthermore, the 'relative isolation' of many small firms from pre-existing business networks meant that many TECs were having to mobilise the networking ethos from an under-developed stage (Parker and Vickerstaff, 1996). To overcome these barriers a number of TECs attempted to implement specially targeted approaches to small business, with the most common activities concerned with raising general awareness, providing subsidies and loans on preferential terms, providing access to business advisors, and focusing on marketing issues (Vickerstaff and Parker, 1995).

The ability and willingness of small firm owner-managers to become involved in local business networks in the UK was further explored during this period by Curran and Blackburn (1994), who suggest that the majority of small business owners in the UK are not joiners of local organisations except where there is a very direct economic benefit, and that the level of embeddedness of business owners in the local community is in general very low. They believe this is partly due to the 'fortress enterprise mentality' of many small business owners, that is, owners have a view of their business as being an expression of their personal independence and autonomy, which necessarily works against most networking activities (Curran and

Blackburn, 1994). They argue that although they found evidence of business-to-business relations in all their study areas:

> 'whether these functioned at a superficial level to promote strong local networks........which might be seen as giving a locality a nucleus around which identification with the locality in a wider sense promoted, is doubtful.' (Curran and Blackburn, p. 167).

They further implied that despite the considerable amount of resources devoted to such initiatives, TECs had already largely failed in their local network approach to small firm development (Curran and Blackburn, 1994). However, Curran and Blackburn's (1994) findings were based on evidence gathered during the very early stages of the development of TECs, and as such promote a rather pre-conceived view of both the resources made available and the effectiveness of their implementation.


## The Arrival of Business Links

Whether or not the result of the perceived success or failure of TECs, the Conservative Government further introduced (between 1994 and 1996) a system of more than 200 local business support networks, known as Business Links (Business Connect in Wales), consisting of partnerships involving TECs, local authorities, chambers of commerce and enterprise agencies. These networks aimed to act as a local 'one-stop-shop' providing all firms, but particularly targeted at growth potential SMEs, with a single point of access to a range of business support services, including those offered by TECs. Business Links, like TECs, quickly came under scrutiny, with it suggested that many organisations were essentially been coerced into working in partnerships due to reductions in their individual budgets and resources, as Government funding being linked more to the quality of local partnerships and networks and less to indicators of 'need' (Martin and Oztel, 1996).

The mechanism for facilitating Business Link support comes mainly through Personal Business Advisors, who act as a key contact point for individual firms, supported by a number of Innovation and Technology Counsellors (ITCs), Design and Export Counsellors, and a Diagnostic and Consultancy Service. Already, a number of reservations have been expressed concerning not only the quality of counsellors, but also the difficulties faced by counsellors in their ability to network effectively, share contacts, and avoid service duplication when they are often attached to 'competing' organisations (Blackburn and Jennings, 1996). However, since 1996 all DTI business and enterprise programmes were delivered through the Business Link network, and as TECs were the key lead agents, the implementation of support at the local level fell squarely on their shoulders (Coopers and Lybrand, 1994). The introduction of Business Link as the direct deliverers of these initiatives further emphasised the increasingly strategic nature of the role that TECs had assumed, with many TECs attaching such significance to business support that they were increasingly allocating funding from their own surpluses to further develop such services (Coopers and Lybrand, 1995; GHK, 1995).

TECs were central to the establishment of Business Links, being responsible for drawing together the proposals on behalf of local areas and in all cases acting as budget holders via one of three broad administrative structures: owners of respective Business Link; contract holders; or key partners (Hutchinson et al., 1996). Furthermore, TECs took an important liaison role with the regional Government Offices responsible for allocating public funding to economic development projects, through the integrated Single Regeneration Budget (SRB) that superseded the previous 'patchwork quilt' of funding streams in England. In Wales, it should be noted that the system of eight Business Connects has operated rather differently, with funding coming from the Welsh Office and being routed through a number of Business Connect partner members, i.e. TECs, enterprise agencies, unitary authorities, and the Welsh Development Agency. This is in part due to Business Connect being set-up as a 'first-stop', as opposed to 'one-stop-shop', intended to provide a co-ordinating and sign-posting facility to other organisations.

It is to the credit of TECs that the Labour Government has made it clear that it wishes the Business Link 'brand' to be maintained despite the institutional changes in the structure of policy provision and delivery that are to come about from 2001. It will be the Small Business Service that takes on the role of delivering 'core' Business Link initiatives, with it hoped that the duplication and confusion in delivery mechanisms that previously existed (and is discussed in chapter 6) is removed.

## Conclusions

TECs were introduced by the Conservative Government with a vision of them becoming hybrid local support organisations operating on commercial terms and acting as facilitators of training and enterprise support. However, an almost inevitable gap opened between the rhetoric and the early practices of TECs. The initial under-efficiency of TECs meant that they continued to rely heavily on central government funding, which weakened their potentially powerful role as agents of local regeneration. Subsequently, commentators were critical of TECs from a very early stage, with many of the most critical surveys being undertaken within the first few years of their existence, a period when the UK was in heavy economic recession. During this period a push began to occur towards TECs taking a more holistic approach to local economic development, mainly led by TEC directors. This push was recognised by the Government who consequently guided TECs towards a role which may be described as that of mini-development agencies. The local economic development role focused primarily on service provision to support the growth of the SME population of localities.

A crucial aspect of the Conservative Government's guidance to TECs was the emphasis on the development of partnerships and co-operation at the local level, with TECs becoming the key node of a policy to enhance competitiveness through a culture of collaboration. The outcome of this was that a networking approach gradually permeated the local economic development strategy of TECs, both as a specific policy tool and as a mechanism for increasing the effectiveness of other support instruments. Although there are undoubtedly many problems in attempting to implant local networks, considerable variation in these difficulties are bound to exist due to the various pre-existing strengths and weaknesses of local economies - an issue which is empirically explored in chapter 5. Also, the over-reliance on income from central government - which is assessed from a TEC perspective in chapter 6 - certainly contributed to reducing the reflexivity and influence of TECs at the local level.

A criticism of local-networks policy is that efforts to enhance local capacity have little relevance to national competitiveness (Curran and Blackburn, 1994). However, this appears to overlook the fact that the most successful national economies have been built on a cohesive local strength that has led to strength in the global marketplace. Furthermore, Curran and Blackburn (1994) criticise TECs for failing to deliver to the small firm population. However, as this chapter has shown, although TECs placed an increasing emphasis on interacting with small firms, there were a number of long-standing external factors working against them. These perceptions of market failure and constraining factors form the basis for the empirical analyses in chapter 5-8. Chapter 7, in particular, focuses on the actual deliverables of a range of network-related initiatives from the point of view of participating SMEs.

# 5 Business Co-operation and TECs - Developing Networks

## Introduction

The concept of networks has become popular in theorising and describing contemporary organisational relationships, particularly linkages between firms situated within the same geographic locale. Typically, it is argued that the existence of established inter-firm networks is one of the key reasons why a number of the most successful localities and regions throughout the world have become or remained more industrially competitive than those which have not adopted such an approach. The 'discovery' of these 'networked spaces' has increasingly attracted the attention of policy makers as a potential instrument to promote the competitiveness of local, regional and national economies (Fahrenkrog, 1994). In the UK, increasing government awareness during the 1990s of the potential role of local networks can be witnessed by numerous White Papers (e.g. HM Government, 1994b; 1995; 1998) which sought to encourage partnership among local firms and institutions. Furthermore, chapter 4 indicates that it was TECs that have became the key policy node in an effort to implant a culture of competitiveness through co-operation.

This chapter empirically assesses the role of TECs as cultivators and catalysts of inter-firm, or business, networks in their respective localities. The chapter focuses on the awareness among TECs of inter-firm networks, and the effectiveness of the instruments used by TECs to generate such networks. It further evaluates: the consequential outputs of, and barriers to, networking; the level of involvement encountered; and existing regional disparities. It draws on the results of a postal survey of TECs in England and Wales undertaken in 1996, which represents the middle period of TECs' existence - a time where they gained a degree of relative stability and establishment. The survey obtained the opinions and views of as wide a range of all the TECs in England and Wales as possible, and obtained a final response rate of 78 per cent (63 out of the existing 81 TECs) - see Huggins (1998a) for a fuller discussion of the applied methodology.

**Table 5.1    Relative Effectiveness and Provision of TEC Initiatives as Catalysts for the Development of Inter-firm Networks**

| Programme/Initiative | % of TECs Providing | Effectiveness Ratio |
|---|---|---|
| Business networking | 77 | 0.817 |
| Business forums | 92 | 0.804 |
| Investors in People | 100 | 0.791 |
| Sector-based groups | 69 | 0.753 |
| Business clubs | 67 | 0.737 |
| Manufacturing initiatives | 81 | 0.697 |
| Management development | 93 | 0.680 |
| Collaborative training | 80 | 0.668 |
| Small firm clubs | 62 | 0.663 |
| Supplier chains/links | 75 | 0.663 |
| Business start-up clubs | 62 | 0.646 |
| Export clubs | 61 | 0.645 |
| Quality/Standards | 85 | 0.579 |
| Innovation | 74 | 0.547 |
| Product development | 54 | 0.542 |
| Technology clubs | 41 | 0.516 |
| Technology transfer | 64 | 0.461 |
| Venture capital/access to finance | 53 | 0.408 |

**Network Instruments and Outputs**

The starting point of the survey entailed quantifying the programmes and initiatives provided by TECs either independently or as part of consortia, in particular Business Links, and rating their effectiveness as catalysts for the development of inter-firm networks. The rating was undertaken on a scale of highly (score of 1), moderately (0.66), slightly (0.33) or not at all (0) effective, with the scoring system assisting the calculation of the relative (i.e. not absolute) average effectiveness of programmes and initiatives with regard to network generation. Therefore, those with an average ratio of 0.66 or above are said to be performing moderately or better, while those with a score lower than 0.66 were less than moderately effective. As shown in

Table 5.1, programmes concentrating specifically on developing business networks amongst local firms were perceived as the most effective, followed by the development of business forums. Investors in People (IiP), sector-based groups and business clubs also scored relatively highly. Business network programmes most often involved a system of network brokerage encouraging firms, usually SMEs, to co-operate with other companies in order to develop and market joint products and services or access resources, such as market intelligence, training, research and development, marketing and finance. The system operates via TEC (or Business Link) appointed Network Brokers, who act as the network catalysts through a process of assessment, feasibility, planning, budgeting, agreements and implementation with participating firms. The process was most prevalent among TECs in the South West region where at the time of the survey the DTI funding a pilot programme to assess the effect of such networks on local company performance. Although the South West pilot was based on a model transferred from the seemingly successful experience of Denmark in developing business networks, initial evaluation work (Chaston, 1996a) suggested limited impact. Other initiatives included TECs setting up their own Business Network Centres (again operated through a brokerage system) as well as business networking forming a part of other TEC programmes.

Business forums operated as informal social events, often comprising working breakfasts and lunches in which different local business issues are discussed. TECs consider that such forums are not only very important 'triggers' to stimulating networking but also ensure a platform for embedding and integrating businesses into the local community. One example is that of a London TEC which established a 'Business Leader Team' consisting of four sub-groups relating to local transport, the Millennium, education, and a 'Sense of Place'. Forums also generated new networks, such as an Asian Business Forum organised by a TEC in the South East which resulted in networks being established to promote a culture of training amongst relevant firms. The importance of TEC generated business forums is echoed by studies undertaken in Scotland, where similar forums are an integral part of Scottish Enterprise's efforts to nurture a networked economy, providing regular meetings to foster links and promote networking amongst local business people (MacLeod, 1996).

The IiP programme is provided by all TECs and is - as has already been mentioned - a system of accreditation and quality control for employer-based training, leading to an award to the employer similar in nature to that of a 'kitemark'. Within this process TECs essentially 'piloted' the effectiveness of inter-firm networking through IiP clubs, which have been used as a tool for providing firms committed to gaining accreditation with an additional impetus through the dissemination of best practice, resource sharing and mutual support. Sector-based groups and business clubs were provided by more than two-thirds of TECs and were usually financed via TEC or local chamber of commerce affiliated membership schemes. TEC sector groups were aimed at developing the local business infrastructure covering issues such as training, skills shortages and labour market information. The most frequently mentioned sectors were manufacturing (as a whole), engineering, textiles, IT, food, legal and financial, care homes, retail, agriculture and rural industry, as well as local (potential) high growth sectors. Groups were increasingly having a more strategic role in assisting TEC development policy for their particular sectors, with networks consisting of business people from within the local sector together with training suppliers, trade unions and other relevant representatives. Business clubs had also evolved to meet the various needs of the local business community, although a number were new incarnations of previous local chamber of commerce operated networks. They had similar functions to that of sector groups but usually covered a more diverse range of local issues on a cross sectoral level, as well as functioning as social networks for members.

The second range of programmes consisted of: manufacturing initiatives; management development programmes; collaborative training; small firm clubs; supplier chains/links initiative; business start-up clubs; export clubs and quality/standards programmes. Manufacturing initiatives, undertaken by 81 per cent of TECs, involved benchmarking and best practice groups aimed at replicating and encouraging methods such as continuous improvement, particularly through the DTI's 'World Class Manufacturing' initiative. This initiative was first piloted and further developed by TECs in the North West region and combines training events, in-house diagnostic consultancy, the brokering of links into appropriate academic and research institutions, group training and visits to good practice case study companies. TECs often selected small groups of companies to participate which they consider have the capacity to become involved in mutually beneficial collaboration. Collaborative management development consists of workshops, forums and groups of local managers developing projects to assess the needs of their businesses or to enhance their personal business skills. By-products of these groups included the development of inter-trading and new collaborative projects beyond the specific programme. Similarly, collaborative training incorporated schemes such as Modern Apprenticeship (MA) clubs for those companies taking on apprentices under the TEC MA scheme, or National Vocational Qualification sector networks.

Small firm and business start-up clubs encompass self-help groups and enterprise programmes which draw on support services, such as marketing and quality assurance, as well as enabling entrepreneurs to share experience. Supplier chain programmes included the TECs' own links with the Regional Supply Network programme, which supported the development of local sourcing by bringing customers and suppliers together through database searches. A number of TECs had also set up their own local purchasing initiatives to encourage inter-trading at a TEC-area or intra-regional level. Export clubs usually consisted of informal meetings of local business people keen to develop strategies relating to trading overseas, while quality/standards initiatives concerned clubs which were often a part of other programmes, such as IiP and management development, aimed at implementing quality standards among SMEs.

Programmes relating to innovation, product development, technology transfer, technology clubs and venture capital or access to finance were the least effective for network generation. This reflects the high levels of trust and commitment by firms necessary to facilitate the development of reciprocal relations within these particular types of networks. As Dickson (1996) has found, successful technological or scientific collaboration among firms in the UK is closely related to the pre-existence of informal and personal ties. However, a significant number of TECs did operate innovation or technology clubs encouraging businesses to develop new product ideas or services, while other initiatives focus on the transfer of technology by identifying and promoting innovation, technology and business centres. Approximately one-half of TECs operated schemes connected with venture capital or access finance, with TECs usually acting as brokers between potential investors or business angels and companies which are seeking to sell equity or raise funding. Some TECs formed networks of both local companies and/or business angels through the Local Investment Network Company (LINC) scheme which maintains a national database matching service. Although TECs considered funding and finance related programmes to be the least effective in relative terms for generating networking, research focusing specifically on DTI-funded pilot TEC business angel networks suggests that they can be considered successful in terms of mobilising a significant pool of investment capital and stimulating SME demand for equity finance (Harrison and Mason, 1996).

As well as those programmes already operating, 71 per cent of TECs claimed that they were planning to introduce new initiatives aimed at enhancing the level of inter-firm networking in their locality. However, TECs were usually rather vague as to what these programmes would entail and how they were to be administered, although a small number of TECs highlighted new joint initiatives between the TEC, local chamber of commerce and the local Business Link. A more notable strategic aim was to enable many of those networks already initiated by TECs to eventually become self-sustaining. At the time of the survey fees were charged to firms for participation in the programmes outlined above by 48 per cent of TECs, although the majority of fee-charging TECs (77 per cent) did make financial assistance available. Therefore, the initial 'buying-in' to programmes was not a major financial obstacle for most firms.

In total, 90 per cent of TECs had established at least one inter-firm network in their local area, with a mean average of seven per TEC. However, this figure is undoubtedly skewed due to a few TECs setting up a considerably larger number of networks; a better guide is the median of five networks per TEC. The majority of TECs had formalised between three and ten inter-firm networks, although 12 TECs had developed 11 to 20 networks. The mean number of firms per network was 24, but this is again distorted by the unusually large number of firms associated with business forum networks, and a more accurate reflection is the median of 15 firms per network. Furthermore, the median of total firm involvement suggests that an average TEC has approximately 100 firms connected to programmes related to enabling inter-firm networking.

The large majority of firms involved in the networks were SMEs, with a fairly even coverage of micro, small and more medium sized firms. Companies with more than 500 employees accounted for only 3 per cent of the total number of firms involved. Firms with between 1 and 100 employees were responsible for 76 per cent of the total participation in networks, which concurs with evidence from other TEC studies (e.g. Vickerstaff and Parker, 1995; PACEC, 1995; Parker and Vickerstaff, 1996) which highlight the emphasis TECs have placed on targeting such firms. In terms of sector, the companies participating in network related programmes were predominantly from the manufacturing sector, with 92 per cent of TECs mentioning firms in this sector. Approximately one-quarter of TECs highlighted involvement by firms in the financial and business services, information and communication technologies, and tourism and leisure sectors. A regional dimension to sector participation existed, with a number of TECs referring to those industries with which their regions or localities have been traditionally associated, for example: automotive engineering - West Midlands TECs; textiles - East Midlands TECs; financial and business services - London TECs; agriculture - rural TEC areas; high technology industry - Cambridge TEC; ceramics - Staffordshire TEC.

According to TECs, the interaction between firms in networks is spilt almost equally between relatively formal and informal relationships. A variation in formality is to be expected as it reflects the differing levels of social embeddedness and ties within networks, and the differing aims and objectives of such associations (Granovetter, 1985). Informal social linkages are often seen as acting as a precursor for more economically embedded ties (Uzzi, 1996). For example, TEC formulated clubs and groups, particularly for specific sectors, usually have a visible network structure, with their primary strategy being to bring businesses together to pursue the common aim of economically developing their locality. On the other hand, for programmes such as management development, manufacturing or training initiatives interaction is often an output additional to the initial objective.

**Table 5.2     Outputs of TEC Facilitated Inter-firm Networks**

| Output/Deliverable | % of TECs (n=51) | Importance Ratio (n=31) |
|---|---|---|
| Collaborative Learning | 71 | 0.74 |
| Process Development | 55 | 0.48 |
| Purchasing/Subcontracting Relations | 53 | 0.36 |
| Joint Marketing, Sales or Distribution | 49 | 0.44 |
| Product Development | 39 | 0.28 |
| Technology Transfer | 35 | 0.24 |
| Corporate Venturing/Access to Finance | 28 | 0.20 |
| Joint R&D | 26 | 0.19 |

The outputs of TEC inter-firm networks are shown in Table 5.2, indicated by both prevalence and relative importance (consisting of respondents ranking outputs). By far the most common and important output was the role of networks in aiding collaborative learning among businesses. This learning is linked to the fact that many TEC activities within business clubs and sector groups are geared towards increasing local training levels with a number of networks involved in the establishment of training centres, particularly for manufacturing, as well as the development of programmes which stimulate and influence the dissemination of a learning and training culture, such as IiP. Secondly, process developments involved the dissemination of best practice and benchmarking through programmes such as manufacturing and management development initiatives, primarily aimed at improving logistics, quality and planning for increased competitiveness and performance.

Purchasing, marketing, sales and distribution partnerships are mainly the outputs of those business networks which have been set up through regional supply initiatives, small business clubs, export clubs, as well as specific businesses network programmes. Outputs relating to product development, technology transfer and collaborative research and development although significant were less prevalent, confirming the relatively low effectiveness of associated initiatives already indicated. Approximately one-quarter of TECs stated that networking had aided local firms in accessing finance, particularly through joint venture partnerships and alliances. The lower efficacy attached by TECs to finance and funding initiatives is undoubtedly due to the higher risks involved this form of facilitated networking.

## Receptiveness, Success and Constraints

An analysis of responses to the issue of the significance attached by TECs to networking confirmed that the majority of TECs considered networking *per se* to be an important contributing factor to enhancing local competitive advantage, and that it was a salient part of their agenda to act as catalysts and developers of inter-firm networks. Indeed, 44 per cent of TECs considered that networking was an important contributory factor towards increasing local competitive advantage, with a further 62 per cent stating that they considered themselves to be important network catalysts. One TEC in Eastern England cited the formation of networks as the cornerstone of its competitiveness strategy, while others pointed to a growing momentum towards networking policy with a gradual realisation that it is often the best way for organisations to 'learn'.

This commitment shown by TECs towards the development of inter-firm networking does not equate with the perceived success of these networks. In general, there was a very mixed response, and although 44 per cent of TECs claimed that encouragement had been fairly successful, a further 42 per cent stated that it had been either fairly unsuccessful and 8 per cent unsuccessful outright. This suggests that the performance of TECs as network generators was low by their own expectancy criteria, a factor which to some extent resonates with other evaluation work which criticises TECs as underachieving in many of their key aims, particularly with regard to support for SMEs (Peck, 1993; Peck and Emmerich, 1993; Curran and Blackburn, 1994; Adam-Smith and McGeever, 1995).

TECs perceived the lack of success to be due to a number of specific barriers, the most considerable being that network involvement by local firms was hampered by a lack of managerial and staff time, cited by almost a half of all respondents (Table 5.3). For example, one TEC in London stated that extended commuter patterns meant that many SMEs were 'too busy surviving', while other TECs indicated that although small firms are usually the target of network initiatives they are predominantly operated by owner-managers who do not have the resources to offer long term and consistent commitment. A lack of awareness and perception of the benefits of networking by firms was also seen as an important barrier, with some TECs arguing that there was a need for marketing strategies which highlight that the necessary time and costs can prove to be an investment if chosen wisely. Similarly, other TECs pointed out that most firms are looking for 'quick fix' solutions rather than the long term benefits that are normally associated with inter-firm networks, with those firms who do offer a commitment often becoming demotivated at an early stage unless a common focus and vision becomes transparent. Such barriers again reiterate the findings of other TEC studies of small firms involvement (i.e. Curran and Blackburn, 1994; Adam-Smith and McGeever, 1995; Vickerstaff and Parker, 1995; Parker and Vickerstaff, 1996).

**Table 5.3    Barriers to the Development of Inter-firm Networks**

| Barriers | % of TECs |
| --- | --- |
| Lack of managerial/staff time and resources within firms | 49 |
| Lack of awareness/Perception of benefits by firms | 35 |
| Lack of TEC resources and time to match firm needs and access appropriate partners | 27 |
| Fear by firms of compromising competitive position/confidentiality | 21 |
| Lack of interest from firms | 16 |
| Geographical barriers | 6 |
| Competition from other local providers offering similar services | 6 |
| Unwillingness of firms to give long-term commitment | 5 |

Other demand side barriers concerned a fear by firms of compromising their competitive position, resulting in what was referred to by one TEC respondent as the 'myopic outlook and defensive nature of many SMEs'. These short-term fears were often more pronounced when networks were focused around one particular sector or industry segment with, as a TEC in the South West argued, there being a 'dependence culture' prevalent in the UK which mitigates against the self-help and the collaborative ethos of networking. TECs also pointed to a number of constraints focusing on their own limitations with regard to stimulating networking, in particular their lack of time and resources. To a lesser extent, 'competition' from other local providers offering similar services was seen by some TECs to be resulting in market saturation with 'too many cooks spoiling the broth', thus diluting overall effectiveness. A number of TECs cited a lack not only of financial resources given their already wide agenda, but also of skilled personnel capable of fully developing and co-ordinating successful programmes and initiatives.

Other constraints concerned geographical diversity in a small number of TECs areas, with a TEC in the North East suggesting that the orientation of business towards a small spatial area of their locality hampered the wider development of networks in the area. One TEC on the English coast reasoned that many local firms were more oriented towards setting up links with firms on the European continent rather than those within their locality. Similarly, within one London TEC area many firms had an international rather than a local focus thus weakening embeddedness and local business identity, heightened by the fact that many employers and employees did not live in the vicinity. Although such factors are not strictly barriers they do suggest that the often endogenous policies of TECs sometimes conflict with the wider exogenous outlook of local firms.

The most important attitudinal constraint normally associated with networking is that of a lack of trust between the network protagonists. The concept of trust has been fully discussed in chapter 2, and in this case can be said to refer to situations in which there is 'the mutual confidence that no party to an exchange will exploit the other's vulnerability' (Sabel, 1992, p.215). TECs experienced considerable problems in generating trust amongst firms, with only 16 per cent of TECs giving a positive response. The large majority of TECs found engendering trust difficult or at least fairly difficult to establish, indicating that it is seen as a deep-rooted problem in many localities. The issue of trust was closely related to the constraint of compromising competitive position, and a North West TEC cited that it is the key change in attitude required if the embryonic 'new-style networking' in the UK is to be as potent as the 'old-style' Marshallian industrial districts that previously existed within this particular TEC's locality. Indeed, neo-Marshallian studies of the new industrial districts in the textile industries of the so-called 'Third Italy' suggest that it is precisely the 'collective capital of trust' (dei Ottati, 1994) that has acted as the precondition for the competitive success of such localities by introducing a dynamism through the removal of the fear of risk (Sengenberger and Pyke, 1992).

The enthusiasm of firms to the concept of becoming involved in TEC established inter-firm networks was also fairly poor, with more than two-thirds of TECs reporting low receptiveness amongst companies. This reflects a number of the barriers highlighted above as constraining development, particularly the existence in the majority of TEC-areas of a company culture that is reluctant and fearful of becoming involved in activities which involve a sharing of information based on mutual trust. However, TECs considered that they should continue to act as catalysts for network formation and demonstrate value, although they did point to a greater participation within those networks already functioning being best fostered by 'network ownership' increasingly being held by private businesses rather than TECs, thus increasing commitment and responsiveness, and facilitating more open communication.

### Endogenous Suitability and Existing Linkages

As TECs are geographically-based institutions it is of interest to look at the perceived importance of the local delivery perspective of initiatives relating to the development of inter-firm networks. The large majority of TECs viewed the local delivery aspect of networking programmes to be either very or fairly important to their success. It could be argued, however, that such an interpretation by TECs is to be expected given the previous Conservative Government's emphasis on this particular 'innovative' aspect of the TEC system. Therefore, it may imply little about the overall efficacy of locally delivered support programmes. Furthermore, 85 per cent of TECs stated that there are also other actors involved in promoting local inter-firm networks, with the most often cited being chambers of commerce and Business Links - other organisations cited included local authorities, private business organisations (including technology centres, banks, accountants), enterprise agencies and development agencies/regional supply offices.

Although TECs have experienced a number of barriers to setting up inter-firm networks less than a third of TECs considered the local economic and industrial structure to be unsuitable for network development. Of the 30 per cent of TECs that did state negative suitability the most frequently mentioned reason was a lack of communality between businesses, as well as a dearth of indigenous businesses. These factors were more acute in peripheral regions where there is often a higher level of dependence on foreign-owned companies, resulting in networking being dominated by local subcontract relationships between these companies and smaller local firms.

In general, TECs considered it to be easier to develop existing networks, particularly those already driven by local employers where there is a structure and common interest, than to set up new ones from scratch. By far the most important existing linkages which TECs concluded they could build upon were those business and sector forums and clubs already operating at the local level (38 per cent of TECs), including: manufacturing forums; small business clubs; trade and professional associations; exporters associations; as well as a small number of TECs (4 per cent) mentioning local investment networks. A further 13 per cent of TECs pointed to the local chambers of commerce  - with which a number of TECs in England eventually merged - as the existing prime movers of local inter-firm linkages through their own business clubs and forums.

The existing local supply infrastructure, coupled with that stimulated through regional supply offices, was cited by 14 per cent of TECs as being important to enabling further linkages. The most advanced regional supply networks existed in Wales where TECs in collaboration with the Welsh Development Agency had implemented a number of local supply networks based around large foreign-owned firms who had a regional presence. Surprisingly, only a small proportion of TECs cited linkages between firms established by enterprise agencies and local authorities as significantly contributing to the existing local business network infrastructure, again suggesting the prevalence of commitment rather than effectiveness. A comparison between involvement and contribution to networking by local agents, i.e. local authorities, chamber of commerce and enterprise agencies, infers that the capability of existing local organisations which have attempted to act as catalysts of inter-firm networks has been limited. This further affirms the doubts raised earlier concerning the efficacy which has been attached to the local delivery message associated with TEC programmes and initiatives.

## Exogenous Networking and Institutional Participation

Although the primary focus of TEC networks concerned development networks within localities, 62 per cent of TECs stated that they were providing, or part providing, programmes aimed at stimulating non-local interaction. The most significant being regional supply networks cited by 20 per cent of TECs, as well as manufacturing and sectors initiatives (16 per cent) with, for example, the 'World Class Manufacturing' being operated on a regional basis. Other initiatives also undertaken at a regional level included sector clubs for modern apprenticeship companies, a clothing and textile network in Yorkshire and Humberside, an oil and gas group in the North West and the South West's defence contractors network (discussed in detail in chapter 8). Regional funding and planning groups were stated by 13 per cent of TECs as a form of regional inter-firm networking, most often involving companies in projects seeking Government (through the Single Regeneration Budget and 'Challenge' based initiatives) or European funding. Trade missions to develop export linkages and regional 'Meet the Buyer' events were mentioned by 8 per cent of TECs.

It is reasonable to assume that certain inter-firm networks have non-firm institutional partners (i.e. other than those organisations acting as catalysts or promoters) and this was confirmed by the fact that TECs indicated a number of active institutional partners. The most frequently cited example was the inclusion of local further education colleges in collaborative training networks (41 per cent of TECs) or the consultancies and providers giving expertise to firms within networks (35 per cent) (Table 5.20). With regard to college involvement, two reports (CIHE, 1996; Rawlinson and Connor, 1996) highlight the potential of TECs to act as brokers between local employers and colleges facilitating training. However, they conclude that there is a lack of awareness among TECs about the actual extent of existing firm/college interaction and the growing importance of colleges as suppliers of vocational training to local employers. This is an important issue in light of the forthcoming merger of the further education and TEC training portfolios, within the new Learning and Skills Councils. If these are to succeed it is vital that there is a full recognition of the role and capacities of each of the existing actors, so that differing levels of provision are placed within these partnerships in the most appropriate and strongest position. Indeed, during their early years it is likely that intra-council 'brokers' will be required to network the varying divisions within the councils.

Universities were cited by a third of TECs through participation in innovation, technology, and product development clubs and projects. The role of regional development agencies (22 per cent), local authorities (18 per cent), chambers of commerce (11 per cent), and trade unions (3 per cent) was usually considered to be one of co-ordinating partners. Only a very small number of TECs cited the involvement of banks, accountants or professional institutes as networks partners.

**Regional Variation**

Aggregating the overall inter-firm networking effectiveness of the programmes and initiatives operated by responding TECs it is possible to calculate relative effectiveness at a regional level in England and Wales, as shown in column 2 of Table 5.4. Although this ratio should be treated tentatively, as it is necessarily of a self-reporting nature, it does give a broad indication of those regions that are performing above (100+) or below (less than 100) the relative average. In this case, it can seen that the highest performing regions were London, Eastern England, the North West and the South West, while the North East, Wales, and Yorkshire and Humberside were the lowest.

**Table 5.4    Relationship between Regional Effectiveness of TEC Networks and Firm Density, Gross Domestic Product (GDP)/Head, Density of High Technology Firms and Number of Firms Involved**

| Region | Effectiveness Ratio | Regional Firm Density | Index of GDP/Head (UK=100) | Density of High Technology Firms | Average No. of Firms in TEC Networks |
|---|---|---|---|---|---|
| London | 105.75 | 4852 | 125.7 | 178 | 171.0 |
| Eastern England | 105.06 | 3242 | 97.9 | 228 | 247.8 |
| North West | 105.05 | 3144 | 90.1 | 152 | 98.6 |
| South West | 103.24 | 2484 | 95.5 | 178 | 111.6 |
| South East | 101.83 | 3414 | 100.6 | 299 | 131.5 |
| East Midlands | 99.79 | 3024 | 96.7 | 147 | 78.0 |
| West Midlands | 99.24 | 3141 | 93.1 | 159 | 147.8 |
| York & Humb | 93.38 | 2854 | 89.9 | 122 | 135.8 |
| Wales | 91.81 | 1990 | 82.7 | 135 | 90.0 |
| North East | 90.68 | 1376 | 88.9 | 70 | 70.0 |
| **Spearman's Correlation Coefficient** | 1% Sig. = 0.75    5% Sig. = 0.56 | **0.81** | **0.79** | **0.78** | **0.61** |

Source: Gallagher et al. (1994), Office for National Statistics (1996)

Speculating on the possible explanation for the greater effectiveness of some regions compared to others, it may to some extent be the case that TECs in some regions have been greater beneficiaries of Government funding relating to network development, in particular the cases of the

North West's pilot of the 'World Class Manufacturing' initiative and the South West's pilot of the DTI's Business Networking programme. Although these factors may have played a part, Table 5.4 suggests that there are more structural reasons for the disparity indicated by the fact there is a high degree of correlation between the effectiveness of TEC facilitated networks and other external factors. Using Spearman's ranked correlation coefficient it can be seen that the regional effectiveness of networking is related to a high 1 per cent level to regional firm density (0.81), Gross Domestic Product/Head (0.79) and the regional concentration of high technology activity (0.78). The link with these three regional measures, which are themselves significantly correlated, implies that despite their being wide spread encouragement among the majority of TECs, networking has been most effective in those core regions with larger numbers of firms operating in higher value-added markets (for instance high-technology-based activity) thus generating greater regional prosperity. This gives further credence to the hypothesis that the ability of TECs to generate effective networks has so far been constrained and limited by the socio-economic structure in which they have operated.

Therefore, the intervention of TECs, as catalysts of inter-firm networks, appears to have actually consolidated the position of the UK's more competitive regions. These geographic areas, particularly those within more advanced metropoles, are the best representation in the UK of so-called 'learning regions' (Asheim, 1996b; Florida, 1995) or 'global regions' (Huggins, 1997), where there is a growing salience among constituent firms that as well as being integrated into local networks, participation in wider national or international networks of knowledge, information and innovation is a key condition for competitive advantage (Amin and Thrift, 1995). These networks have further concentrated expertise and know-how in activities such as high technology industry in these regions. The results of the survey analysed in this chapter, which show a relationship between the efficacy of TEC networks and the prevalence of existing linkages and the encouragement of non-local networking, further supports the importance of these factors. However, despite there being structural barriers working not only against networking generation but also more general economic development in the UK's less favoured regions (LFRs), this does not necessarily mean that the situation is irreversible. For example, it is encouraging to note that the majority of the relevant TEC personnel - who will undoubtedly form the 'backbone' of the staff in the new Learning and Skills Councils and the Small Business Service - were becoming increasingly aware that 'networking solutions' are long term rather than a 'quick fix', with a number of TECs in LFRs instigating some of the more innovative networking projects that may yield greater benefits in the future.

## Concluding Remarks

Despite a strong commitment by TECs towards the development of inter-firm networks, participation was limited, with approximately only 100 firms involved per TEC area. The success and effectiveness of those networks that have been generated by TECs often fell short in terms of the TECs' own criteria. This lack of success was due to a number of factors, the most considerable being that network involvement was hampered by a lack of managerial and staff time among local firms. A lack of awareness and perception of the benefits of networking by firms was also seen as an important barrier, with TECs considering there to be a further requirement for marketing strategies which highlight that the necessary time and costs can prove to be an investment if chosen wisely. TECs pointed out that most firms are looking for 'quick fix' solutions, rather than the long term benefits that are normally associated with inter-firm networks. Other demand side barriers concerned a fear by firms of compromising their competitive position, with a lack of trust among firms seen as a deep-rooted problem in many localities.

Building networks inevitably involves processes of trial and error, due to the difficulty in identifying participants and formulating relevant common issues. Also, a shortfall in resources may hinder progress when the benefits are not as high as expected. This chapter has shown that within the TEC environment there is considerable variation in these processes for differing initiatives and programmes. In general, three pertinent and differing network types emerged, consisting of: (1) learning networks; (2) commercial networks; and (3) innovation networks. Learning networks were the most effective and successful, with business clubs and sector groups increasing local training levels, as well as those programmes stimulating and influencing the dissemination of a learning and training culture, such as IiP. Process developments are also a feature of learning networks, with the dissemination of best practice and benchmarking through programmes such as manufacturing and management development initiatives, primarily aimed at improving logistics, quality and planning. Purchasing, marketing, sales and distribution partnerships can be characterised as commercial networks involving regional supply initiatives, export clubs, as well as specific business network programmes. Commercial networks further involve accessing finance, particularly through joint venture partnerships and alliances, and 'business angel' programmes. Product development, technology transfer and collaborative research and development take place through innovation networks. However, TEC generated innovation networks were not highly prevalent and the least effective, reflecting the high levels of trust and commitment by firms necessary to facilitate the development of reciprocal relations within these particular networks.

# 6 The Evolution of TECs and Networked Economic Development

## Introduction

At its most fundamental level, the capacity to network constitutes the disposition to collaborate to achieve mutually beneficial ends. In particular, networks in the local economic development arena consist of various partners who pool specific resources - such as financial and human resources, competence and know-how, etc. - through relations based on trust and reciprocity. As already indicated, TECs have a dual, but overlapping, capacity in their networked approach to economic development: (1) to act as a catalyst for the generation of new networks, predominantly of an inter-firm nature; (2) to create partnerships and communication networks between themselves and other local institutions and businesses. The previous chapter further found that although TECs have been committed to the development of inter-firm networks they have faced a number of barriers which have limited progress. This chapter assesses how the concept of networking has been gradually and practically applied to the economic development policies of TECs within the framework of this dual capacity.

Commentators such as Bennett et al. (1994) and Smits et al. (1996) found that the economic development 'community' in the UK generally viewed the primary role of TECs as being to increase co-ordination, integration, coherence and linkages through public, private and public-private networks at the local level. This chapter analyses what role TECs actually consider themselves to have in the economic development arena; how this has incorporated network concepts, at a number of levels, in their regeneration and competitiveness strategies; and the influence of the previous Conservative Government's policies, with regard to the associated funding regime. Furthermore, the chapter considers the practicalities and problems that TECs have encountered in facilitating the building and sustaining of local inter-firm networks, primarily among SMEs, in a number of differing scenarios. The research approach adopted for this chapter consisted of a semi-structured interview-based method. Nine TEC-site visits were undertaken in differing regions of England and Wales, with in-depth interviews carried out with 18 key individuals (two in each TEC-area) who were either senior TEC employees or in some way attached to their economic development activities - see Huggins (1998b) for further details.

## TECs and Local Economic Development Strategy

The Conservative Government envisaged TECs as having a dual role in local economic development. Firstly, as strategic partners responsible, with others, for generating and implementing a shared framework; and as developers, deliverers, funders and influencers responsible for ensuring the effective provision of specific initiatives within this framework (DfEE, 1995a; GHK, 1995). All the TECs interviewed concurred with this view of their role as that of local economic development strategists working in partnership (or in some case merging) with what they considered to be the operational deliverers of services. These include: chambers of commerce; Business Links; enterprise agencies; regional supply offices; and local authorities. This positioning of TECs in a strategic role was related to the Government's guidance, 'TECs: Towards 2000' (HM Government, 1994a) and 'TECs: Beyond 2000' (HM Government, 1996), which discussed TECs as being at the 'strategic heart' of economic development, and avoiding compromising this position by acting as a large-scale programme and initiative deliverer. However, the authority that Government vested in TECs to act as the key catalysts in local economic development partnerships and networks has resulted in considerable local tension and friction.

Haughton et al. (1997) argue that as TECs have sought to carve out a distinctive economic development role, organisations such as chambers of commerce and local authorities have become fearful of their own role being usurped. This, they suggest, has resulted in local partnerships being a mask for underlying 'turf wars' in which TECs are accused of 'organisation machismo' (Haughton et al., 1997). These fears have in many respects proved to be an over-reaction and misinterpretation of what has essentially emerged as a position in which TECs act primarily as co-ordinators of local public-private networks. As Strange (1997) has illustrated in his work on Sheffield, the influence of TECs in building coalitions has been to legitimise and state-sanction the role of local private business communities in economic development policy delivery. Furthermore, the arrival of Business Link as providers of business and enterprise support has further emphasised the position of TECs as strategic co-ordinating partners. This distinction between the policy and delivery side was seen by all the surveyed TECs as defining an operational role for Business Links.

This led to relationship between TECs and Business Links coming under considerable scrutiny, often focusing on the friction that has emerged between the Boards of both bodies, largely due to TECs being responsible for the allocation of budgets through its role as a contract manager to Business Links (Chittenden et al., 1995; Robertson, 1996b). TECs act as the strategic conduit for Government funding, in particular from the Department of Trade and Industry, to Business Links and others. However, they are very much reliant on these contractors making an impact in local markets if their own policies are to be realised (Coopers and Lybrand, 1995). Interviews carried out with TECs and Business Links confirm the existence of tensions, which have become even more heightened as TECs have pressed forward with their agenda to become key 'movers and shakers' in the business community. Furthermore, Business Link Boards have felt frustrated at having to contract with the local TEC rather than directly with Government. As Bryson (1997) argues TECs have remained the anchors for Business Link and in many cases are considered as merely their 'enterprise arm'. This is supported by the fact that the majority of TECs viewed Business Link Boards of Directors as being a duplication of resources, since policy in the first place was being steered by the TECs.

Blackburn and Jennings (1996) contend that although Business Links have the potential to be a successful 'one-stop-shop' business intermediary, they have not attained credibility within the business community. TECs also accepted that the Business Link concept could a have positive effect on local business performance, but there was a general feeling that the long-term future of Business Links lay in their gradual subsumption by TECs. In retrospect, however, the Labour Government has introduced almost the converse of this situation, by removing TEC branding and enhancing Business Link brands through the Small Business Service. To a large extent, this is unsurprising given that the Labour Party always claimed credit for initially developing the 'one-stop-shop' model.

Five of the nine case-study TECs indicated that the process of establishing a Business Link had been fraught with difficulty, primarily because of the nature of the partnership that needed to be put together, i.e. involvement from the whole local enterprise support community. These TECs further criticised Business Links for subsequently emphasising this entity as an individual 'company', which TECs considered detracted from their original partnership approach and mission, and increasing the accompanying amount of necessary resources. Martin and Oztel's (1996) work confirms that the introduction of Business Links has in many cases been counter-productive due to a further fragmentation of provision. A situation that some Business Link Boards have exacerbated by attempting to create a separate identity and demanding separate representation on bodies such as EU Structural Fund monitoring and advisory committees (Martin and Oztel, 1996). Most TECs echoed these sentiments and further argued that the Government's imposition of the Business Link model had side-tracked them from developing their own 'locally customised' economic development model, which the Government had charged them with generating.

**Table 6.1    Views of Case-Study TECs on Strategy and Business Links**

| Contention | Agree | Disagree | Unsure |
|---|---|---|---|
| Role of TEC is that of strategist as opposed to operational deliverer | 9 | 0 | 0 |
| TEC had arms-length relationship with local authority | 6 | 3 | 0 |
| Operational delivery is the defining role of respective Business Link(s) | 9 | 0 | 0 |
| Business Link Boards of Directors are a duplication of resources | 7 | 1 | 1 |
| Business Link can become self-sustaining | 3 | 4 | 2 |
| Business Link should merge with TECs | 6 | 1 | 2 |
| Business Link implementation had been very problematic | 5 | 4 | 0 |
| Regional Supply Networks were proving ineffectual | 6 | 2 | 1 |

**Note: For Wales case-study TEC views refer to Business Connect**

**Conservative Government Funding Regime**

The basis and tangibility of government policy to a large extent lies in the levels and types of finance and funding made available. Funding is therefore inextricably linked to policy and vice-versa and, in particular, its level and capability are necessarily key barometers of the importance attached to economic development policies. The Conservative Government was often attacked by TECs for decreasing their overall budgets during the early years of their development, although the issue was somewhat alleviated by the introduction of the TECs' 3-year operating licenses.

However, those TECs surveyed criticised the short-term nature of the bidding process introduced by the Government's 'challenge'-based funding, particularly through the Single Regeneration Budget (SRB). Those projects receiving funding were often perceived as 'Government's flavour of the month' initiatives. The SRB, which is an integrated budget of already existing Government programmes promoting economic regeneration, and local competitiveness and sector challenge funds have increasingly become the key mechanism by which TECs seek funding for economic development. Testimony to this is the fact that in recent years TECs have been involved in more than three-quarters of winning SRB partnership bids (Tilson et al., 1997).

Due to their direct relationship with Government, TECs have undoubtedly become adept at preparing such bids (GHK, 1995); however others argue (for example, Haughton et al., 1997) that TEC co-ordinated bids have been looked on favourably by Government, with other partners involving TECs purely to 'legitimise' their bids. Whatever criteria the Government used for choosing bids, the majority of TECs did not consider that the overall focus was correct. For example, the 'Competitiveness White Papers' (HM Government, 1994b; 1995) were criticised for promoting a mind-set that encouraged projects perceived as primarily 'new' rather than effective. This has engendered a reactive rather than pro-active posture among TECs, whereby they are often competing along highly prescribed guidelines within short time periods for funding that is not always linked to their overall local economic development strategy. As highlighted by Vere (1993), this resulted in a situation whereby there is a fundamental tension between the need for the accountability of funds and the scope to use them flexibly and innovatively.

Whether through design or necessity, a key outcome of the reduction in TEC budgets and the introduction of a funding regime based on a bidding process has been to limit the ability and capacity of TECs, particularly those in smaller localities, to tackle economic development on their own. Therefore, a networked approach, through the generation of local partnerships, has increasingly become a key feature of the economic development landscape. Budget enlargement has necessarily been one of the key motivations towards forging partnerships, and there is the inherent risk that those relationships formed will result in ineffectual and shallow relationships (GHK, 1995). However, the majority of TECs in receipt of substantial Challenge and SRB funds indicated that such funds had actually facilitated the creation of useful networks. These networks are seen as being particularly appropriate for creating a 'brainstorming arena', and the 'Sector Challenge' initiative was highlighted as a good mechanism for bringing together individuals from similar industrial backgrounds to discuss relevant issues. One negative factor associated with this approach is that participation is usually concomitant with the possibility of 'tapping-into' Government funding streams, and therefore the life-span of the networks may be restricted to the funding period.

In general, SRB funding has been quite disparately spread, and apart from those networks created through this bidding process the three most important sources of funds for creating networks, particularly those of an inter-firm nature, have been: the DTI (mainly the Business Enterprise Support budget); the EU; and the chambers of commerce. The DTI and EU funding is often of a joint nature with Government financing being matched by EU Structural Funds, in most cases via the European Regional Development Fund (ERDF). According to Lloyd and Meegan (1996), this funding has become increasingly coherent as local and regional agencies, such as TECs, take a role in shaping and delivering policy with 'new' (post-1993) EU regulations ironing out local-national-European tensions.

However, most TECs indicated that a problem of EU funding is that it has exacerbated the unevenness of development, even within some TEC-localities. This is primarily due to there being a split between those areas that are being designated as beneficiaries of EU Structural Funding, particularly the Objective 1, 2 and 5 ruling areas (and thus DTI matched funding), and those that are ineligible. For instance, one TEC stated that it undertook a greater level of economic development activities in those districts covered by the Objective 2 ruling than those without it, and that it was easier to put together networks and partnerships due to the existence of the 'EU funding pot'. In particular, the TEC highlighted its small business service as an example of an initiative where opportunities have been restricted to Objective 2 districts since the demise of central Government funding for new start-up firms. Unsurprisingly, those TECs in receipt of significant amounts of EU funding conversely argued that EU funding had been correctly targeted towards the most needy socio-economic areas, compared with the distribution of Government funding. TEC links (and in a number of circumstances merger) with the local chamber of commerce are a smaller but nevertheless significant source of funding, with TECs often taking a share of the subscription fees of joint membership groups and other 'networking' events. Other funding for network development has mainly been restricted to TEC discretionary funding or financing from their own reserves.

Despite the criticism made by TECs of the prescriptiveness of the Government's funding model, a number of TECs did stress that since the introduction of Business Links and the Government Offices a significant degree of flexibility was gradually beginning to evolve. Government guidance to TECs stressed that regional Government Offices were to become key players in promoting a coherent approach to the preparation of funding bids (HM Government, 1996), and recent evidence suggests that the introduction of these bodies has been partially successful in linking central Government policy closer to the machinery of local and regional agencies (Jacobs, 1997; Mawson and Spencer, 1997). The majority of TECs, however, remained sceptical of this new flexibility, claiming that the Government was paying lip service to local approaches and discretion while funding still remained contingent on satisfying a standard national model. Ward (1997) has argued that for real flexibility to emerge processes such as the SRB must become more transparent, as well as there being a relaxing of the output-related funding regime. One TEC pointed to the generic nature of Business Link executives as an example of this continuing, although more covert, prescription.

With the revitalised importance given by the Labour Government to regional policy, and the introduction of regional development agencies (RDAs) in England, it was of interest to seek the views of TECs on whether funding was best allocated locally or at a more regional level. In general, the TECs indicated that although they primarily had a local focus, there was also an additional need for them to work regionally at a trans-TEC level, through improving their own inter-TEC networks. For instance, a TEC in the North West argued that if they were themselves better networkers they would be in a far stronger position to generate a national lobby for assistance, particularly with regard to the SME sector. Examples of the type of regionally funded projects operating include a consortium of TECs in Eastern England working on the development of the biotechnology sector in the region, and the Manufacturing Challenge programme provided by TECs throughout the West Midlands which focuses on developing best practice and benchmarking amongst automotive and associated firms to produce 'learning economies of scale'. A possible explanation for the success of these projects is that being sector focused they also incorporate a common sense of industrial and regional identity.

All TECs considered that one of the problems involved in operating projects at a regional level is that bidding processes mitigate against it, due to proposals often having to be submitted to the Government at short notice. They also considered that sector networks would be far more sustainable at a regional rather than the local level. In general, a regional approach was advocated where the nature of programmes and initiatives engender a feeling of collective unity through a focus on themes and issues, such as mutual industrial sectors or changes in shared infrastructure. These perceptions confirm and add testimony to the new 'fashionability' and revival of interest in regional issues and policy (Mawson, 1995; Mawson and Spencer, 1997) away from what had increasingly become merely a method of perpetuating inter-area competition and inequality (Ball, 1995; Evans and Harding, 1997). Almost paradoxically, this increasing momentum towards the regionalisation of economic development, coupled with policies to merge of post-16 education and training, has acted as the catalyst for the eventual demise of TECs.

A consensus existed among TECs that the overall distribution of funds was uneven due to several key factors. Firstly, as mentioned earlier, TECs in areas designated by the EU as 'less favoured' have access to a larger 'funding pot'. Similarly, as TECs were introduced in a period of economic recession, central Government funding was weighted towards those areas suffering economic decline at this point. On the other hand, the ability to access commercial funding from large companies is more likely to take place in TEC-areas in more favoured regions, i.e. where the decision-making head offices of large firms are usually located. A further factor concerned the embeddedness of TECs and the fact that their introduction was staggered, giving older TECs a head-start in the 'funding stakes'.

As well as the embeddedness of TECs, it was also suggested that some TECs are simply smarter than others at the competitive bidding process. Certain TECs appeared to be better at what was termed 'reading the way Government was thinking' at a particular time, and being able to successfully predict 'flavour of the month' projects. However, the most contentious funding issue concerned budget allocations being based on the number of VAT registered businesses within TEC-areas. This system of funding, introduced through the regional Government Offices, was worrying to a number of TECs because they considered that it had shifted the allocation process from being means-related to size-related. It was argued that this policy favoured urban areas and the large business agglomerations of the South East of England, compared with those areas with a smaller business stock.

The above suggests that there are a number of determinants concerning the inequitable distribution of funding; although some are based on seemingly arbitrary criteria, others concern the funding of areas of industrial decline that claim more regeneration related finance but lose out elsewhere. In the light of this discussion it is worth noting Gray's (1997) labelling of these funding arrangements as being of a 'contract culture' relying on certain quantitative indicators that distort and undermine the social and economic purpose of the policies at stake.

## Policy Delivery

TECs and Business Links are undoubtedly attempting to create fee paying services. This approach has met a number of difficulties and more often than not services seem to be discounted on a fairly easy going and ad hoc basis. The main problem with subsidising services was, as one TEC suggested: 'Its the old adage. If you charge peanuts, you end up getting monkeys.' In other words, the prevalent attitude is that although TECs (or Business Links) take whatever payment they can get for their services, they are also aware that this undervalues the product or service 'sold' to the business 'customer'. The fact that a charging structure is on the TEC agenda indicates that they are moving away from the dependency culture of 'something for nothing'. This fits with Storey and Strange's (1992) argument that the Conservative Government orchestrated a shift from the characteristic of dependency within the UK SME economy, to one where success and financial benefits were related to a willingness to be involved in some degree of risk-taking. For example, a TEC which previously gave cash sums, through hand-outs, to individuals attempting to start their own business now channels this finance into advising, supporting and training those willing to invest their own capital. Similarly, another TEC indicated that they were seeking to trade on a business-to-business basis, moving away from a 'grant-aid mentality' in which TECs are perceived as part of the 'grant-aid society'. The same TEC highlighted that they still used the option of incentivising programmes and initiatives to firms that were 'less able to see the direct benefits', but which once committed were obliged to input significantly larger amounts of their own resources. The main problem facing TECs is that companies which are receptive to business development are those that have already realised that it is in their vested interest to be involved and are participating in projects without financial incentives, while those firms which should be involved are unreceptive, despite initial 'incentivisation'.

An important point made by the TECs concerning financial assistance was that many companies participating in programmes and initiatives were actually unaware that their involvement was being subsidised by TEC funding, for example, through project co-ordination and the use of external consultants. There does appear to be a degree of validity to this argument, and research by Smits et al. (1996) and Smits and Rushing (1997) makes reference to the 'almost-invisible hand' of TECs, whereby their 'behind-the-scenes' involvement attracts little public attention. They further argue that a lack of the full recognition of TEC accomplishments actually threatens their long-term sustainability (Smits et al., 1996).

The apparently parochial and myopic outlook of SMEs also appeared as a key theme that TECs felt they had difficulty in overcoming. TECs contended that there is a need for such companies to be educated into taking a vested interest in the development of their local economies in order to reconcile this complacency. This apathy is rooted in two dichotomous explanations. Firstly, firms situated in localities of relative prosperity and affluence are seen to be rather blasé in their current 'comfort zone'. Secondly, while more successful and large companies are often geographically mobile, the insularity of smaller 'surviving' firms in areas of economic decline is necessarily a constraining factor.

In order to facilitate the education of firms, TECs suggested that in the long-term it would be favourable to shift support away from programmes that are so outwardly publicly-funded initiatives, and of which the majority of the business community are still deeply sceptical. A number of TECs were considering moves for more initiatives and networks to become self-sustaining, although in most cases they were still acting as the main funders and facilitators. Some TECs were working towards a 50/50 split between their own support and that from the private sector, involving joint membership with income being generated through subscription and fees, but in most cases this was not proving to be an easy goal to attain and was seen very much as a long-term objective.

One of the main problems highlighted by TECs, particularly with regard to the self-sustainability of networks, is that in the UK there is simply not a culture within indigenous business of investing in information or learning. TECs further considered, especially those situated in older industrial regions and localities, that it will take a long time for small business owner-managers to realise the need for investment in their own learning through networks; and even where there is greater awareness, a lack of resources may hinder involvement in a culture of learning. This confirms Gibb's (1997) assessment that, in the UK, there has been little progress over the last twenty years towards building upon small firms as 'learning organisations'. Similarly, Scott et al. (1996) highlight the isolation of the majority of SMEs in the UK manufacturing sector from sources of information and knowledge. A less perceptible, but nevertheless important, constraint on the performance of TEC network groups was the increasing prevalence of individuals who may be termed 'network junkies', which one TEC executive defined as 'individuals who have time on their hands to become involved in talking shops, but when push comes to shove offer little long term commitment in terms of their own resource input'.

The intermediate model that has been most widely adopted so far consists of the sustainability of networks gradually being transferred to the private sector in terms of decision making, but with TECs acting as 'silent partners' in which they continue contributing to those facilitation functions which businesses lack the time to undertake - one TEC referred to their changing role as being 'chameleon-like'. The increasing number of mergers with chambers of commerce is also seen as influencing network development and may in time be beneficial to increasing pro-activity. However, TECs were aware that they must be careful not to duplicate networks and ensure that the time of business people is not wasted by asking them to attend unnecessary meetings and functions. For example, the case-study TEC in Wales found that many of its business groups were duplicates of those being marketed by the Welsh Development Agency, suggesting a lack of regional institutional networking.

## Evolving Business Networks

The academic discussion of business co-operation and networks is often undertaken in fairly abstract terms; the objective of this section is to add some realism through 'on-the-ground' examples of inter-firm networks in which TECs have acted in a facilitating and supportive capacity. The TEC National Council (1997) has highlighted that TECs must be increasingly 'client' (i.e. local company) focused, with inter-firm networks playing an important role in 'developing co-operation, mutual assistance, trade and the sharing of expertise and good practice between local businesses, strengthening supply chains and to help maximise the benefits to all parties from this process' (p. 18). The following examples are by no means to be taken as evidence of TECs attaining great success in these processes, but more as an indicator the range of networking developments in which TECs have sought involvement. It was shown in chapter 5 that despite TECs under-performing in their network development activities there are nevertheless three pertinent TEC facilitated network types around which research may be focused, i.e. learning, commercial and innovation networks. Learning is the process whereby skills, knowledge, habit and attitudes are acquired (Gibb, 1997). Learning networks, therefore, can be said to be interactive processes aimed at generating the exchange of these human resources. These networks are the most common and effective form of TEC supported inter-firm collaboration with the examples identified here concerning the following initiatives and programmes: Investors in People clubs; performance improvement networks; manufacturing initiatives; sector groups; and business forums. Purchasing, marketing, sales and distribution partnerships are characterised as commercial networks, with the discussion concentrating on support for joint marketing groups and regional supply networks. There was little evidence of the prevalence or effectiveness of TEC facilitated innovation networks - i.e. promoting product development, technology transfer and collaborative research and development - although two interesting examples of innovation-related co-operation are a rapid prototyping group and a local manufacturers' group.

## Investors in People Clubs

The majority of TECs operate clubs for those companies that have committed themselves to achieving the Investors in People (IiP) accreditation. These clubs consist of a series of workshops (often monthly) where companies can share their learning experiences and move further towards recognition. They have been highlighted by the Government as a particularly effective form of information and knowledge dissemination (QAD, 1995). However, the data gathered in this study suggests that the workshops have had mixed success, often dependent on the range of firms participating in any given yearly cycle. Some TECs have encouraged participants to 'pair-up' and to work together on a fully collaborative basis towards recognition. A TEC that had introduced 'pairing-up' commented that although this is a highly genuine form of networking, in terms of the potential to create synergy, it was in practice very difficult to implement. The same TEC has also set-up a network to encourage longer-term interaction between local companies. The IiP Achievers Club, as the name suggests, is a network for companies that have achieved accreditation, and was designed to support companies - a mix of SMEs and a smaller number of larger firms - maintain and further best practice human resource development through a strategy of continuous improvement.

The nature of the Club has meant that it has served as a focus for relationship and synergy building among the most successful companies in the locality, acting as a mutual self-help group through the identification of both good and bad practice. The Club, which has been in operation for two years, has concentrated on issues such as lifelong learning and business excellence, with the agenda formalised by a small steering group. Although the TEC was keen that a member of the Club should act as the chair of the steering group, it in fact assumed this role itself as the participants considered they did not have the necessary time to commit to what are basically mundane administrative duties. The TEC IiP manager admitted that in this respect he had failed abysmally in shifting network ownership from the TEC to the members.

*Performance Improvement Networks*

The national expansion of the 'World Class Manufacturing' initiative has resulted in a number of TECs operating what may be termed as performance improvement (PI) networks. PI networks facilitate group learning through introducing and implementing particular best practices amongst manufacturing firms in a locality, while at the same time reducing the costs of 'one-to-one' manufacturing management consultancy. One TEC acted as a pilot for the feasibility of PI networks aimed specifically at enhancing the performance of suppliers rather than manufacturing assemblers. The networks consist of regular 'interactive' workshops, initially operated over a six-month period, that are the culmination of awareness seminars and specialised focused groups. The awareness seminars are a first chance for the TEC to highlight to firms, in particular SMEs, the advantages of exchanging ideas and the demonstrable benefits of working outside of isolation. It is also an opportunity to find out whether or not any companies are in direct market competition, in which case they may be allocated to separate focus groups and workshops. The TEC are keen not to force the network development and the focus groups act as a forum for the development of ideas and issues, which although termed 'specialised' are often fairly generic and cross-sector in nature, for example environmental legislation, quality standards, management development, access to finance and enhancing R&D capabilities.

The ensuing workshops typically consist of 5-7 firms meeting 10 times over the six-month period, working towards a specific common output, as well attending larger seminars with the members of other workshops. The TEC considers PI groups to be its most successful inter-firm networking project, and although the TEC and Business Link take responsibility for the administrative 'paperwork' of the networks, the chair of each group is allocated from the network participants. One insight from the TEC/Business Link network co-ordinators concerned the fact that in most cases it is the same core of pro-active companies that are involved in many of their programmes and initiatives. However, with regard to network sustainability this was seen as being a positive factor, since these firms gradually gain more and more trust in each other and knowledge of the work of other participants.

*Manufacturing Initiatives*

One TEC played a leading role in developing the 'Manufacturing Challenge', which is a West Midlands company 'mentoring' programme designed to up-rate the competitive performance of participating SMEs.

The Challenge gives SMEs access to industrial sponsors and one-to-one demonstrations of best practice examples, supporting them in making their own specific manufacturing practices more effective. The Challenge has attempted to overcome a conception that many network initiatives often become nothing more than means for 'industrial tourism', whereby members visit each others premises but gain little or no new usable information and knowledge. The main network actors consist of a number of successful local firms who act as 'mentors' for firms with specific problems. The interaction involves individuals from the 'problem' company spending time with their mentor assessing and analysing best practice techniques, with company and TEC representatives devising a project action plan.

The Challenge seeks to create 'whole manufacturing' solutions, but is essentially project-based and geared towards making a number of significant improvements within a reasonably short time-scale. Therefore, the relationships are necessarily and usually temporary in nature, with the aim of the TEC being for a number of those companies that have taken part in problem solving to themselves eventually become mentors. The programme is now offered by all TECs in the West Midlands, operating specialised theme groups such as exporting, environment, information technology, benchmarking, and small firm start-ups.

*Sector Groups*

Sector groups were considered by TECs to be catalysts for change whereby organisations identify and resolve issues, and undertake activities collectively that would be difficult for any single organisation to carry out in isolation. The groups are intended to develop long-term initiatives and stimulate relevant joint action for meeting differing interests within the local business community, with many having a local planning role focused on business growth and training plans. Their key task is usually to analyse issues affecting their own local industry sector and the resultant training and employment implications, thus defining strategically the way forward for human resource development. In many ways sector groups exemplify the increasing trend towards the ethic of corporate community involvement (CCI) by which companies, usually fairly large concerns, apply human (and/or financial) resources to solving a variety of local socio-economic problems (Grayson, 1994).

TECs are seeking to introduce initiatives with a significant degree of CCI (TEC National Council, 1997), for example, one TEC had facilitated sector groups for IT, manufacturing, tourism and leisure, financial services and construction, with a stipulation being that all individual members are local employers. The most active group was that concerning the IT sector, which had produced a detailed plan to develop and introduce a local 'technology village' for vocational training development and promoting new start-up companies. This group has been particularly active due to the locality having a core of large computer companies that have subcontract links with small locally-owned companies. Internal trust has been fostered between companies that are often market-place competitors by an agenda that does not compromise sensitive issues. Some of the projects undertaken include setting-up computer networks in local schools, the enhancement of computer-related qualifications for NVQs and GNVQs, and the generation of new IT start-up firms. For small firms, participation means an expansion of their 'stakeholder web' (Jennings and Beaver, 1997), i.e. organisations which have a vested and personalised interest in wishing to see them succeed.

*Business Forums*

One large-scale business forum studied was a network of about two hundred and fifty companies situated on a business park. The local merged TEC/Chamber has taken the key role in facilitating this cross-sector network, initially undertaking a 'needs-analysis' to identify from members the role they saw the Forum playing; i.e. to making it a demand rather than supply-led association. The companies involved range from small engineering firms to large technology-based inward investors. The TEC suggests that it had little problem in actually creating the Forum, with its main challenge being to sustain it. Sustainability, however, has been promoted by the members all being situated in close proximity, which, the TEC argues, has created a 'family atmosphere' facilitating contact on a basis far more frequent than the regular Forum meetings. Forum issues have included waste management, with a number of members utilising the by-products of the others manufacturing processes, that has been mutually cost beneficial to those involved. The Forum has further generated a commercial role through the development of a joint purchasing network in which a group of twenty members have undertaken to bulk purchase a number of common products, in order to gain economies of scale.

The TEC emphasises that it views this Forum as an example of a 'best practice network', stressing that attempts to set-up similar networks on other business and technology parks have been less successful, gaining little initial momentum. The TEC attributes this to the fact that the original Forum had a strong cross-sector mix of companies, resulting in a non-competitive threatening environment that allowed relationships to develop from one of mutual learning to more commercially-based interaction.

*Joint Marketing Groups*

Little evidence was found of TECs catalysing joint purchasing networks, that would give SMEs buying power through accessing the economies of scale associated with large organisations. Instead, joint marketing groups were the most common form of TEC facilitated commercial networks, most often formed by a TEC or Business Link network broker. For example, one TEC had brokered a consortium of five local companies in the field of commercial facilities management. The firms involved consisted of: a commercial office cleaner; site security; building and decorative services; grounds maintenance; and catering services. Following market research undertaken by the TEC, the group members identified a trend whereby their existing clients were rationalising their supplier base. As the members were primarily specialists, rather than 'multi-trade' and 'complete package' suppliers, they were in danger of losing work to large trade companies. Also, the companies were increasingly finding it necessary to substitute short-falls in turnover due to the recent curtailment of public sector expenditure on their services. The concept of the network, therefore, was to pool services and resources, and to market and tender jointly for appropriate business opportunities, particularly within the private sector.

The network further aimed to act as a 'one-stop-shop' disaster recovery service for insurance companies and loss adjusters in cases of sudden and unexpected damage to commercial and industrial property. A head-start was gained by the network due to a few of the companies already having some common customers that were able to act as test-bed for the new networked package. From these customers a number of 'package' contracts were gained, acting as a catalyst for the development of new business. The companies involved have all reported a substantial increase in turnover coupled with the creation of a small number of new jobs, as the economies of scale generated have allowed the firms to compete on a more level playing ground with larger facilities management organisations. Initially instigated by a TEC network broker, the group has since become self sustaining, appointing its own marketing co-ordinator.

*Regional Supply Network*

Supply and sourcing linkages are focused around the DTI's Regional Supply Network (RSN) initiative that was launched in 1995 to bring together local companies with larger local, regional and national buyers seeking new suppliers. The service, operated by a series of ten regional supply offices, offers advice on potential suppliers and sources of supply, new business opportunities for suppliers, and to trace convenient supply sources for potential purchasers. The offices, and the accompanying national company profile database that matches suppliers with potential purchasers, are partly supported, co-located and operated by the TEC and Business Link infrastructure. The database covers key financial information of supply firms as well as their quality accreditation and existing base of customers. The RSN has taken a sector approach, whereby regional executives specialise in a specific sector within their region or locality. One advisor outlined his primary role as being to visit local companies and gain an insight into their purchasing strategies, provide introductions and project continuity. His particular sector focus concerned food and drink companies, and as well as handling enquiries from potential supplier and purchasers he had also taken the lead in organising introductory functions, whereby the buying teams of national supermarkets had the opportunity to meet small specialist food drink suppliers, that proved successful in initiating a number of new contracts.

Although the RSN has been relatively successful in capitalising new contracts for SMEs, with a total of more than £100m of new business generated as a whole in the first two years of operation, there is little evidence that it has encouraged the growth of integrated local supply chains and inter-firm networks that are a feature of the Welsh model. This, in part, is undoubtedly due to RSN executives being briefed to remain focused towards the requirements of purchasers rather acting as an extra sales resource for supplier firms. The interviewed RSN executive indicated that this had led to inevitable tensions in his role as an intermediary, and although he referred to the development of long-term purchasing/sourcing relationships it was also made clear that a number of the buyer-supplier relationships were still extremely price-sensitive. It was interesting to note that in some circumstances he considered potential purchasers had initially used his services purely and only as a price-checking exercise.

*Innovation Networks*

TEC support for innovation is primarily geared towards funding programmes delivered through the Business Link model, in particular the resources committed towards the employment of innovation and technology counsellors. The counsellors act as local 'trouble-shooters' and as a sign-posting agency for SMEs that are seeking to introduce product and process changes. Although the counsellors do often operate fact-finding seminars, the majority of contact is on a one-to-one basis, working in brokerage capacity before a specialist consultancy or agency is contracted to undertake one-off project work. TEC and Business Link personnel indicated that innovation programmes, that in most cases are initially DTI-funded initiatives, are not generally instigated through collective processes. However, there are a limited number of interesting, if isolated, examples of innovation occurring through TEC supported networks.

One TEC network brokered network focusing on innovation is that of an engineering rapid prototyping group (RPG) involving three small companies - an engineering design consultants, a traditional model maker and a precision casting company - as well as the local university. The RPG is a complete design and prototyping service using stereolithography, which as individuals firms they would not be able to offer due to the overall expense of installing a complete technological prototyping system. The key player in the network is the university, which houses a large proportion of the most expensive and up-to-date machinery, with the companies benefiting greatly from access to technology that was previously under-utilised. The nature of the prototyping sector is such that not only is the machinery constantly being up-dated, but there is also a continual learning curve with regard to developing and utilising new techniques. The university was again crucial in this respect, as they were keen to pass on technical skills and contribute to raising the technological standards of participating firms. The advantage to potential clients is that the network provides a combination of academic, practical and commercial engineering skills, incorporating both traditional and advanced prototyping techniques. Among the projects completed is a mobile communications system that has been adopted by a large regional police force, which the network brought to market in eight weeks. This involved developing the electronics and external casings for an advanced logistics system for emergency service vehicles enabling remote tracking. The co-ordinating role of the TEC network broker was increasingly scaled down, with group becoming self-sustaining.

A less dynamic, although nonetheless useful example, of a TEC supported group that has facilitated technological innovation is a local cross-sector manufacturers' group, involving SMEs as well as larger organisations, aiming to promote and spread best practice within the indigenous manufacturing sector. The group is co-ordinated by a full-time manager who arranges monthly meetings, as well as undertaking the 'profiling' of member firms as a tool for increasing local sourcing and as a marketing device for the local manufacturing sector as a whole. The most interesting facet of this network is that the interaction generated by firms has resulted in a number of innovation-related collaborative activities. The best practice projects, for example, take place in what are called 'action groups', with one recent group spawning a relationship between a small technology-based firm and a CD-ROM manufacturer to develop a multi-media package.

The group also played an important role in facilitating the merger of two member firms, one a packaging firm and the other a service engineer, as they became aware that the knowledge of one company complemented the manufacturing resources of the other. Through merger the new company pooled its human and capital resources to develop a new high quantity stretch-wrapping machine, becoming only the third UK producer of such technology. The manufacturers group was able to arrange substantial financial support to cover the design and training costs of the project and also contributed to the development of the new machine. The company estimates to sell approximately 2,000 machines a year and has taken on three extra production staff.

## Networks of Mediocrity

The aforementioned examples suggest that the most effective and sustainable networks are initially based on informal relations, such as those developed through voluntary attendance at 'learning' workshops and seminars. As trust emerges and bonds are gradually gained these arrangements may evolve into more formal and long-term associations, based on a degree of contractual or 'dotted line' agreement (Ibarra, 1992), such as joint marketing and purchasing networks. Through informal networks social exchange occurs between parties giving them the opportunity to demonstrate their trustworthiness to each other, which in the long-term makes possible more formal mutual commitments (Forsgren et al., 1995). In this way social capital (Putnam, 1993) is built by individuals moving from a position of isolation to one of connectivity in their professional and/or public activities (Wilson, 1997).

However, similar to the development of other relationships, such as that from courtship to marriage, a desirable or sustainable relationship is not always the end outcome. As Miles and Snow (1992) argue, the effectiveness of the majority of organisational networks declines rather than improves over time, mainly due to mistakes in their design or operation. Similarly, TEC networks brokers and other personnel responsible for the development of more formalised networks indicated that significant problems existed in generating an environment for dynamic and sustained co-operation, with many of the emergent networks being only mediocre in terms of motivation and ambition. The irony of many co-operative developments is that although financial motives are commonly the key reason for network participation, firms are still reluctant to actually input any significant amount of their own resources, be it time or money, unless financial gain is guaranteed.

Most of the network-types that TECs and others are attempting to evolve to a large extent resemble other forms of business propositions - being necessarily speculative and variable in success and based on differing degrees and types of trust relations - and although they additionally imply an actual sharing of the necessary resources and associated risks, many emergent networks are dissolved if immediate benefits for little input are not forthcoming in the very short-term. Perhaps, this is to be expected, more than might be considered, given that many of the companies involved are small concerns working to tight budgets and time-frames. It can also be hypothesised that the sustainability of networks is directly related to the initial expectations of the participants. For example, groups such as business clubs/forums and sector networks are able to retain a high degree of membership and sustainability because the expectations in terms of immediate financial benefits are relatively low. Within these networks the motivation for involvement is related more to: socialisation; avoiding local business isolation; and heightening the feeling of self-worth in the local community.

Although such business and sector groups and forums may spawn more formal networks, through interaction with associates, the anticipation of financial rewards are nevertheless lower than in groups that are designed purely for such purposes. Networks are, therefore, means to numerous ends, and it is possible that TECs have over-sold their potential achievements, particularly in more formalised processes, to interested parties at too early a stage in development and to the detriment of long-term progress. This implies that economic development policies aimed at catalysing and implanting networks in the business community should initially focus on fostering trust in an informal environment. Furthermore, participants should lead the 'issues' agenda, thus directly influencing their own expectations levels, that although in the first instance may be fairly conservative will eventually become more ambitious as relationships are embedded in more formal ties. Interestingly, Chaston (1996b) has argued that in the UK 'demand' for networks is much more oriented to informal structures, with formal networks appearing significantly less compatible with the norms and practice of small indigenous firms.

Obviously, conflicts of interest will result in relationships breaking down even in informal structures, but in such circumstances firms may well have been involved in a worthwhile learning process or awakened to ideas which they can instigate in-house. One broker described successful network development as 'squeezing' together companies that are driven by a common motive, through inter-facing them on an informal but regular basis and waiting for something to 'pop-out' amongst the most dynamic members, while the demotivated firms cease their links. However, one TEC had experienced so many problems in developing formal networks that it had dissolved its business network programme, with the allocated resources being concentrated on entities such as the more viable business forum and small or start-up business clubs. The TEC indicated that although firms in networking projects were initially brought together informally, barriers still existed due to an inability to reach a common consensus on opportunities or ideas that would increase the competitiveness of all participants. In such circumstances the end result, particularly for projects attempting to develop supply networks, often consists of two companies that were not originally aware of each other undertaking some form of short-term subcontract work. According to this TEC, network support projects are still perceived in their locality as being part of a 'dependency' rather than a 'self-help' and 'mutual assistance' culture, with firms willing to become involved if there was the incentive of a subsidy or grant and without themselves having to contribute.

Further problems encountered by TEC brokers entailed the restrictions of working within a locality that they considered did not possess a core of SMEs with common interests, as well as problems concerning the local socio-economic structure being over-reliant on a small number of key large organisations. This led them to conclude that greater success may have been attained if the projects had been initiated at a regional or even cross-regional level. Similarly, Forsgren et al. (1995) argue that although it is difficult to influence the 'life-cycle' of networks the involvement of companies in wider geographic network structures has a positive effect on their commitment to collaborative processes, as well as their own potential for development. However, such networks have their own particular set of problems with regard to the need for increased organisational capacity.

Others argue, for example Pyke (1994), that close geographical proximity means that firms are more likely to have known each other over a long period, and may therefore have 'organically' engendered trust and a propensity to co-operate. Nevertheless, the brokers claim that wider spatial networks would go some way to alleviating parochialism and intra-local competitiveness, such as the reluctance that emerged among small local engineering firms to co-operate within a congested local subcontract market serving larger firms. Related to this example, it should be made clear that the majority of TEC facilitated networks involve horizontal relations, where there is often a high level of intra-network competition between participants occupying the same supply-chain position, which itself is a contributing factor towards catalysing conflict and disruption (Sydow, 1996).

The experiences of this particular TEC highlight a number of fundamental and prosaic barriers to formalising inter-firm networks, such as poor attendance at meetings, that indicate a lack of genuine commitment by firms, most commonly derived from difficulties in reaching agreements on common objectives. This stems from the differing needs of the various companies, which are often irreconcilable. Although a number of groups did survive a few meetings due to the enthusiasm of a core of initiating companies, the networks inevitably collapsed when the participants were asked to pay for specific activities or to meet the costs of the TEC broker; implying that at this point they did not attribute any worthwhile value to the groups. The brokers suggested that as network development was taking place during a recessionary period many companies had reduced human and mechanical resources to survival levels and simply had no spare capacity or drive to re-grow their businesses in an under-performing economy.

Other examples of barriers to network sustainability experienced by the TEC included: partners becoming involved in a dispute over a business matter divorced from the networking project; impetus and enthusiasm waning as members became frustrated by lack of progress when a key partner was involved in negotiations that eventually led to the company being taken over; and a lack of confidence in the business prospects of a number of partners. Therefore, as formal network development is a process that is inevitably complex and time consuming, concerning organisations that are discrete legal entities with their own objectives and missions coming to mutually acceptable compromises, the TEC suggested that only 'financially-sound' companies should be considered as network partners. Similarly, it was seen as advantageous for the actual individuals involved to have a significant degree of personal autonomy and authority so that decision making was not continually referred back to within the companies.

## Concluding Remarks

The chapter has focused on the effects of governmental attempts to vest in TECs the role of local strategists; the subsequent imposition of a prescriptive funding regime; and how policy delivery has increasingly encompassed a networked approach at both an inter-institutional and inter-firm level. It has been shown that the approach adopted by TECs, based on developing networks with other partners, has suffered in many circumstances due to the governmental restrictions placed on them, in particular the necessity to constrict activities to arenas that are often overly localised. Also, a key outcome of the reduction in TEC budgets and the introduction of a funding regime based on a bidding process has been to limit the ability and capacity of TECs to tackle economic development on their own. This has resulted in the concept of networking, through the generation of local partnerships, becoming an even more important component within the economic development landscape. It appears that better co-ordination and closer collaboration within the bidding-related bureaucracy is required, in particular that surrounding the Single Regeneration Budget. The TEC perspective presented in this chapter suggests that the Labour Government should take greater responsibility for funding projects based on sound and long-term objectives, rather than an over fascination with prescribing funds towards short-term 'flavour of the month' initiatives. These are lessons which should be heeded by both the Learning and Skills Councils and the Small Business Service.

The findings of this chapter indicate that TECs appear to have had an almost 'invisible hand' in shaping and administering policy, with often the most minimal of resources. The arrival of Business Link as deliverers of business and enterprise support further emphasised the position of TECs as strategic co-ordinating partners. However, the dual existence of both TECs and Business Links further fragmented an often already confused, duplicative and counter-productive system of business support, in which Business Links have faced credibility problems in the business community. Furthermore, although TECs and Business Links have attempted to create fee paying services, this approach has met a number of difficulties and more often than not services seem to be discounted on a fairly easy going and ad hoc basis.

The chapter further considered the practicalities and problems that TECs, often in the shape of 'network brokers', have encountered in facilitating the building and sustaining of local inter-firm networks, primarily among SMEs, in a number of differing scenarios. It was found that the most effective and sustainable networks are initially based on informal relations, such as those developed through voluntary attendance at 'learning' workshops and seminars. The evidence suggests that the initial focus of projects should consist of expanding the level of interaction and contact between SMEs through learning networks that focus on building the stock of social capital. Also, it appears that gaining sufficient reserves of social capital should be considered prior to the planning of any formal 'dotted line' commercial or innovation-based relations. While this chapter has viewed network developments from the perspective of TECs, chapter 7 evaluates TEC facilitated inter-firm initiatives considered from the point of view of those companies participating in this mode of economic development policy.

# 7 Evaluating Network Policies

## Introduction

The existence of a large and growing mass of literature on inter-firm, or business, networks, and their perceived value to economies, would suggest that much is already known about how they are actually created and what are their key constituent characteristics. However, the network metaphor is now being applied to such a wide array of activities that there appears to be a gap emerging between the academic discourse of inter-firm networks and an understanding of what company managers are actually doing when they are described as joining, or already being a member of, a network. As Bosworth and Rosenfeld (1993) state, there is a danger that the term 'network', particularly in public policy discourse, will slip directly from obscurity to meaninglessness without an interesting period of coherence. Furthermore, as Bessant (1995) suggests, networks are still a comparatively new addition to the policy maker's 'toolbox', and despite there being considerable excitement about their potential there is a risk that they will be used widely but not necessarily appropriately. The objective of this chapter is to go some way to meeting Bessant's (1995) recommendation that there is a need to further explore the strengths and weaknesses of inter-firm networks as a public policy resource which has necessarily required experimentation and adaptation.

The focus of the chapter is an evaluation of the inter-firm network initiatives operated by TECs and their partners (i.e. Business Links, chambers of commerce, enterprise agencies and other private support agencies) from the point of view of the companies participating in these initiatives; which, in this case, are overwhelmingly SMEs. It has already been suggested, in chapter 5, that the networks generated through these initiatives can be categorised into three types - learning, commercial and innovation - depending on the expected and actual outcomes. This chapter evaluates how network initiatives contribute to these outcomes through two differing channels: (1) informal network initiatives; (2) formal network initiatives.

As discussed in chapters 2 and 6, informal network initiatives refer to policies that bring together firms to share information, solve common problems, or acquire new skills through voluntary contact and interaction.

A further distinction has been made between informal - general network initiatives, where the interaction primarily consists of information and knowledge exchange which is usually of an on-going and 'non-goal' specific nature (for example: business clubs); and informal - task-specific initiatives, involving a form of workshop-based learning aimed at achieving some common end result, such as company accreditation (for example: benchmarking and best practice clubs). Formal network initiatives consist of efforts to bring together firms to co-produce, co-market, co-purchase, or co-operate in product or market development through contractual agreement. Such contractual agreement refers to a commitment by participating companies to routinise these business activities as a collaborative endeavour, through mutually binding consent. Formal network initiatives in the UK have primarily been based on the importation of the key elements of the Danish network programme, that has already been discussed in chapters 3 and 5, consisting of the employment of 'network brokers' as the primary operators of the initiatives.

The chapter focuses on the results of a survey of companies that have participated in the following network initiatives operated by TECs and, where stated, their partners: (a) informal - general - (1) Local Manufacturers Group (involving local chamber of commerce and Business Link); (2) Local Sector Group; (3) Venture Capital Seekers Group (involving Business Link); (4) 'Corporate' Business Club; (5) Business Start-up Club (involving local enterprise agency); (b) informal - task-specific - (6) Investors in People (IiP) Club; (7) Management Development Forum (involving private agency); (8) Manufacturing Challenge 'Cluster' Groups (performance improvement/best practice networks involving private agents); (9) Export Club; (c) formal - three large scale formal network initiatives involving Business Links and private consultants. The previous research, detailed in chapters 5 and 6, enabled access to be granted to the databases of a number of TECs, with five TECs being chosen to participate in the survey; one from each of the broad regions of the North of England, the Midlands, the South East, the South West, and Wales. These five TEC-areas incorporated a mix of both rural and urban locations, manufacturing and service sector structures, and rates of economic growth.

*Research Design*

Questionnaires were posted to 531 companies (including initial piloting in one TEC-area) who had participated in one of a total of 12 network initiatives, as illustrated in Table 7.1. After following-up non-respondents through reminder letters, a total of 267 responses were obtained, a response rate of 50.3 per cent. This response rate compares favourably with the rates obtained by other surveys of SMEs, for example Bryson's (1997) study of Business Links obtained a company response rate of 10 per cent. It is also fairly comparable to Curran and Blackburn's (1994) much applauded response rate of 59 per cent for a survey of small firms.

**Table 7.1     Distribution of the Types of Inter-firm Network Initiatives and Number of Firms Surveyed by TEC area**

| TEC | Type of Inter-firm Network Initiatives Surveyed | No. of Firms Surveyed | No. of Responses | Response Rate |
|---|---|---|---|---|
| TEC A | (1) Investors in People Club; (2) Management Development Forum; (3) Local Sector Group | 84 | 63 | 75.0 |
| TEC B | (1) Business Start-up Club; (2) 'Corporate' Business Club; (3) 'Formal' Business Networks | 210 | 79 | 37.6 |
| TEC C | (1) Local Manufacturers Group; (2) 'Formal' Business Networks | 95 | 58 | 61.1 |
| TEC D | (1) 'Manufacturing Challenge' 'Cluster' Groups (Performance Improvement/Best Practice Networks) | 40 | 24 | 60.0 |
| TEC E | (1) Export Club; (2) Venture Capital Seekers Group; (3) 'Formal' Business Networks | 102 | 43 | 42.2 |
| **Total** | **12 Initiatives** | **531** | **267** | **50.3** |

The differing numbers of firms surveyed by TEC-area, shown in Table 7.1, reflects the range of initiatives, with some having far more participants than others. The differing response rates is a further reflection of the fact that while TECs listed a large number of firms as being attached to certain initiatives, especially for formal network initiatives, in reality this involvement had been restricted to a visit from a TEC manager or network broker and/or attendance at an 'awareness' seminar. For example, the relatively low response rates in TECs B and E are due to the operation of formal network initiatives that initially canvassed a large pool of companies, through visits and seminars, that subsequently did not follow through their involvement. Therefore, the majority of non-respondents can be assumed to have actually 'dropped-out' of the initiative at a very early stage. A small number of firms returned their questionnaires stating that they had only been involved in the initiative for a very short-period of time. These respondents were eliminated from the final analysis.

The majority of participating firms were of small size, and more than one-half of the sample – 53 per cent firms - were micro-firms of ten or less employees (11-25 employees = 15 per cent firms; 26-100 = 18 per cent; 101-200 = 9 per cent; 201-500 = 2 per cent; 501+ = 3 per cent). There was a relatively broad overall breakdown in terms of sector with 48 per cent of firms involved in manufacturing and 52 per cent in service sector activities. The high response rate is in itself a good indication of the reliability of the responses to the overall sample. However, this reliability was also assessed in relation to the representativeness of responses to the sample in terms of company sector and size. By applying the overall response rate to each size of firm band and sector, chi-square tests indicated that the probability of the sample and response distribution being different was less than 5 per cent.

## Creating Interaction and Co-operation

Initially, the survey assessed the extent to which the inter-firm network initiatives facilitated by TECs and their partners attempted to create and engender interaction between participating firms. The majority of participating firms considered that the co-ordinators and operators of the initiatives (i.e. network brokers; workshop leaders; company mentors; initiative managers; trainers; etc.) did give a high (37 per cent of all participating firms), or at least moderate (43 per cent), importance to the stimulation of company interaction. It was further found, perhaps surprisingly, that it is the co-ordinators of informal networks - i.e. those groups where no contractual and/or binding agreement exists between the members - that have given the highest importance to stimulating interaction; with 29 per cent of the participants in formal network initiatives claiming that brokers had placed a low importance on stimulating interaction. This finding can be explained by the fact, as illustrated by Chaston (1996a), that processes of facilitating formally implanted networks in the UK have been primarily on the Danish network development model, whereby there is initially a fairly lengthy period of firm assessment and feasibility analysis, based around one-to-one company-broker planning sessions, involving little actual interaction between firms. Also, due to the necessity for higher commitment levels by companies involved in formal network initiatives, often in the form of commercially binding agreements, there are far higher 'drop-out' rates compared to those associated with informal network initiatives.

Despite the importance placed by co-ordinators on stimulating interaction, more than two-thirds of firms reported that actual interaction was in reality either fairly unintensive (44 per cent of firms) or non-existent (27 per cent of firms). Although less than a third of firms were involved in intensive company interaction, 5 per cent of participating companies did indicate that more could have been gained from the initiative if the interaction had been of a more intensive nature. Firms that were involved in initiatives where the facilitators had placed a high importance on stimulating interaction were more than five times as likely (60 per cent compared to 11 per cent) to be involved in intensive interaction, compared with initiatives where the facilitators had given less importance. Therefore, it is clear that it is primarily the facilitators and brokers, rather than the firms participating in network initiatives, that initially hold the key in the crucial outset period to producing interaction that can subsequently lead to the formation of embryonic networks. In other words, if facilitators do not prioritise from an early stage the creation of some form of contact between those firms that are exposed to network initiatives, there is little chance of the emergence of sustainable networks based on co-operation.

Significantly, more than three-quarters of firms that reported a degree of interaction with other companies stated that it had been either very co-operative (29 per cent of firms) or fairly co-operative (60 per cent) (Table 7.2). This implies that where company interaction occurs it does not, in most cases, have any detrimental effect on the potential for the development of closer and more collaborative relationships between firms. However, there was a marked deviation in the level of co-operation achieved by informal and formal initiatives. Whereas only 8 per cent of firms involved in informal networks reported unco-operative interaction, this rose to 32 per cent in the case formal network initiatives. This confirms the evidence of other recent evaluations of formal network initiatives in both the United States and New Zealand, which found that there are often serious difficulties to be encountered in generating an environment of compatibility between firms (Perry, 1995; Rosenfeld, 1996; 1997b; Welch et al., 1997b). These compatibility factors most often concern an inability to appeal to the self-interest of all participants, as well as a lack of a critical mass of individuals who are both sufficiently knowledgeable and empowered to make decisions on behalf of their firms (Rosenfeld, 1996).

**Table 7.2**     **Level of Co-operation Between Participating Firms (% of Firms)**

| Type of Network Initiative | Very Co-operative | Fairly Co-operative | Fairly Unco-operative | Very Unco-operative |
|---|---|---|---|---|
| Informal - General | 27.1 | 61.4 | 10.6 | 0.9 |
| Informal - Task-Specific | 42.9 | 55.4 | 1.7 | 0.0 |
| Informal (All) | 31.8 | 59.9 | 7.7 | 0.6 |
| Formal | 4.0 | 64.0 | 32.0 | 0.0 |
| **All Network Initiatives** | **28.7** | **60.0** | **10.8** | **0.5** |

A lack of compatibility among participants was recognised, as shown in Table 7.3, by 19 per cent of firms (21 per cent in the case of formal network initiatives) as a key barrier limiting interaction and co-operation. However, by far the most common barrier is the well documented (see for example: Curran and Blackburn, 1994; Adam-Smith and McGeever, 1995; Vickerstaff and Parker, 1995; Parker and Vickerstaff, 1996; Rosenfeld, 1996) constraint associated with networks, as well as more general business support, initiatives; i.e. the lack of time participants are prepared to invest in initiative involvement (mentioned by 60 per cent of firms), particularly small owner-managers. Rosenfeld (1996) similarly found in his study of networks initiatives in Oregon that the most significant barrier to development concerned the claim by managers that daily business pressures made it physically difficult for them to actually leave their company's plant.

The issue of trust as a key constraining factor was mentioned by only 3 per cent of firms, rising to 6 per cent in the case of formal network initiatives. This figure, which does not indicate that significant levels trust were engendered between the majority of participants, partly reflects the fact that the majority of informal networks, based around non-competitive (in terms of inter-group conflict) collective learning and information exchange processes, do not usually require high levels of trust to be generated, as there is a virtually negligible commercial 'risk' element. Indeed, the 'type' of trust required to generate and maintain interaction in these circumstances is akin to 'weaker' and more easily attainable forms, such as the 'competence' and 'swift' trust identified, respectively, by Sako

(1992) and Meyerson et al. (1996). Therefore, there is little need in these circumstances to guard against 'free-riders' and 'free-loaders' (Telser, 1987; Putnam, 1993). In the case of formal initiatives, it appears that the majority of networks have simply not been sustained long enough for issues concerning the uneven distribution of power, exploitation and opportunism - and thus the requirement for 'strong' trust' - to become a significantly relevant issue.

Some degree of trust, as contended by Granovetter (1992), is a basic necessity for the normal functioning of economic actions. It is suggested, therefore, that the lack of company investment in network initiatives, measured in terms of the time that they are willing to allocate for involvement is indicative of the fact that they consider the costs, and associated risks, of producing the type of strong trust necessary to create sustainable networks to be too expensive. That is, firms have not placed enough value on the initiatives and have, therefore, not pursued the type of 'studied trust' identified by Sabel (1992; 1994), which is catalysed through systematic investments in processes of learning how and why to trust. As Sako (1992) found, 'studied trust' is by no means 'cheaply' acquired, being subject to high set-up costs that may actually be detrimental to the efficiency of companies in the short-term.

The relationship between trust and the success or failure of network initiatives is further explored, in a more qualitative manner, in chapter 8; however the fairly unintensive nature of much of the interaction reported by firms in this survey suggests that in most cases the type of trust generated by these networks initiatives resembles a relatively weak form, which can be related to the concept of 'swift trust'. Swift trust is most closely associated with temporary groupings involving actors that have no presupposed reason to trust each other acquiring a form of trust involving a degree of mutual commitment, but which also simultaneously hedges against the risks of betrayal (Meyerson et al., 1996). Instead of focusing on the creation of 'tacit' agreements to trust and co-operate, swift trust identifies more 'codifiable' arrangements centred around the undertaking of definable roles and duties.

Other barriers limiting interaction included: (1) a lack of clear guidance, preparation, objectives and measures of success by initiative facilitators; (2) a lack of tangible early benefits; (3) a number of firms considering themselves to be too specialised to benefit from a network. The most bizarre problem concerned a company that considered the table seating arrangements at meetings to be continually unsatisfactory.

**Table 7.3    Barriers Limiting Interaction and Co-operation According to Participating Firms (% of Firms)**

| Type of Network Initiative | Lack of Trust between Participants | Incompatibility of Participants | Lack of Time | Other |
|---|---|---|---|---|
| Informal - General | 3.2 | 19.0 | 61.1 | 12.7 |
| Informal – Task-Specific | 0.0 | 15.9 | 61.9 | 9.5 |
| Informal (All) | 2.1 | 18.0 | 61.4 | 11.6 |
| Formal | 6.1 | 21.2 | 54.5 | 15.2 |
| **All Network Initiatives** | **2.7** | **18.5** | **60.4** | **12.2** |

**Frequency, Density and Mode of Inter-Firm Contact**

As indicated in Table 7.4, a disappointingly high 58 per cent of firms (rising to 72 per cent for formal network initiatives) reported that their frequency of contact with other participating companies was less than once a month, with a further 31 per cent of firms in contact once a month, 11 per cent at least once a week. These figures illustrate the high 'drop-out' rates associated with network initiatives (particularly for formal structures), and for business support in general, which are often associated with the lack of early benefits accruing from such programmes. However, the sustainability issue appears to be particularly acute for these initiatives, as it can be inferred that more than one-half of all participants effectively exit the initiative before the development or building of any inter-company relationships. This suggests that social capital, or the relationships and norms which facilitate co-operation and collective action (Putnam, 1993), has not been effectively nurtured by facilitators in the design of initiatives. It is undoubtedly problematic, as well as impossible mechanistically, to build social capital due to its intangibility. However, it does appear that initiative facilitators should increase the emphasis within their programme design on creating the 'nuts and bolts' of social capital (Wilson, 1996; 1997); that is, communication and relationship skills relating to attributes such as listening, understanding, respecting, empathy and honesty. At present, the low frequency of contact implies that most company ties can be described as being 'weak' in terms of the level of bonding, and will only evolve into 'strong' ties if sufficient levels of social capital are built-up.

**Table 7.4    Average Level of Interaction and Contact Between Participating Firms (% of Firms)**

| Type of Network Initiative | Daily | More than Once a Week | Once a Week | Once a Month | Less |
|---|---|---|---|---|---|
| Informal - General | 0.8 | 1.7 | 10.0 | 31.7 | 55.8 |
| Informal - Task-Specific | 0.0 | 1.7 | 10.2 | 33.9 | 54.2 |
| Informal (All) | 0.6 | 1.7 | 10.1 | 32.3 | 55.3 |
| Formal | 0.0 | 0.0 | 6.2 | 21.9 | 71.9 |
| **All Network Initiatives** | **0.5** | **1.4** | **9.5** | **30.8** | **57.8** |

Participating firms stated that they were in 'direct contact' with an average of 6.2 other companies through network initiatives (6.6 for informal networks; 4.0 for formal networks). This figure can be taken as a good estimate of the actual size of functioning networks, which on average can said to consist of 7.2 member companies (1 plus average number of direct contacts). This is significantly lower than the average of 15 firms claimed by TECs in chapter 5, which is undoubtedly more representative of the average number of participants that at some point are exposed to a network initiative. The difference between the two figures is consistent with the aforementioned estimated 'drop-out' rate for initiatives of 58 per cent. It also illustrates the gap between the size of business clubs/forums and the like, and those relationship-structures that evolve within initiatives which can be constituted as being definably an inter-firm network. Those firms involved in interaction that was at least fairly intensive were in direct contact with an average of 13 other firms, while this fell to an average of only 3 firms for initiatives where the interaction was relatively unintensive. This suggests that the density of networks, in terms of the number of company connections, is a direct function of the level of interaction that facilitators and brokers are able to achieve.

It was found that interaction was largely cross-sector in nature, with only 15 per cent of firms indicating that they had interacted solely with companies from within their own particular sector. This figure rose to 31 per cent for formal initiatives, indicating that formal network development, focusing on commercial or innovation outcomes through member binding agreements, was seen by facilitators as being best promoted by bringing together firms where it was assumed there was a higher degree of communality. The seemingly poor overall performance of formal initiatives, however, suggests that many participating companies were wary of compromising any competitive position that they may have held over other participants.

**Table 7.5    Mode of Interaction and Contact Between Participating Firms (% of Firms Reporting Differing Types)**

| Mode of Interaction and Contact | Informal - General | Informal - Task-Specific | Informal (All) | Formal | All Network Initiatives |
|---|---|---|---|---|---|
| Self-Initiated One-to-One Meetings | 34.7 | 29.3 | 33.0 | 20.0 | **31.4** |
| Organised Workshops | 25.0 | 44.8 | 31.3 | 7.7 | **28.4** |
| Forums/ Conferences | 21.8 | 46.6 | 29.7 | 19.2 | **28.4** |
| Written Contact (e.g. letters/fax/ e-mail/etc.) | 25.8 | 24.1 | 25.3 | 20.0 | **24.6** |
| Social/ Recreational | 17.7 | 10.3 | 15.4 | 0.0 | **13.5** |
| Organised Group Company Visits | 8.9 | 15.5 | 11.0 | 7.7 | **10.6** |
| Organised One-to-One Meetings | 11.3 | 6.9 | 9.9 | 11.5 | **10.1** |
| Self-Initiated Group Meetings | 4.8 | 13.8 | 7.7 | 8.0 | **7.7** |
| Other | 1.6 | 3.6 | 2.2 | 4.0 | **2.4** |

The most common form of interaction and contact reported by participating firms, as indicated in Table 7.5, consisted of self-initiated one-to-one meetings, taking place either face-to-face or via the telephone (indicated by 31 per cent of participants). This reflects the fact that although networks are a group endeavour, the 'on-the-ground practicalities' of 'networking' necessarily consist of behaviour that is often more dyadic in nature. Further evidence of this is confirmed by the finding that only 8 per cent of firms were in contact through self-initiated group meetings. Other common types of interaction occurred through organised workshops (28 per cent), forums and conferences (28 per cent), and written contact (25 per cent). Interestingly, only 14 per cent of firms indicated that they were in contact with other participating firms through social or recreational pursuits. This suggests that the level of 'local embeddedness' in the areas where these initiatives were operating is relatively undeveloped, with only a small number of participants engaging in informal social linkages. This further confirms the earlier finding that only low levels of social capital are currently being built within the initiatives. Indeed, 46 per cent of all participants (66 per cent in the case of formal initiatives) stated that their involvement in network initiatives had not made them feel any less isolated from the rest of their respective business communities. These factors can be partly related to the fact that the majority of small business owners and managers do not actually appear to consider pursuing informal 'embedded' linkages as being worthy of any significant degree of their time.

**Network Outcomes on Firm Performance**

The survey assessed the relative benefits of participation in inter-firm network initiatives on the learning, commercial and innovative capabilities of companies, using Likert-scales to gauge perceived improvements. In general, the benefits recorded by firms have been modest, with benefits to 'learning' capabilities proving by far the most effective, confirming the relative outputs as indicated previously by TECs in chapter 5. Learning capabilities were assessed by asking participating companies whether or not improvements had been made, through involvement in the initiative, in training, skills, expertise, know-how; as well as the ability to access management and quality benchmarks, and best practice standards. Table 7.6 indicates that more than one-half of firms (53 per cent) considered the initiatives to be at least moderately beneficial to their learning capabilities, with 15 per cent of firms considering them to be highly beneficial. Informal task-specific initiatives, such IiP Clubs and performance improvement networks, were the most effective with 27 per cent of firms indicating that they were highly beneficial.

The relative effectiveness of learning benefits, compared to the commercial and innovation capabilities indicated below, confirms that the comparative strength of TECs and their partners in the area of business support lies in training and skills improvement, rather than direct commercial or technological innovation support. It also concurs with a recent evaluation of inter-firm network initiatives in the United States, where it was found that the strongest positive effect of policies was on improving the skills level of management and employees (Welch et al., 1997).

**Table 7.6     Relative Benefit of Inter-firm Network Initiatives on the Learning Capability of Participating Firms (% of Firms)**

| Type of Network Initiative | Highly Beneficial | Moderately Beneficial | Slightly Beneficial | Not at all Beneficial |
|---|---|---|---|---|
| Informal - General | 11.3 | 37.1 | 34.7 | 16.9 |
| Informal - Task-Specific | 27.4 | 45.2 | 22.6 | 4.8 |
| Informal (All) | 16.7 | 39.8 | 30.6 | 12.9 |
| Formal | 3.1 | 28.1 | 34.4 | 34.4 |
| **All Network Initiatives** | **14.7** | **38.1** | **31.2** | **16.0** |

In terms of the benefits to direct commercial capabilities, firms were questioned as to the extent to which inter-firm network initiatives had increased, consolidated or diversified sales and total market shares, or facilitated access or expansion into new markets. As Table 7.7 shows, such benefits were in general very small, with 44 per cent of firms indicating no tangible benefits, and only 23 per cent of firms reporting at least a moderate benefit. Furthermore, it is noted that formal network initiatives were by far the least beneficial, in terms of the number of companies indicating some gain, with 61 per cent of firms stating that the initiatives were not at all beneficial. To some extent, this appears to be the result of the facilitators of formal network initiatives 'over-selling' the potential for commercial benefits, leading to participating companies construing these benefits as being attainable in the short, rather than the long, term. In these cases, companies have become disillusioned when such benefits were not forthcoming in the short-term. This confirms the hypothesis, suggested in chapter 6, that the sustainability of network initiatives is directly related to the initial expectations of participants, with informal initiatives often being able to retain a higher degree of participation precisely because the expectations in terms of immediate financial benefits are relatively low.

**Table 7.7** **Relative Benefit of Inter-firm Network Initiatives on the Direct Commercial Capability of Participating Firms (% of Firms)**

| Type of Network Initiative | Highly Beneficial | Moderately Beneficial | Slightly Beneficial | Not at all Beneficial |
|---|---|---|---|---|
| Informal - General | 4.2 | 20.8 | 35.0 | 40.0 |
| Informal - Task-Specific | 4.9 | 13.1 | 39.3 | 42.7 |
| Informal (All) | 4.4 | 18.2 | 36.5 | 40.9 |
| Formal | 0.0 | 22.6 | 16.1 | 61.3 |
| **All Network Initiatives** | **3.8** | **18.8** | **33.5** | **43.9** |

**Table 7.8** **Relative Benefit of Inter-firm Network Initiatives on the Innovation Capability of Participating Firms (% of Firms)**

| Type of Network Initiative | Highly Beneficial | Moderately Beneficial | Slightly Beneficial | Not at all Beneficial |
|---|---|---|---|---|
| Informal - General | 3.4 | 12.7 | 23.7 | 60.2 |
| Informal - Task-Specific | 6.8 | 15.3 | 23.7 | 54.2 |
| Informal (All) | 4.5 | 13.6 | 23.7 | 58.2 |
| Formal | 0.0 | 12.5 | 15.6 | 71.9 |
| **All Network Initiatives** | **3.8** | **13.4** | **22.5** | **60.3** |

The scenario concerning benefits to company innovation - i.e. introducing and developing new products and production processes, or increasing R&D activity - is even more disappointing than the small number of firms benefiting from changes in commercial capabilities. As indicated in Table 7.8, only 17 per cent of firms reported at least a moderate increase in innovation capabilities, with a further 60 per cent stating that there had been no benefits at all to innovation processes. It could be argued that innovation enhancement is not one of the primary roles of TECs and their partners; however, as innovation is now acknowledged as the key factor in sustaining competitive advantage (Porter, 1990; Freeman, 1994), it is considered that more policy emphasis, for both network initiatives and business support programmes in general, should be placed on developing the innovative capacity of firms. Although, this has partially been recognised through the introduction of Business Link innovation counsellors, many of their programmes are operated on a one-to-one basis. This detracts from the growing evidence indicating that innovation is most effectively undertaken as a collective and collaborative process; that is through networks (Clark and Staunton, 1989; Camagni, 1991; Lundvall, 1993; Dodgson and Rothwell, 1994; Powell et al., 1996; Simmie, 1997; Braczyk et al, 1998).

The generally poor benefits accrued by participating firms is summarised in Table 7.9, which shows that 43 per cent of firms (61 per cent for firms involved in formal initiatives) did not consider the initiatives to be of any value as a means of improving competitive performance. Although 34 per cent of firms reported that it had some slight value, only 23 per cent stated at least a moderate value. This compares relatively poorly with evaluation from the Danish network programme, which found that 75 per cent of participating firms had increased their competitiveness (Rosenfeld, 1996). The figures bluntly indicate that the inter-firm network initiatives operated by TECs and their partners have yet to have a widespread influence on the competitive advantage of firms in the UK. While certain learning benefits are occurring, these have in most cases failed to be translated into economically measurable indicators. The large majority of participating firms are not utilising the network initiatives as a 'stepping-stone' for processing learning benefits into innovation gains, through the development of self-sustaining networks.

Although companies appear to be joining initiatives with the common purpose of attempting to improve their competitive position, the 'glue' that is necessary to sustain co-operation over a significant period is more often than not absent due to the lack of value companies subsequently place on the initiatives. Therefore, it must be concluded that such initiatives have yet to be perceived by most companies as a systematic way of sourcing innovation through information and knowledge exchange. As well as reflecting on the abilities and methods employed by network co-ordinators, it is also suggested that it is an indication of the 'mind-set' of those firms that become involved in such initiatives. That is, many companies have yet to prioritise the means by which innovation is attained. Interestingly, 46 per cent of firms which stated that the nature of interaction had been at least fairly intensive did perceive the initiatives as being at least moderately valuable to improving competitive performance; while only 12 per cent for those firms that stated there had been little or no interaction reported the initiative as being of such value.

**Table 7.9    Relative Value of Inter-firm Network Initiatives as a Means of Improving Competitive Performance (% of Firms)**

| Type of Network Initiative | Highly Valuable | Moderately Valuable | Slightly Valuable | Not at all Valuable |
|---|---|---|---|---|
| Informal - General | 1.7 | 21.0 | 33.6 | 43.7 |
| Informal - Task-Specific | 8.3 | 21.7 | 38.3 | 31.7 |
| Informal (All) | 3.9 | 21.2 | 35.2 | 39.7 |
| Formal | 0.0 | 6.5 | 32.3 | 61.2 |
| **All Network Initiatives** | **3.3** | **19.0** | **34.3** | **43.4** |

These findings strongly suggest that network initiatives should not be seen, or promoted, as stand-alone policies, but as part of integrated economic development strategies. For example, IiP Clubs and similar quality-based initiatives have had a relatively beneficial effect, but as part of a more 'total' approach to business improvement. This confirms Marshall et al.'s (1995) assertion that the most successful projects stimulating business growth are those that integrate both manpower and business development. In their study of network initiatives in the United States Malecki and Tootle (1997) contend that the most successful network initiatives are those that have facilitators or brokers who act as community or civic entrepreneurs, essentially having 'their fingers in many different pies', enabling network policy to be integrated into other mechanisms for generating and maintaining economic development. However, the UK experience indicates that network policies are often in competition with other business support programmes that are operated by a host of intermediaries, as well as being subject to the same arbitrary evaluation and funding mechanisms. In funding terms, network initiatives, and other business support programmes, are also still the 'poor relation' to what are often portrayed as low-grade training schemes that primarily recruit trainees into occupational sectors such as hairdressing, catering, and administration (Jones, 1997). A number of respondents indicated that one of the reasons for the limited impact of networks initiatives concerned inadequate funding in terms of effective databases and other follow-up resources.

One of the key problems with network development policy is the lack of 'hard data' that has been generated by previous evaluation work into the actual effects and outcomes of initiatives (Rosenfeld, 1996). Therefore, this study attempted to gather certain quantifiable data by questioning firms on what changes had occurred in their economic make-up that could be directly attributed to involvement in the initiatives. This process obviously has the capacity for a degree of bias, due to it being based solely on the views of participants, with the possibility that respondents may either over- or under-emphasise the actual effects. However, it would appear to have more value than some other evaluative work, for example that undertaken in assessment of the Danish network programme, which analysed changes in the economic indicators of participating firms without allowances for dead-weight factors and other potential externalities that may have accounted for the movement (Gelsing and Knop, 1991; Jakobsen and Martinussen, 1991).

**Table 7.10    % of Participating Firms Reporting Economic Changes that can be Directly Attributed to their Involvement in an Inter-firm Network Initiative**

| Type of Network Initiative | Increase in Turnover | Increase in Productivity | Decrease in Costs | New Employees |
|---|---|---|---|---|
| Informal - General | 14.4 | 14.5 | 7.6 | 13.7 |
| Informal - Task-Specific | 22.2 | 35.8 | 22.6 | 15.4 |
| Informal (All) | 16.9 | 21.2 | 12.3 | 14.2 |
| Formal | 9.4 | 8.6 | 10.7 | 10.7 |
| **All Network Initiatives** | **15.0** | **18.7** | **12.1** | **13.7** |

As indicated in Table 7.10, the survey found that for all participating companies the following percentage reported a positive change that could be attributed to their involvement in an inter-firm network initiative: 15 per cent of firms achieved an increase in turnover; 19 per cent an increase in productivity; 12 per cent a decrease in costs; and 14 per cent had increased total employment. Although these figures are, once again, very moderate they do indicate that network initiatives can have a positive impact on firms and subsequently economic development. However, this currently appears to be restricted to about 1-2 firms for every ten that participate. The largest number of participants reporting positive changes were those involved in informal task-specific networks with: 22 per cent of firms achieving an increase in turnover; 36 per cent an increase in productivity; 23 per cent a decrease in costs; and 15 per cent had increased total employment. This relative success can be partly related to the fact that such informal groupings often form part of wider initiatives focused specifically on achieving best practice and reaching benchmarks that should necessarily lead to production increases or cost decreases. In their study of models facilitating the adoption of concepts such as total quality management, just-in-time and zero inventories among SMEs, Gunasekaran et al. (1996) similarly found inter-firm networks to be an integrated part of models for improving productivity and quality.

Those firms stating they had achieved some positive changes in the above indicators were further asked to estimate the actual amount of movement. The average changes, as shown in Table 7.11, are: a 15 per cent increase in turnover; a 15 per cent increase in productivity; an 11 per cent decrease in costs; and an average 5.8 new employees. These figures undoubtedly offer a degree of optimism and are, more or less, of a similar order to those recorded by the evaluations undertaken in Denmark and the United States. For example, in Denmark it was found that approximately 20 per cent of participating firms had achieved an increase in turnover of at least 10 per cent and a decrease in costs of at least 5 per cent; in the United States members of network initiatives reported an average net increase of 4.7 jobs as a result of participation (Gelsing and Knop, 1991; Jakobsen and Martinussen, 1991; Welch et al., 1997).

**Table 7.11    Average Movement in Economic Indicators by Firms that Reported Tangible Change Directly Attributable to an Inter-firm Network Initiative**

| Type of Network Initiative | % Increase in Turnover | % Increase in Productivity | % Decrease in Costs | Number of New Employees |
|---|---|---|---|---|
| Informal - General | 16.4 | 22.3 | 11.0 | 4.8 |
| Informal - Task-Specific | 10.9 | 9.5 | 4.1 | 6.1 |
| Informal (All) | 14.4 | 15.6 | 7.6 | 5.3 |
| Formal | 20.0 | 15.0 | 26.7 | 15.0 |
| **All Network Initiatives** | **14.6** | **15.2** | **10.6** | **5.8** |

## A Cost Per Job Assessment of Networks as an Economic Development Tool

In order to assess more fully the effectiveness of inter-firm network initiatives as an economic development policy tool it is useful to estimate the average cost of those jobs created. As with any other cost per job assessment, it is naturally subject to certain qualifying judgements and caveats. In this case, the absence of reliable and readily available information concerning the funding and resourcing of initiatives meant that the two most important judgements made related to: (1) the actual costs of administering and operating network initiatives; and (2) the time period in which benefits are assumed to have accrued. The actual costs of operation will necessarily vary significantly between the type of network policy (i.e. informal - general; informal - task-specific; formal) implemented, and as to whether financial assistance is provided to participants, or if finance is actually raised through membership fees, such as in the case of business clubs. The study found that the majority of informal - general networks raise some funding through memberships fees, while informal task-specific and formal network initiatives commonly offer a subsidy during the first year of operation of approximately £1,000 per participating firm. In these circumstances, it was assumed that any jobs created were the result of expenditure in the first year of operation, i.e. the period during which the largest public funding contributions are made.

It can be estimated that the total public expenditure associated with operating network initiatives, on a first-year basis, consists of: the costs of employing a network facilitator/broker (taken as the average total cost, including overheads) - approximately £40,000; general operating costs (such as the additional use of buildings, equipment and consultants) minus any subscription fees - approximately £15,000; average amount of subsides (average number of participants - active or non-active - that received £1,000 grant - a proxy of the number of average participants according to TECs, as given in chapter 5, has been used) - approximately £15,000. The estimated total yearly operating cost of approximately £70,000 is fairly comparable with the costs of operating network initiatives in the United States and Denmark, which have been estimated at approximately US$100,000 and £100,000 a year, respectively (Huggins, 1996; Welch et al., 1997). The cost per job can be estimated as a proportion of the average amount of employment generated by each initiative as follows:

Cost per job created =
(average operating costs of networks) / (per cent of firms experiencing employment growth) (average increase in number of employees) (average 'active' network size [1 + average number of direct firm contacts])

Cost per job created =
(£70,000) / (13.7 per cent) (5.8) (7.2 )= £12,235
(Note: in this case there is no need to assess dead-weight factors as firms have already stated the jobs created are a direct result of participation in the initiative)

This figure of an average cost per job of £12,235 is obviously quite crude, being subject to a number of untested assumptions, in particular concerning the fact that those jobs created are the result of only one (the first) year's funding. Nevertheless, it does provide a broad guide by which to make a comparison with other economic development policies. In general, the cost appears to be higher than the average for small firms policy as a whole, for example Hart and Scott (1994) have estimated the cost per job of these policies to be £8,032. It also substantially higher than the £4,380 which PACEC (1995) estimated, as indicated in chapter 3, to be the average cost per job of all TEC services (although this figure has been debated). However, the figure appears to be fairly 'competitive' compared with the cost of jobs created through European Union structural funding, which have recently been estimated as costing anywhere between approximately £10,000 and £25,000, depending on the region where the funding was spent (Shutt, 1996; Huggins, 1998c). Most importantly, the figure indicates that network initiatives are not a prohibitively expensive economic development tool, in terms of costs to the public exchequer. Indeed, as has been shown, the most substantial costs that need to be met are usually those that are borne by the participating firms, in terms of investments in time and effort.

**Sustainability and Formalisation**

The positive growth figures shown in Table 7.11 indicate that where network initiatives are able to draw-in a critical mass of committed firms over a sustainable period, networks can act as an effective and important instrument for economic development. Furthermore, it shows that it is those firms which have committed themselves to sustained membership of formal networks that have achieved the highest economic growth and increases in efficiency - an average 20 per cent increase in turnover; 27 per cent decrease in costs; and an average of 15 new employees (Table 7.11). This emphasises what Amin and Thrift (1995) term the 'power of networks', with it being formalised groups that are their most potent form in the long-run. The key problem for TECs and their partners is that the positive effects of network initiatives are still highly marginal and restricted.

The problem facing policy makers and facilitators is compounded by the fact that only 22 per cent of firms had actually had any form of contact with other participating companies that had evolved beyond the immediate confines or life-span of the initiative. Also, only 11 per cent of firms had entered into any formal contractual agreements with other participating companies that would not have occurred without contact through the initiative. This again implies that approximately only 1-2 firms for every ten participating in these initiatives have entered networks that have generated their own momentum and become, to some extent, 'free-standing' and self-sustainable. Companies involved in either informal or formal network initiatives that subsequently evolved sustainable formal contractual agreement between some of the participants were those that most commonly attached some positive value to the initiative. For instance, more than twice as many companies (22 per cent compared to 9 per cent) reporting the initiatives to have been of at least moderate value to competitive performance had evolved formal agreements out of the initiatives, compared with those firms stating that the initiatives had been of little value to competitiveness.

The data do not allow for an accurate calculation of the overall death-rate of the networks set up within initiatives; nevertheless, the aforementioned figures on 'spontaneous contact' implies that approximately 80-90 per cent of the networks generated have not become sustainable. However, perhaps the most optimistic finding from the survey is that 65 per cent of the small number of firms that had actually evolved 'free-standing' networks outside of the initiative did consider them to be sustainable in the long-term. Such sustainability is closely related to exposure to interaction within the initiative that had been at least fairly intensive, with 49 per cent of firms involved in intensive interaction forming new links, compared to only 10 per cent where the interaction was unintensive.

## Concluding Remarks

This chapter has evaluated the network initiatives facilitated by TECs and their partners from the perspective of participating firms, predominantly SMEs. It was found that the effectiveness of network initiatives, in terms of the ability to create and sustain co-operative inter-firm networks, is closely correlated to the level of contact and interaction that is facilitated between participants. However, the majority of participants have not generated the strong trust relationships necessary to sustain such networks. Most of the interaction that has taken place within the initiatives has been of a fairly unintensive nature, reflecting the fact that any trust which has been generated is usually relatively 'weak' in terms of its ability to build social capital. This is further reflected by the low frequency of contact between participants, which indicates that in most cases only 'weak ties' exist within the initiatives. The variance in the strength and density of the ties also appears to be closely linked to the ability of network facilitators and brokers to stimulate interaction during the early stages of the initiative.

The majority of the interaction that did occur was usually of a dyadic, or one-to-one, nature. There was generally a lack of interaction through spontaneous group action or via socially-based contact and linkages. This indicates that the existence of embedded and social capital 'rich' ties are not a common feature of the network initiatives. The outcome of this has been to limit the benefits accrued by firms through participation. Those benefits which companies have gained are usually of a 'learning', rather than of a commercial or innovation, related nature, reflecting the fact that the relative support strength of TECs and their partners facilitators is skills and training based. However, the lack of comparative strength in areas concerning focused and collaborative innovation support has seriously limited the ability of the initiatives to impact on the overall competitive advantage of participating companies. These companies have subsequently undervalued the ability of networks to enhance learning benefits as a means of achieving innovation. Despite a general under-achievement the initiatives indicate that inter-firm network policy, if correctly implemented, can be a cost-effective instrument for economic development. Chapter 8 further explores the reasons for the relative success or failure of differing network initiatives that policy makers have attempted to implement.

# 8 The Success and Failure of Implanted Networks

## Introduction

Chapter 7 found that the success or failure of public policy inter-firm initiatives is related to a number key factors, such as the motivations and expectations of participants, coupled with the ability of initiative facilitators and brokers to create valued interaction and exchange between participants, and to instigate a 'contact process' within which trust relationships are generated. These were most successfully delivered through informal, or non-contractual, processes; although it was found that the potential for the most substantial economic gains for network members were to be made through formal groups with focused objectives, related to which there was some form of contractual agreement. This final empirical chapter examines in more depth the processes and causes of network success and failure, defined in terms of the ability of the network to become a sustained and valued form of business activity for its members.

The chapter examines four different case-study network initiatives (drawn from the initiatives surveyed in chapter 7) as follows: (1) a failed informal 'new entrepreneurs network'; (2) a successful informal 'local cluster group'; (3) a failed formal 'defence contractors network'; (4) a successful formal 'small-firm technology group'. The case-studies draw strongly on the actual narrative explanations given by managing directors of their involvement, and the subsequent events that took place, within the networks initiatives, which as Pitt (1998) contends can to an extent be treated as quasi texts containing implicit and personal theories of their managerial action, particularly in relation to the 'type(s) of rationality' - i.e. social and/or economic - employed. These actions and events within the network initiatives were corroborated by there being two informants for each initiative which enabled the clarification of any 'fuzzy' issues. The case-studies explore the motivation and rationality of SME managing directors to join the network initiatives, and the importance they place on collective business action in general. They further assess the role of the initiative facilitator/broker and the actual mechanics of exchange and interaction during the critical early stages of network formation.

The four cases were developed in a qualitative manner, consisting of a series of in-depth interviews undertaken with the managing directors of companies that had participated in one of four inter-firm network initiatives. The case-studies are not proportionately representative of the overall success and failure of network initiatives, but were chosen to provide further insight into the actual processes concerned with building and sustaining of networks through policy intervention.

## New Entrepreneurs Network

The new entrepreneurs network is an initiative funded by a TEC and operated in partnership with an enterprise agency under the banner 'Enterprise Connect'. The TEC has funded the initiative for three years with the aim being to: (1) train prospective entrepreneurs in the basic skills and practicalities required to operate a business, for example book-keeping, employment law and tax payment; (2) to help new entrepreneurs overcome the fear and isolation often associated with new business venturing; (3) to facilitate, if possible, the exchange of the goods and services produced by each member; i.e. to act as a 'first market-place'. The operation of the network primarily took the form of weekly groups focused around some facet of new business management, and led by personnel connected either with the TEC or the enterprise agency. In addition, there was a mix of monthly and other one-off social and speciality events. The network has also produced a directory listing all the member entrepreneurs in a business profile format. The aim of the directory was to both facilitate interaction between members and to act as a marketing tool for their businesses.

There were no membership or joining fees associated with the network, and the actual number of participants turned-over fairly steadily as new members joined and others dropped-out. At any one time it appears that total membership was approximately 50, although the entrepreneurs interviewed stated that they were actually in contact with about 5 or 6 other members on a regular basis. At the time of the interviews the two entrepreneurs were still operating their businesses, which in both cases were, by choice, sole proprietorships. Both entrepreneurs had previously served a considerable period of time working for large organisations within their own industries. The first was involved in quarry engineering and materials handling, and had started his own business, Seminex Services, as a result of the large rationalisation within the quarrying industry. The second operated a portable appliance testing service, Centurion Inspection Services, and had started the business due to his perception that there was a market niche which he could exploit.

It was suggested in chapter 2 that motivation for joining an inter-firm network consists of either a social and/or economic rationality on behalf of the members. In this case, the new entrepreneurs interviewed described intrinsically different reasons for participating. The owner of Centurion stated that the key motivating factor was the financial assistance that was available to participants, as well as the possibility of marketing his services to other members:

> 'All I did it for basically was the cash, the start-up assistance. I was quite clear in my mind where I was going and what I was going to do. I produced a business plan that was acceptable and it followed along fairly well according to that.' (Centurion)

> 'I didn't want to know how to run a business. I've got the books, and the accounts, tax and pensions were all under control. I just wanted to meet somebody who might want to use the services I provide.' (Centurion)

Whereas as the owner of Centurion was seeking some direct economic gain, the motivations of the owner of Seminex are based more on a social rationality. As a new entrepreneur with little business experience the owner claimed that he often felt isolated and fearful, which he hoped could be overcome by 'meeting people in a similar situation' through joining the network. The owner did utilise the network in fulfilling a knowledge function, in terms of learning the rudiments of business management. However, the key motivating factor was the seeking of 'social guidance' to alleviate the fears that are often associated with new entrepreneurs, rather than in terms of directly improving business performance. In practice, the owner of Seminex felt that he gained very little from his contact with other members apart from a small degree of reassurance concerning, for instance, the fact that they were also experiencing similar problems with slow-paying customers. Although he attended the network meetings for six months he did not maintain contact with any of the other participants beyond this period. This he stated was due to two main reasons. Firstly, he had very little in common with the other members, particularly as there were very few members directly involved in engineering. Secondly, he felt that a number of members appeared to be 'rather untrustworthy characters', and in particular he highlighted an anecdote describing the actions of an aspiring estate agent.

The owner of Centurion similarly described little positive gain apart from the financial assistance. He felt that as the proceedings, being primarily dictated by the public sector operators, were slow and thus gained little momentum, with meetings taking a form of 'meeting for meetings sake', rather than gaining a definable direction. He further described the production of the network's directory as taking an inordinate amount of time to finish (15 months in total). At the time of joining the owner had been hopeful of carrying out some portable appliance testing for other members, but in reality this failed to materialise. He partly saw this to be a result of the meetings and social functions of the network not lending themselves to useful social exchange:

'There was a social side to it, but it usually involved you participating in something which you usually did within a little group.... there was no cross-fertilisation of ideas and little contact beyond the exchange of business cards.' (Centurion)

Neither owner stated that they would be willing to pay for membership of the network, beyond a token subscription. The owner of Seminex stated that there was a large cross-section of individuals involved in the initiative which often hindered the meetings, and that a more sector-specific focus may have strengthened the outputs. He saw a further drawback as being the fact that some of the other aspiring entrepreneurs seemed to be of a 'poor calibre', and subsequently held back the more dynamic members:

'There were people from all walks of life. Older semi-retired people who were making rubber ducks or snakes and things that they wanted to sell on markets stalls. There's no connection between them and my own specialism.........Maybe its the case that any real new successful entrepreneurs haven't got time to be involved in initiatives like this in any case.' (Seminex)

The owner of Centurion also acknowledged that the success of the network was very much down to the type and attitudes of the members. He stated that although the framework provided by the network operators may not have been the most conducive to producing interaction, the members did not attempt to adapt it to suit their needs. Interestingly, both owners outlined that they had strong socio-centric networks within their own business sectors which they consciously maintained, i.e. business contacts and colleagues that they had nurtured a relationship with from their previous employment. For example, the owner of Seminex acts as an intermediary between certain members of the quarrying industry, building-up trustworthy relationships with a large number of individuals within the sector. He considers this network to be a vital factor in the successful setting-up of his business and, therefore, works hard at maintaining it. Also the owner of Centurion has nurtured a number of key contacts that contract portable appliance testing in the insurance broker sector.

When asked what could have improved the overall success of the initiative the interviewees highlighted the following requirements: (1) a degree of sectorisation and more focused activities within the network model; (2) the ability to 'access' successful local entrepreneurs who could act as role models from whom lessons can be learnt (and if possible some who have 'failed'); (3) a more practical and less theoretical approach - some of the initiative facilitators were seen as being rather 'flowery' and of a 'lecturer-nature', detached from the realities of business; (4) there should be more strategic emphasis on interaction and contact with other members - 'there was a need for members to understand that they should not just talk to people willy-nilly, but to pin-point those who are actually in a position to possibly help them' (Seminex); (5) more professionalism from both the facilitators and members of the initiative. With regard to the issue of professionalism, the owner of Centurion highlighted that although the committee steering the network contained a number of member entrepreneurs (as he himself was), many individuals would often not be in attendance at key meetings, which resulted in the slowing down of potential projects.

The operating costs of the initiative have proved to be higher than forecast, and after funding the initiative for three-years the local TEC is ceasing to allocate any further finance towards it. Coupled with a lack of definable outputs this has led to abandonment of the network, with no structure currently being implemented to take its place.

## Local Cluster Group

Local cluster groups consist of a number of self-help networks that have been successfully piloted by a TEC in the West Midlands. The groups provide facilities for the representatives of up to 10 companies to work together on finding human resource solutions to common business problems and carry out development work. The groups are further able to draw on the support services, for example marketing and quality assurance, of the TEC and Business Link. The TEC has funded the groups since 1995/96, with the day to day management of the groups being undertaken by a local management consultancy. Members further contribute an annual subscription fee of approximately £250 per company. The operation of the groups consists mainly of monthly meetings and a series of organised company visits. However, the participants are generally in contact with each other approximately once a week via telephone, written contact and self-initiated one-to-one meetings, in order to arrange and discuss new and potential projects. Furthermore, there is considerable ad hoc contact with the management consultancy operators and the TEC/Business Link service providers. In this case, the cluster group studied consisted of a network of manufacturing firms located in a relatively small area of the West Midlands, i.e. the ten member firms are in fairly close proximity to each other. The two interviewees were the managing directors of a small metal fabricator producing vehicle brake components - Midlands Metal - and a small iron foundry - Goodirons, which are both well established local companies.

In both cases the motivation for joining the network was that the managing directors felt that it would be worthwhile to extend their contacts with other local companies. Goodirons stated that their relationships with other local companies until joining the cluster group had become 'clannish'. The company was only directly interacting with companies that were involved in the foundry sector, with the managing director considering that the time was right for a broadening of horizons and for the company to learn and innovate through interaction with other manufacturing sectors. Both companies also considered that the format of monthly meetings, with a relatively small group of companies, leading to additional interaction could be useful and beneficial. In the case of Midlands Metal, the firm had actually already been looking to join such a group:

> 'We already wanted to join a group of local businesses where we could share problems, solutions and get to know people in the area...........As it was put to us [the formation of the group], we felt it was worthwhile at least seeing how it went, and it has proved interesting. I don't attend every single one of the sessions, sometimes another colleague of mine goes in my place; sometimes I take another one along with me.' (Midlands Metal)

> 'Our first priority was to gather information as to what's going on in the area and pick up ideas to discuss.......the iron foundry industry is a bit clannish and I think we should talk to different people, not just stick to the [a foundry association] and other organisations.... I was intrigued that as it's a small group you can get almost like a one-to-one situation which, I think, is very, very beneficial. It's a relaxed atmosphere as well, which is very useful for discussion. It's different, you know, not so formal as a lot of these seminars run by different organisations.' (Goodirons)

According to the companies, the key to the success of the group has been that although they are all involved in manufacturing within the same locality, none are actually within the same production or market sector. Therefore, they have been able to discuss and develop similar subjects and projects which affect them individually as companies but does not compromise them competitively. As the managing director of Goodirons stated, the companies involved are all of a 'similar ilk', being manufacturing firms within a small locality, but differentiated enough to encourage a free flow of information and exchange experiences with the rest of the group:

> 'We were happy to chat and discuss things from day one, it was as though we'd been in it for a long time......You don't have to be in the same industry to apply similar ideas. If you're in manufacturing, you're in manufacturing.' (Goodirons)

The companies further pointed to the success of the group being partly related to the energy of the management consultant, who has effectively acted as the network broker, encouraging companies to attend meetings and co-ordinating and administering projects that are interesting and relevant to all members. The close spatial proximity of members has meant that not only is travel time kept to a minimum, but also that the companies were already aware, and in most cases had already had some form of previous contact, with each other. In other words, there was a degree of embeddedness which was positively drawn upon. The meetings have taken place at an easily accessible site, during the late afternoon when the participants have felt that they have had sufficient time to complete their normal business, and that the meeting was not encroaching into their leisure time. Both companies initially joined the group for one year, but in both in cases they continued and renewed their membership beyond this period. As new projects arise the business support managers of the TEC/Business Link are usually brought on-board to oversee their facilitation. Midlands Metal highlighted the example of a 'tooling project' that had been developed to reduce the costs of producing and supplying a particular engineering part utilised by a number of the members. The group appears to have been particularly successful in nurturing an environment that has steered relatively free of friction or animosity between members, with power tending to be evenly distributed and trustworthiness forming easily and incrementally overtime. Also, as it is predominately managing directors that are involved, they are usually among the most dynamic people within their organisations, as well as being empowered to 'get things done':

> '....there's no direct competition [between members]. I think, when you look at the people who actually go to the meetings, they're not the sort of people who aren't able to make decisions, they're all mainly at director level.' (Goodirons)

'There's no friction or anything like that. No, it's a good group of people. Everybody who comes there is free to discuss points and we all join

in.......Nobody takes over the chair and we all have a reasonable  input.'
(Midlands Metal)

Both firms emphasised that the monthly meetings had developed a social element with food and drinks being served, generating an environment whereby the members are able to relax in what they considered to be comfortable yet professional surroundings, making them amenable to freely discussing ideas and exchanging points of view. The managing director of Goodirons indicated that it was during periods of social interaction that opportunities, both of a one-on-one business nature and ideas for collective action, had often occurred, with the frequency increasing as the personal relationships between members strengthened. This social factor, coupled with a commonality in terms of locality and the manufacturing emphasis, resulted in the group quickly gaining momentum and becoming a valued collective forum for the members:

> 'I think that the better you know people, the more people open up to you and the more you get to know of the general business climate in [the locality].....Our particular product isn't made by anybody else in [the locality], so I can't relate our product to the rest of the group; but in terms of the employment of people in the area, the people issues, we have similar problems, situations and we can learn from each other how we've dealt with those situations. So, there are good areas  where we have cross-fertilised ideas.' (Midlands Metal)

Although the members currently pay an annual subscription fee of £250, Goodirons and Midlands Metal suggested that they would actually be willing to pay more, further stating that they saw the current costs, which are subsidised by the TEC, as 'good value for money'. The companies stated that the group had been of most importance in supporting them to: (1) overcome local business isolation, by facilitating communication with other local firms; (2) gain a deeper knowledge of local and national trading climates and labour market issues; (3) learn certain new techniques and practices in the area of business management, in particular quality assurance, best practice and benchmarking issues (both companies considered that they may not have taken on-board these issues if they had been presented in another less accessible format). It is interesting to note that both managing directors displayed a strong sense of belonging and ownership when discussing the cluster group, and they indicated that relationships with other members had become far stronger than the ties they had with the members of their respective chambers of commerce and trade associations to which they are affiliated. The managing director of Midlands Metal also suggested that the group was operated and managed on a level that was more professional than that he had experienced with other business groups.

The managing director of Goodirons had previously spent a number of years working in the Far East, and he suggested that the cluster group was being to resemble some of the more 'open' co-operative practices that he had witnessed in Japan. In particular, he highlighted the openness with which business and technical issues were discussed, as well as the ability to actually access and enter the plants of other firms. Furthermore, he considered that although arms-length relationships are still predominant in British industry, a culture change is slowly but surely taking place:

> 'I've been a manager since 1973, working for quite a few companies all over the world. I spent six years in the Far East, and as far I could tell co-operation is precisely why the Japanese succeeded. In this country [the UK], the way I see things is that companies have been too against one another, to the detriment of British industry as a whole....I think we're more co-operative now, particularly in manufacturing, because manufacturing is tough and it's getting tougher. To me, you've got to put yourself out; we try and help people and we hope people try and help us. If another foundry want to come and see m place I have no problem whatsoever with that. Years ago, no way would people allow so-called competitors around their site.... I'm trying not to look at things in the old fashioned way of 'screw the other companies'. We're all in it together. The old fashioned management style is changing, and hopefully British managers will be talking even more by the time I retire. Even the iron foundry industry is no longer the old-fashioned, backward-looking industry it was.' (Goodirons)

The attitude and outlook of the managing director of Goodirons, summed-up in this revealing quote, appears to epitomise the notion of entrepreneurs as network builders disposed to generating trust and social capital with their competitors. It is also interesting that his influences and perceptions have been learnt through interacting with the culture of Japanese industry. It would seem that his own personal approach may have undoubtedly had a positive influence on a small network such as the cluster group. This indicates that not all small companies in the UK are operating within a 'fortress' mind-set and mentality of 'us and them'. In particular, this company has recognised the benefits of securing trustworthy ties that have the potential to accrue economic gain through social exchange, not necessarily in the short-term but more probably in the long-run.

In general, this 'enlightened' attitude appears to be a key feature of the types of individuals and companies involved in the cluster group. Indeed, the managing director of Goodirons specifically stated that he considered the strength and sustainability of the group to be closely related to the fact that it has operated with member managing directors who as individuals have been pre-disposed to achieving innovation through collaborative means. So far the group has steered clear of entrepreneurial opportunism that could act to the detriment of the group as a whole, i.e. 'free-loader' or 'free-rider' syndrome. This can be related to the indication by both companies that they felt the benefits of membership to be 'tacit'; that is, the knowledge and information exchanged is only of specific use if there is already a degree of commonality and social capital built-up between those exchanging it. In other words, valued exchange only takes place after a degree of trust has been generated:

> 'You do get this cross-fertilisation. You do find out things from other employers in the area that you weren't aware of, and that's extremely difficult to quantify because it can pop out in any discussion. You can't measure it......It's only when you get together, if you don't get together you're never going to have that opportunity, so the odd comment here or there can be important to you.' (Midlands Metal)

The managing director of Midlands Metal further suggested that the generation of trust, and the avoidance of 'free-loaders', may be partly due to none of the companies involved being direct competitors in the marketplace. Indeed, although he stated a similar co-operative outlook to that of Goodirons, he did admit that the situation might be different if they were directly competing with any of the other members:

> 'You do get a sense of feeling that you'd like to help if somebody is in trouble. If they've got issues they're not sure of and we've gone through the same problem say last year and found a resolution, then I'd have no qualms about passing on advice and information.......Yes, it would make a difference if you've got two people sitting in the group as direct competitors and you were talking about something that could affect your trading. That certainly could be an issue, but we haven't had that sort of situation.' (Midlands Metal)

## Defence Contractors Network

The Defence Contractors Network (DCN) project, operated through a consortium of TECs and subsequently Business Links in one English region, is arguably the most resource intensive attempt in UK to set-up a formal inter-firm network through policy intervention. The DCN was originally conceived by a TEC/Business Link network broker and was based on a seemingly successful inter-firm network in France. By the standards of most network initiatives the DCN managed to mobilise considerable finance through both public sector contributions and private sector subscription fees, and was given a high market and media profile at its launch in 1996. The primary aim of the DCN was to promote and enhance the volume and quality of domestic and international contract opportunities available to a group of regionally-based high technology defence contractors. These companies were targeted for support due to a recognition that in recent years they had suffered significant contractions in their markets as a result of the high level restructuring that occurred in the defence sector. After a 'recruitment campaign' managed by the network broker, during which a group of complementary firms were sought, the DCN was officially launched as a consortium of twenty defence contractors that had signed a legally binding 'collaboration agreement'. In total the group members had a combined turnover of £80 million and employed 1,100 people. The marketing of the DCN consisted of the distribution of 'glossy brochures', 'trade-fair' events, and the organisation of meetings with the leading buyers for large defence companies and agencies. The prime potential contractors were seen to include organisations such as the Ministry of Defence, British Aerospace; GEC Marconi and McDonnell Douglas.

The network broker subsequently took on the role of the network's business manager, and in addition to the joining and membership fees the member companies further contributed a monthly fee of £1,800 towards the operating costs. Part of the marketing strategy consisted of the DCN being portrayed not as a trade association but as a business enterprise in its own right within which member companies were themselves making a significant contribution. It was further indicated that the DCN would operate a service that could: (1) offer a rapid and collective response to tender requirements; (2) act as a single point of contact for the administration of multi-source contracts; (3) deliver 'cradle to grave' project management. The 'collaboration agreement' incorporated the network as a company limited by guarantee, with the twenty member companies acting as the shareholders. According to the company memorandum this agreement would seek actively to 'maximise for the benefit of members the commercial opportunities in the network field through the pooling of knowledge, ideas, skills and experience co-operation and teaming amongst members'.

From this 'mission statement' the members identified five key areas where they considered that the DCN could have a potentially important role within their current business activities (in order of importance): (1) delivery of tendering opportunities from prime contractors; (2) delivery of market intelligence, such as identifying project/technical managers within the defence supply chain who have problems to be solved or equipment to be developed; (3) development of inter-membership activities, such as product development, design and technical consultancy, with the active promotion of these capabilities through the completion and interactive use of a DCN internet web-site; (4) representation at industry events; (5) representation of all member companies within individual markets. In practice and reality the DCN, in the final instance, failed to deliver on the most important aspect of its reason for being - the gaining of new contracts - which ultimately led to the breakdown of the network in 1998. There are a number of lessons to be learnt concerning both the construction and operation of such a formal network which, in this case, will be assessed through the views of two former members, XYM Microcam and Eastco Analytics, both involved in computer engineering.

The managing directors of both companies indicated that the initial approach to join the DCN by the network broker had involved a 'hard-sell' technique, whereby the companies felt, in their own words, partly coerced to join through a fear instilled by the broker that if they did not agree to join the group immediately then there was another company already waiting to take their place:

> 'We were approached by the broker by letter and by coming here to talk to us about joining the network. It was put in such a way that suggested there were a limited number of organisations being approached, and because of our former interest with military applications and the defence sector generally; as well as because we had moved into two specific areas - GIS and document management - that we had a core skill that we could bring to the partnership.... Now, I have to tell you that, in that conversation, he [the broker] said that there was another company based in [the locality], who were interested in joining the group and also had the same core skills and had military connections. The implication being that if we didn't agree to join there and then, there was someone else who would take that up. So, you felt that maybe there was a bit of pressure.' (XYM Microcam)

Despite this pressure, both companies were aware that due to changes in the defence sector there was a need to diversify and find new markets. Therefore, both companies agreed to join the DCN in the hope of stimulating a process of business substitution. In particular, the managing director of Eastco Analytics had previously been a member of a self-initiated network of five technology-based firms that had successfully produced and marketed an interactive software package. In this case, the managing director considered one of the positive points of the DCN to be that a business manager, in the form of the broker, was going to be remunerated for constructing, administering and maintaining the network; a task which in his previous experience the managing director had found to be highly time consuming:

> 'On the one side of the equation we felt there was some coercion, but at the same time we grasped that here we were now seeing a major chunk of our business eventually going to peter out. So we were looking for other opportunities and therefore the idea of joining a group of companies of similar background, and similar problems, if you like, seemed like a good idea....I might say, it was not for the first time that we as a company had done this and so the principles of such a group were known to us, with both the benefits and downsides being appreciated.....So, here I am saying to myself 'Yes. We've done this once before and it can work, and this time we're not going to have to be involved in its construction.' (Eastco Analytics)

As the setting-up of the DCN involved the formation of a new company it was necessarily a fairly formal process, with little actual interaction during these early stages between member companies. The companies described the broker as taking the role of an intermediary and conduit of the overall information and knowledge contained within the group. In hindsight, the companies considered that the broker appeared to be taking an approach whereby he was able to control, monitor and even censor information exchange within what was a very embryonic structure. It is also now the opinion of the two companies that the seemingly 'secretive' nature of the broker hid at an early stage a number of key constraints which influenced the break-up of the network. In other words, the broker adopted an approach which in itself is the antithesis of the trust and social capital building associated with successful inter-firm networks, i.e. it was broker who appeared to be committing many of the 'cardinal sins of co-operation'. Nevertheless, the network initially appeared to be progressing effectively with an official launch that received widespread and high profile media (including television) coverage, involving ratification by a government minister. However, this superficial hype only served to paper over a number of cracks that can be identified as some of the key reasons for inter-firm network failure.

Apart from bringing the companies together for a couple of pre-launch meetings, the broker appeared to overlook the fact that trust can only be gained, and valued information and knowledge exchanged, when an environment that stimulates interaction between participants is generated. That is, the broker essentially by-passed any 'trying-out' and 'getting-to-know-you' processes. It was only after the launch that member firms were brought together in meetings to discuss and formulate strategies and targets, by which time the companies had already signed the legally binding collaboration agreement. As a result of these formulation meetings it soon become apparent that there was an incompatibility between some of the members firms, particularly with regard to the provision of overlapping products and services:

> 'There wasn't a particularly favourable environment and it certainly didn't seem strong enough for the network to actually succeed.......The mix of companies was wrong, which led to a lack of communication between us.' (Eastco Analytics)

Also, the fact that there were twenty companies involved appeared to further hinder relationships within the network, with too many interests and opinions needing to be represented. For instance, a key output of the formulation sessions was that the DCN should approach prime contractors via a series of face-to-face presentations and meetings. However, the fact that only a small proportion of the members could actually attend these presentations led to further antagonism between the members and the broker, who assumed responsibility for choosing those companies that were to be present:

> 'I suppose that the first indication to me that things were not likely to work out quite as well as we might have hoped was when there was a meeting being set up with British Aerospace. The numbers of people who were entitled to go along from the group was limited to three, or perhaps four, organisations. I remember talking to [the network broker] about his plans for the meeting, and they didn't appear to include us.....In this case, and with our background I really felt we had something to offer. If part of the strategy [of the DCN] is to lead the small organisations to become a supplier to a major international company, I thought we should know about it and be part of it......You couldn't help but feel that there was just a faint whiff of favouritism. I didn't feel too happy with that at all.' (XYM Microcam)

According to both companies a key factor in their joining the DCN was the promise made by the network broker that he had the necessary connections to access and create opportunities in new markets on behalf of the members. The reality, however, appeared to be that although the broker did possess a number of key contacts in the defence sector, these did not amount to gateways to new markets. Indeed, the broker's targeting appeared to consist of the very markets where the restructuring was taking place:

> 'The process consisted of the broker selling the fact that market opportunities would be uncovered which were too large for any single company to undertake on their own. The companies were sold on the idea of

a collaborative method to enter these markets.....There was a general lack of orders, especially from the MOD [Ministry of Defence], which seemed to be the primary target market.' (Eastco Analytics)

'The original expectation was that we would be introduced to opportunities through [the network broker]. He was ostensibly being paid by the group to create opportunities and open doors, but in the end these weren't forthcoming.......There's no question in my mind that these were the expectations and remit of [the network broker], and they just didn't materialise.' (XYM Microcam)

These problems resulted in a breakdown in the relationship between the DCN members and the network broker, as well as the Business Link co-ordinators. In a series of written exchanges (made available for this study) the members accused the broker of a lack of management control, and for side-lining the membership from a significant part of the programme of actions. It was further considered that the broker had taken on a number of extra commitments outside of the group, which had an adverse effect on his role as the DCN's business manager. At this point the members approached Business Link concerning a proposed re-crediting of six months fees (a total of £10,800). A compromise was reached whereby the monthly fee was reduced by one-third. However, a short while later the members again became concerned that the broker had not undertaken work that could substantiate a monthly fee of £1,200. This correspondence further added that:

'Our businesses only pay fees for services that are understood, agreed and delivered, therefore why should we continue to allow DCN to be run as a cash-cow and pay for services we have not had the benefit of. Services, which to establish control over we will have to constrain in the future, so ensuring the Business Manager's activities are targeted to meet first and foremost the Shareholders requirements.' (DCN Memo)

The dissatisfaction of the group was manifested by almost half of the members leaving the DCN at this time. This had the subsequent effect of substantially increasing the average monthly fee required to be paid by each member company. Therefore, although the DCN may have been able to function better as a smaller group, the operational costs meant that emphasis was put on seeking new members to substitute for those that had dropped-out. This proved to be a rather impractical process, although some tentative discussions did take place with a network broker situated in another English region. According to the interviewees, the accumulation of problems was a clear indication that sustaining the group was proving an impossible task, particularly as the friction between the remaining members and the network broker mounted. Furthermore, a DCN memo stated:

> 'We have been badly served and even damaged by [the respective Business Link].....Our short committee meetings seem to run as talking-shops to agree points for the shareholder meetings that follow. They do not allow sufficient time for considered debate or time for us to plan and implement actions, so that we remain totally reliant on the Broker, a state of affairs that is unfair and unsatisfactory!' (DCN Memo)

It appears that the broker fostered this situation of reliance in order to construct and maintain a position of power within the group, through operating a system which rather than being based on trust has more in common with 'old-fashioned' adversarial resource dependent relationships. The exact motivation for the broker's strategy of power building are unclear. As he was fulfilling an entrepreneurial function on behalf of the group - in seeking new business opportunities - he undoubtedly needed to maintain a degree of control and centrality. However, the abuse of power is usually associated with a strategy of exploitation, and in this case it is worth noting that the DCN memo referred to above made further reference to the DCN bank account being 'topped-up to make dubious payments'. In general, the catalogue of errors and problems led to the eventual demise of the group, with its overall operation seemingly being constructed along lines that appear to incorporate the exact opposite of the key principles of building inter-firm networks. However, perhaps the key reason for failure of this network is that from the start it was ill conceived. That is, it was set-up as a means of serving a target market which in reality did not exist. The result being that there was neither a social or an economic rationality for the existence of the network.

### Small-firm Technology Group

The small-firm technology group consists of a formal network of four small technology-based organisations. The network, developed by a TEC network broker, has been operating successfully since 1995 and involves a pattern-making aluminium alloys specialist, an advanced products designer, a low volume tool making and moulding specialist, and the commercial arm of a university engineering centre. The companies involved employ a total of 33 employees and have an overall (including the engineering centre) investment of approximately £1 million in equipment, computer hardware and software, with each company having its own fairly specific niche market within which it was already successfully operating. The key objective of the network is to offer a consolidated service to the designers and developers of new products within manufacturing companies to help them reach production and end markets efficiently and effectively. Each of the three companies and the engineering centre specialise in different stages of the design and development process.

Since its launch the network has gained and successfully completed a number of contracts for a range of high profile clients. As was the case with the DCN, the network broker managed to achieve extensive media coverage during the launch period, including TV and radio. Up until the launch period the direct financial costs of setting-up the network were borne entirely by the TEC involved, consisting primarily of the employment of the network broker; after this period the costs were met by the members. The two interviewees approached for the study were the managing directors of the products designer - FM-Design - and the tool maker/moulder - P&P Technology.

The experiences of the two managing directors during the early stages of setting-up the network were slightly different; P&P Technology were directly involved in approaching the network broker to evaluate the possibility of brokering a group involving them, while FM-Design were subsequently approached by the broker with a view to joining the group. The managing director of P&P Technology was primarily motivated to respond to a mailshot from his local TEC due to what he considered to be the technological upgrading taking place in certain niche markets in the tooling and plastics manufacturing sector, in particular the introduction of computer controlled equipment with a high capital value. This technology was only necessary for the firm to serve a small proportion of its market, and being such a small company it was almost impossible to concentrate limited resources. That is, the area of technology requiring upgrading would not give a quick enough return on investment, due to this part of the market not constituting a large enough part of the company's total business. Therefore, it was the need to make advancements into specific areas of technical production, which the company could not finance by itself, that was the key motivating factor for the firm to enter discussions with the network broker. Following these discussions, the broker tasked himself with seeking out appropriate organisations that would potentially consider making a formal arrangement to join a network based around the pooling of both human and capital resources:

'When I saw business networking as a concept I felt that there were opportunities to possibly partner companies who specialised in CAD related technology, and to introduce that aspect of production into our own overall business activities through a network as opposed to an in-house thing.....[The network broker] was able to talk to me on a more technical basis, where he was trying to identify exactly the sort of companies that we could imagine attracting into a network. We discussed many options over a period of months, according to the technical capabilities of the different possible partners and also the varying types of technology that we considered would strengthen a network, if it were ever introduced. [The broker] had already met the director of the engineering centre, and having met him myself we felt that maybe the centre would itself be one of best types of partners that we could look for within the proposed network.' (P&P Technology)

At this juncture the three parties discussed further potential members, in particular the requirement for a design specialist and a metal components company. FM-Design emerged as the only serious design option that was available locally, while the aluminium alloys specialist was also seen as being a locally-based company that could strengthen the overall make-up of the network. Both P&P Technology and FM-Design considered that the broker played a vital and indispensable role in bringing the potential members together at this point:

'The broker was really the main figure in all of this, going round talking to each of us as individuals, exploring the concept of networking and the potential partners that would create what would ultimately be the network. He saw that all four partners were warm not just to the concept of the network but also the other partners that would be involved. I quite clearly remember that the first thing was to get the four companies round the table.' (P&P Technology)

'...so, [the broker] came along and put a project to us and we said yes. We then started to work on that project with [the other organisations].It was not clear as to how it might work out when we kicked off, but we felt it was worth the risk, very much. The broker acted as, if you like, the secretary. He set up meetings, took minutes, distributed minutes, reminded people of things, that sort of stuff. He was very helpful.' (FM-Design)

The early meetings of the embryonic network consisted of the four organisations and the broker discussing the merits and possibilities for collaboration and their overall strength and weaknesses as individual organisations. Therefore, a concept that had originally been triggered by the weakness in the future strategy of one company, in terms of technological capabilities, evolved into a process that was attempting to solve the problems and enhance the market status of four organisations. It appears that a natural bond and a high degree of affinity emerged during the planning stages. As in the case of the cluster group, this can be partly related to the relatively close spatial proximity of the organisations, with them already being aware of each others existence prior to the formation of the group and having an innate respect for the others capabilities:

> 'Well to an extent, as it happens, we did know each other, with the exception of the engineering centre....We're all in a similar marketplace; we're in the same geographical location; we're possibly working for the same companies and we've all been around ten years or so....You do get to know the different companies in your own area, for various reasons. So, straightaway, [P&P] knew me. I knew [P&P]. I knew the [MD of the alloys company] and he knew me. He probably also knew P&P. So there was, at the very least, a knowledge of the companies.' (FM-Design)

Although the companies appeared to possess a degree of embeddedness, none had previously been involved in work with the academic sector. Therefore, there was necessarily a need from the companies' point of view to understand the role of engineering centre and to resolve any cultural differences. However, in reality the industrialists and the academics adapted to each other comfortably and quickly. This appears to be due to the high degree of technical commonality that emerged between the two groups, i.e. they were all 'speaking the same language', as well as it soon becoming clear that centre was keen to adopt as commercial a stance and to be as successful as possible in the industrial sector. As the managing director of P&P Technology suggested, there is still a reluctance in industry to place investment, faith and responsibility in academic organisations, so the fact that the centre can boast direct and close industrial links and partners obviously strengthens their position. Therefore, the nurturing of industrial partners was already a key strategy of the centre. Also, the university was the largest conduit within the network of the most advanced machinery and technology.

Trust and social capital were built-up during these early stages and this facilitated the progression of action. The network was formalised by the setting-up of a marketing umbrella with its own 'network identity' and the signing of a confidentiality agreement. At this point the network was officially launched with the publication of a 'glossy brochure', a series of awareness-raising marketing workshops, and a targeted direct mailshot. By this stage the costs of the marketing campaign and the majority of operational costs, with the exception of the broker's time, were met directly by the member organisations. This was a strong indication that the members valued the process of forming the network, which, in the first instance, had been highly reliant on the skills and experience of the broker. Indeed, the role that the broker undertook appears to resemble what can be described as an exemplary civic entrepreneur:

'[The broker] was able to get to know lots of different companies, not necessarily with networking in mind, but for other roles within [the TEC]. It was often as simple as [the broker] saying, 'Funnily enough, I was down there at [an engineering company] two weeks ago and I noticed that they were experts in CAD technology'... He was centrally placed in a completely non-biased situation where he could take an overview, using all of the TEC's information, their databases, their possible intimate knowledge of certain specialisms within different places and different companies within the region, and, therefore, we just had to face the fact that he had a better and wider knowledge than ours.....The TEC and the broker's role was independent, looking to advantage all the companies, not just one or two. I think it was crucial that they had no interest in promoting one company over another.' (P&P Technology)

This approach, which appears to directly counter that taken by the facilitators of the DCN, also incorporated a high degree of realism with regard to levels of expectancy. For instance, during the first year of operation it was decided that no commercial pay-back could be expected, and was not therefore sought. Instead, the broker co-ordinated a series of small pilot projects that were internal to the network, and operated through twice monthly meetings and written and telephone contact. These projects were essentially contracts that had already been gained by one of the partners, and that they already had the capability to fulfil individually, but which were undertaken through the network entailing no commercial gain for the other partners, in order to further build-up social capital resources through 'trying out' processes. Although, these projects were carried out with some intrepidity they appeared to cement the network as a functioning and visible structure:

'We had to warm to each other and really make some pilot projects through the network to ensure that we were comfortable; not just with the concept of it and that we liked each other as people and business people, but to test that we could actually work together, and that the services were right and the prices were right and all the other stuff that had to be in place to satisfy the market existed. We had to say to ourselves 'Right, this is the job which I'm going to put through the network to see how it actually works.' It is quite a big psychological step to take, because you have to then put your entire trust in your partners to do their part of the job. I can't remember specifically the first job that we did like that, but I was certainly very nervous about it going though without a problem, but you know it must have happened.....It's like anything else, as you start becoming more familiar with it as a potential route and a potential service that you offer on the market the more it works and the more you use it.' (P&P Technology)

This incremental process of trust generation, coupled with the personalities involved, served to raise a number of 'ground rules' which became implicit in the network: (1) not all the members would receive equal shares of the gains of each project, and may not even be involved in all projects if their services are unnecessary - i.e. the avoidance of 'free-loading'; (2) details of the work done for the competitors of a partner company to remain confidential; (3) partners are not directly obligated to use the services of a partner if it is considered that the work is best undertaken elsewhere; (4) 'intimate knowledge' of members to remain confidential; (5) partners to remain autonomous and to introduce the operation of the network to projects where it is considered to be advantageous. However, the network has proved to be such a key asset to the members that they have co-operated with each other far more than they originally anticipated, with the ties between the partners becoming increasingly strengthened:

> 'Our customers like seeing an actual partnership between the sub-contractors, something which sort of links us at the hip. It makes them feel more confident about giving us their business. So we try to promote that image to the market-place and, to a large extent, it's worked to our benefit.' (P&P Technology)

Although this example has shown the strength of formal networks, it has also indicated that there are an array of variables, in terms of the attitudes and competencies of the potential network members, that are required to both complement and coincide with each other if such structures are to be successfully set-up from scratch. In this case, the network broker was instrumental in initially drawing together a complementary group of organisations and sustaining interaction during the early critical stages. Nevertheless, the overriding factor was that the representatives of the individual organisations developed and maintained a strong empathy at both a personal and business level, which resulted in the strengthening and embedding of ties in a fashion which has remained free of power struggles and operated within a 'democratic structure':

> 'No, there's certainly never been any real friction between us. It's been very democratic, and we all obviously supply different parts of the cake. We design it, make sure it comes out the other end in the way it's supposed to. The university produces, directly from our CAD files, models very quickly. [The other two companies] can then produce a few, or hundreds or thousands of the product, by using a variety of different techniques. Therefore we are mutually serving each other and it's been very

beneficial....The team are extremely straight people, most trustworthy, very decent.' (FM-Design)

After the launch period it took approximately eighteen months for the network to settle into, and understand, a trend within which the partners would function. The broker is no longer directly involved in the network, and although this has led to a decrease in 'round the table' activity the partners now express having a deep relationship within which they fully understand the capabilities and requirements of the other members:

> 'We know exactly what we're able to use each other for........We use each other when it's required and beneficial for either our customers or ourselves, and we leave each other alone when it's not. That way, we find that we get the best advantages from each other and we don't distract each other when it's not necessary.' (P&P Technology)

At present the level of contact is approximately one formal meeting a month, to arrange presentations and discuss current projects , as well as on-going telephone and written contact and one-to-one meetings between the partners involved in particular projects. The network is currently reviewing its marketing strategy, in order to target potential new customers more effectively. Also, the group is assessing the feasibility of installing a central 'intelligent telephone' for the network in one of the four member locations, which will be able to relay enquiries to the relevant personnel within the member organisations.

This example has served to indicate the economic potential of formal inter-firm networks. However, it should be remembered that setting-up a successful formal network through policy intervention is very much an exception to the rule, and in this case the early stages of the network were very much based on an informal network structure, i.e. without any binding agreement taking place. Indeed, the interviewees made it clear that although the success of the network had facilitated the sharing of business risk among the partners in the long-term, in the early states they regarded the process as involving relatively high risk. Furthermore, although they acknowledged that due to the success of the group they would in hindsight be willing to contribute towards payment for the services of the broker, they also stated that given the same situation the payment of such services would still be difficult to justify given their knowledge of the high probability of network failure.

## Concluding Remarks

The four case-studies strongly confirm there to be a number of key variables that contribute to the success or failure of policy implanted inter-firm network initiatives. These factors, summarised in Table 8.1, indicate that network initiatives possessing certain characteristics are far more probable to gain a degree of sustainability. In particular, a relatively low number of overall participants and a degree of spatial proximity appears to greatly increase the chance of gaining a critical momentum for collaborative activity. Also, commonality with regard to the nature of the businesses involved is an important factor in developing a sense of belonging and trust and social capital building, within embryonic networks that are 'democratic' in nature. It is the network brokers who are the key catalysts for facilitating initiatives that possess these features. It is paramount, therefore, that networks are brokered in a highly effective fashion. The most important role of the broker is to develop network projects within which the relationships between the participants become valued and defined. These relationships are best facilitated within an environment possessing a degree of informality, allowing interaction to develop within business settings that have a 'social' dimension. A failure by the broker to stimulate such an environment will severely reduce the likelihood of embedded relationships developing, and thus of establishing sustained collaboration and co-operation.

It has been shown that networks in business, be it of an inter-firm or more socio-centric nature, are often consciously developed and maintained by those managing directors who have recognised the importance of co-operative activities for achieving competitive advantage for their companies. It is also a further indication that there at least a small number of SMEs in the UK that are not cocooned within the 'fortress enterprise' mentality identified by Curran and Blackburn (1994). However, exchange and interaction that is valued by the members of networks is only truly generated when trust relationships are formed. Within the network initiatives this was best facilitated by brokers who understood and approached the development of networks from both an economic and social point of view. The best network support consisting of brokers who are able to mix and overlap the 'hard' business and 'softer' social interests of participants. Nevertheless, as far as possible network initiatives in the first instance should be conceived on some achievable and tangible goal. In successful networks this has often been triggered by issues concerning some form of common problem or difficulty.

## Table 8.1    Characteristics of Case-Study Inter-firm Networks

| Characteristic | New Entrepreneurs Network | Local Cluster Group | Defence Contractors Group | Small-firm Technology Group |
|---|---|---|---|---|
| Status of Initiative | Informal/ Failed | Informal/ Successful | Formal/ Failed | Informal/ Successful |
| Number of Firms | 50 (approx.) | 10 | 20 | 4 |
| Direct Costs per Participating Firm | Free | £250 per year | £1,800 per month (shared between the firms) | Free (during setting-up phase) |
| Key Motivation for Involvement | 'Social guidance' on business matters | Extend local contact base in order to exchange information and business experiences | To directly gain new business through collaboration | Technology-based resource sharing to capture niche markets |
| Network Process | Weekly & monthly meetings, one-off social & speciality events | Monthly meetings/ company visits, on-going contact via telephone, written contact & self-initiated meetings | Formation of 'umbrella' company, sporadic meetings, visits to potential customers, written contact | Twice monthly meetings, written and telephone contact |
| Network Environment | Low levels of embedded-ness, trust and interaction | Strong sense of 'belonging' within relationships possessing a significant degree of embeddedness, trust and innovation | Broker dominated, little scope for developing relationships and interaction, lacking trust & social capital | Social capital building through 'trying out' processes, within a highly democratic structure |
| Role of Broker(s) | Information/ Knowledge Provider | Project Co-ordinator | Entrepreneurial Agent | Civic Entrepreneur |
| Effectiveness of Broker | Low/ Medium | High | Low | High |

| **Keys to Success/ Failure** | (1) Low calibre of network members, (2) Too general in focus, (3) Lack of direction & subsequently definable outputs | (1) High degree of commonality, (2) Close spatial proximity, (3) 'Democratically' organised, (4) Importance of informal 'social' contact emphasised | (1) Ill conceived ambitions & outputs, (2) Too diverse a range of firms, (3) Lacking management control, (4) Overly focused on the motivations of the broker | (1) Close spatial proximity, (2) High degree of 'technical' commonality, (3) Strong network identity, (4) Adoption of a long-term approach |
| --- | --- | --- | --- | --- |

The case-studies strengthen the hypothesis that it is formal groups which are the most potent form of inter-firm network, but that it is through an initially informal structure that they are best facilitated. The studies further indicate that both social and/or economic rationalities underlie the processes and motivations of managing directors to involve themselves in company collaboration and co-operation. Indeed, the motivation of most managing directors was embedded in both economic and non-economic interests. The subsequent effects of the processes undertaken within the initiatives are strongly linked to the degree of commonality in interests that already exists between participants, which is in turn a measure of the existing social capital contained within the groups. This includes the attitudes and pre-conceptions that they initially bring to the initiative. It is the ability of the network broker/facilitator to harness these interests and attitudes, in a format and environment that can generate valid interaction and exchange, which is critical to gaining the sustainability of groups. Brokers are further responsible for setting targets which lead to the expectancy levels of participating companies being manageable in both the short and long-term. Finally, the four cases suggest that initiatives where there are relatively small numbers of participants have the most chance of developing sustainable networks, because a less diverse range of interests and opinions are required to be harnessed by the facilitators.

# 9 Conclusions

## Introduction

The central focus of this book has consisted of an exploration of the extent to which public-private partnership bodies such as TECs can act as facilitators and catalysts for inducing companies within their localities to increasingly collaborate and co-operate through inter-firm networks. A number of important findings related to the policy position of TECs as generators of economic development have emerged, as well as a critique of the relevant discourses surrounding the theoretical analysis of inter-firm networks and their formation and sustainability. This first part of this chapter reviews the key findings, in order to place them in a perspective that is pertinent from both a theoretical and policy perspective. In the second part, the findings are further drawn upon to construct a number of recommendations for the future of economic development policy in the UK, and specifically inter-firm network development.

## The Commitment-Achievement Gap

It is clear that TECs consider themselves to be important catalysts of inter-firm networks. They further consider such networks to be a key contributory factor towards increasing local competitive advantage and stimulating economic development. However, it has been shown that TEC generated inter-firm networks have so far contributed little to raising local prosperity. Indeed, an average involvement of only 100 firms per TEC in network activities, which includes high participation membership groups such as business forums and business clubs, as well as small business clubs and start-up groups which were merely inherited from organisations such as enterprise agencies and chambers of commerce, points strongly to a high degree of under-achievement.

Mutual learning is the most important and widespread function of those inter-firm networks that have been generated, followed by the undertaking of shared commercial activities. TECs claimed to be attempting to stimulate innovation through networks, although the actual level of innovation generated was very minimal. As innovation is considered the most important factor towards raising competitive advantage (Porter, 1990), the fact that this is the weakest performing activity of TEC facilitated networks casts further doubts on their effectiveness. Therefore, although TECs indicate that they are committed to network generation as a key component of their local economic development strategies, this commitment has not been transferred into widespread value-adding economic outputs. Such results confirm the weakness in the performance of TECs found by other evaluators, particularly relating to SME support (e.g. Peck, 1993; Peck and Emmerich, 1993; Curran and Blackburn, 1994; Adam-Smith and McGeever, 1995).

An important demand side barrier to inter-firm network development, from the perspective of TECs, concerned a fear by firms of compromising competitive position, with TECs considering a lack of trust among firms seen as a deep-rooted problem in many localities. This finding concurs with Curran and Blackburn's (1994) 'fortress enterprise mentality' - and as Granovetter (1992) and Monsted (1995) state, without trust relations there can be no networks. Also, as Vickerstaff and Parker (1995) suggest, one of the key reasons for a 'knowledge gap' existing between TECs and local business is that the majority of firms are not already part of established business networks, and therefore have a high level of insularity. The empirical evidence confirms that building networks inevitably involves processes of trial and error due to the difficulty in identifying participants and formulating relevant common issues (OECD, 1992), with facilitators most usually having to overcome the entropic outlook of small firms (Perry, 1995). Furthermore, what exactly makes for an effective inter-firm networking strategy is still to be learnt, and a number of TECs in this study highlighted a shortfall in their own resources as hindering progress. As Joyce et al. (1995) suggest, these resource barriers may be best overcome by developing networks very selectively.

In general, TECs have not been able to develop any of the key attributes connected with a transition to the Marshallian 'industrial district model' (Amin, 1994). In contrast, the evidence strongly suggests that there are structural reasons for the disparities in networking performance highlighted at a regional level. For instance, the regional effectiveness of networking was highly related to indicators of firm density, Gross Domestic Product/Head and the concentration of high technology activity. Therefore, it can be argued that despite there being widespread encouragement among the majority of TECs, networking has been most effective in those core regions with larger numbers of firms operating in higher value-added markets, and has constrained the performance of TECs situated in the UK's less favoured regions. These regional disparities echo Bennett and McCoshan's (1993) assertion that the operation of effective networks is closely related to strong spontaneous economic development. However, nearly all TECs considered that they should continue to act as catalysts for network formation and demonstrate their value, pointing to greater participation within those networks already functioning being best fostered by 'network ownership' increasingly being held by private businesses, rather than TECs and/or their partners.

Within the scope of the empirical study it would have been advantageous to assess changes in TEC network generation against pre-existing baselines. This proved impossible due to a number of barriers; for example, many TEC programmes involve networking which is implicit to their overall operation and is not easily visible, and furthermore TECs' own baselines tend to be 'quantity' rather than 'outcome' target driven. An example of this is the formal business network initiatives, most often based on the 'Danish model', where TECs have had a target of creating, on average, 5 sustainable networks within a given 1-2 year period. However, these targets say nothing about the effectiveness or impact of their operation. It should also been borne in mind that networks are not 'quick fix' solutions and it is dangerous to evaluate performance purely over a short-term period. The picture is further complicated by the fact that many of the larger groups such as business clubs were inherited from the previous organisational set-up rather than being new TEC creations.

### TECs as Business Support Strategists

The scope for TEC intervention in business support has been critically and seriously limited by the low level of financial and human resources that TECs are able to commit to their business and enterprise support role, primarily due to restrictive government funding regimes. In particular, more long-term Government funding may have enabled TECs to further overcome barriers associated with poor recognition and awareness of their existence in their respective business communities. The overall proportion of TEC budgets allocated to business support has been insufficient to address the needs of the majority of local businesses. Therefore, the expectations and ambitious objectives for TECs to become more sensitive and business-oriented than predecessor bodies (Bennett et al., 1994; Hart et al., 1996) have not been fully met despite the rhetoric indicated by many TEC directors (see for example Rajan, 1993). It is clear that adequate long-term funding must in future be made available to the Small Business Service, as well as the Learning and Skills Councils. At the time of writing, it is not clear whether the funding levels will be able to provide for new, sensitive and innovative business solutions to economic development problems.

The enthusiasm shown by TECs for developing their enterprise and business support role has been frustrated by a lack of long-term and coherent financial resources, with those activities that have been undertaken often being small-scale and 'symbolic' in nature, rather than indicative of wider intervention and development. Haughton et al. (1995a; 1996b) have highlighted the preference of TEC directors towards involvement in enterprise and local economic development activity as opposed to more 'run-of-the-mill' training programmes, and there is the obvious danger that TECs may be prone to 'talking-up' up their economic development involvement. Peck (1993) argues that the credibility of TECs as local institutions born of their community is crucially undermined by the fact that they are Government imposed. Similarly, Hart et al. (1996) indicate that the over reliance of TECs on the national funding model has weakened their ability to engage in local functions. This is supported by the results presented here, which point to the generally low effectiveness, not only of TECs but also other local business support agencies, and cast doubts on the efficiency of the 'local factor' in programme development and delivery, in terms of the restriction of provision being at a TEC-area level.

TECs, by their own criteria, have under-performed, and the problems identified by the aforementioned commentators have not been adequately redressed. Business support activities are relatively marginal affairs within TECs, particularly when compared to the budgets committed to training. Therefore, as Peck (1993) and Peck and Jones (1995) argue, the mission of TECs of removing bureaucratic red tape and stimulating innovation through levering in private sector involvement and funding has still largely failed. In other words, TECs have not fulfilled the role of civic or local policy entrepreneurs that was envisaged for them, nor have they operated as effective public-private partnerships.

## The Sustainability and Formalisation of Inter-firm Networks

Despite the problems TECs and their partner organisations have encountered, where network initiatives are able to draw-in a critical mass of committed firms over a sustainable period, inter-firm networks can act as an effective and important instrument for economic development. Furthermore, those firms which have committed themselves to sustained membership of formal networks that have achieved the highest economic growth and increases in efficiency. The indication that those committed to formal networks have achieved a decrease in costs of more than one-quarter adds a degree of empirical evidence to the theoretical discourse of inter-firm networks; which contends that companies operating within such structures can achieve substantial discounts on their transaction-costs (for example: Powell, 1990; Cooke and Morgan, 1993; Grabher, 1993).

These transaction-cost discounts refer to comparisons with the cost of buying in the market-place, or attempting to subsume from elsewhere, the commercial and innovative advantages gained through reciprocal network exchanges and adaptations. In other words, the costs of producing, purchasing, developing or marketing the outputs that companies require to increase or maintain competitive advantage are significantly reduced by, or may not even be possible to undertake without, joining a network within which there is a degree of binding agreement and obligation. For those initiatives surveyed, there are a small number of firms (the average number of firms in formal networks is only 4) which are acting in a collective capacity, over a sustained period during which social capital is built-up, enabling them to reap substantial economic gains. In these cases, long-term sustainability becomes a function of the extent to which the transaction costs of members would increase if the network ceased to exist.

The real value-added from involvement in network initiatives does not generally come from direct participation, but from the indirect interaction that subsequently evolves as a result of participation. Facilitators and brokers should place more emphasis on stimulating improvements in both the short as well as long term, in order to partially off-set the high set-up costs that committed companies are required to invest. As with other studies of policy-induced networks, it seems that the most stable structures are those that pursue relatively modest and limited initial goals, with the hope that some early success from relatively short-term and superficial activities will build up commitment to co-operation (Gertler and Rutherford, 1996).

The key problem for TECs, and their partners, is that the positive effects of network initiatives are still highly marginal and restricted. Therefore, the challenge for network policy makers is (at least) two-fold: (1) to increase the number of firms that join network initiatives and subsequently give a significant degree of commitment - in terms of the time, both of an input and elapsed nature, and effort required to achieve quantifiable outputs; (2) to build formal networks through the gradual evolution of informal groupings into more concrete structures - by incrementally increasing the level of connectivity between firms, as well as the level of potential and expected outputs. Actor-network theorists refer to the process of evolving relationships as one of 'translation', involving turning an idea, identified by a problem or opportunity, into reality through a series of moves, or 'passage points', through which actors become enrolled and subsequently locked into a project (Callon, 1986; Knights et al., 1993). The relative success of informal networks suggests that they have the most potential to act as the catalysts for more formal and sustainable network development. These networks have usually brought together firms to solve common problems, exchange knowledge or acquire new skills through social learning practices (Wilson, 1997). As Storper (1995) suggests, in these circumstances economic 'spill-overs' can be expected to become greater as the level of interdependency increases.

The development of trust is undoubtedly a key feature facilitating a social infrastructure that can convert and transfer informal into formal networks. However, the general lack of interaction reported by the companies surveyed has meant that the 'trying out' processes associated with exchange theory - whereby 'minor transactions' eventually evolve into 'major transactions', as trustworthiness is proven and adaptations are undertaken (Blau, 1964) - have not been a common feature of those initiatives studied. In general, binding and interdependent relationships and collaboration have rarely been a part of the outcomes from the policy processes employed. A prisoner's dilemma approach to analysing the study suggests that in the final instance most of the participating companies are more content to 'defect' rather than co-operate within inter-firm network initiatives. This does not imply that they are acting out of ignorance or irrationality, but due to what Putnam (1993) has termed the absence of 'credible mutual commitment'.

Drawing on existing prisoner's dilemma research (see: Cable and Shane, 1997), it can be argued that the majority of participants in the network initiatives studied consider that co-operation is not the best route of action due to one or a mix of a number of factors: (1) companies have not prioritised co-operation as a corporate strategy; (2) the benefits of co-operation are not transparent; (3) a lack of information concerning potential network partners; (4) a lack of existing social connectivity between potential network members; (5) a lack of compatibility in terms of needs, problems and aims. Therefore, by their own calculations, firms consider that the potential outcomes of co-operation are not strong enough for them to forgo the commitments that need to be made in resources of time and effort.

It should be remembered that companies and economies that have successfully embraced inter-firm networks, have usually done so in a spontaneous and organic fashion (Piore and Sabel, 1984; Hirst and Zeitlin, 1989; Cooke and Morgan, 1993; Amin, 1994; Saxenian, 1994; Fukuyama, 1995). However, companies involved in, as well as local and regional economies pursuing, policy-implanted network initiatives are often already among the less innovative and creative in evolutionary terms. This is recognised by the very fact that they are the subject of such policy support precisely because they are usually among the least successful cohort of firms within a national or sub-national economy. The reasons for their relative failure will be varied, but it is now readily acknowledged that small firms, and SMEs in general, often suffer a higher degree of business isolation than more successful larger companies. For example, Donckels and Lambrecht (1995) found that high growth companies are those with considerable external contacts and which do not have a 'living on a desert island mentality'. Scott et al. (1996) have particularly highlighted the isolation faced by the majority of SMEs in the UK manufacturing sector from sources of information and knowledge. At a spatial level, Johannisson, (1995) has found that it is businesses situated in innovative settings that are the most successful at building networks that blend business and social concerns through both individual dyadic ties and larger socio-centric networks.

While 'lead' firms (Lundvall and Johnson, 1994) continually re-position themselves and their networks to maintain growth, it appears that 'laggard' companies are often caught in a vicious-circle. Such firms are not usually members of established business networks and are subject to a significantly high degree of insularity, which in turn makes them sceptical of actually joining networks. As Johannisson (1995) found, most organically formed networks have emerged partly as a result of a social rationality based on moral resources, culture, habits and customs. The 'marketing' of networks facilitated through policy intervention, however, has usually been solely based on accessing and 'tapping-into' a managing director's economic rationality of profit maximisation. The enhancement of economic motivations alone is a key reason behind the early breakdown of many network initiatives. Therefore, there is a need for all those involved in inter-firm network policy to be further enlightened as to the social conditions and environment within which spontaneous business networks have emerged. This does not imply that such conditions can be mechanistically transferred, but recognises the fact that there is still much to be learnt about business decision-making processes concerning the motivation to 'network', which can positively assist intelligent policy-transfer.

## The Socio-Economics of Inter-firm Network Development

The case-studies developed in chapter 8 indicate that despite the prevalence of TEC marketing which has focused on raising the 'economic expectancy' of participants, both social and economic rationalities do form part of the processes and motivations for joining and participating in inter-firm networks and associated initiatives. This concurs with Granovetter's (1985) suggestion that economic action is embedded in behaviour that is a mix of both social and non-social factors - whereby embeddedness is understood to be the effect that all forms of relationships have on subsequent actions. It also resonates with Fukuyama's (1995) thesis of social virtues being an important but often 'hidden' contributor to economic efficiency and prosperity. In particular, social and economic rationalities often appear to overlap. For example, the motivation to join networks may be due to a desire to search, access and pool knowledge that is utilised in ways that fulfil both economic and non-economic considerations. Knowledge, in this case, is defined as an institutional asset represented by both the social knowledge of co-ordination and learning - 'tacit' and 'knowing how' - and explicit knowledge - 'codifiable' and 'knowing about' (Blackler, 1993; Grant, 1996; Kogut and Zander, 1996; Mowery et al., 1996). The importance of knowledge acquisition and management indicates that as an identifiable resource it is now appreciated by theorists and forward thinking business practitioners as being fundamental to making competitive improvements (Lundvall and Johnson, 1994; Lundvall, 1994; Grant, 1996; Powell et al., 1996; Oliver, 1997).

The success or failure of the inter-firm networks studied, in terms of the sustainability generated, is significantly related to the embeddedness and commonality that already existed between members. This focus on existing relationships and cultural familiarity is consistent with the theories put forward by critics of neo-classical economics, who argue that a web of factors are at play within economic action, diminishing the extent to which humans are able, or wish, to act as individual utility maximisers (DiMaggio and Powell, 1991; Biggart and Hamilton, 1992; Fukuyama, 1995). As described by one managing director, members of a successful network saw themselves as being of a 'similar ilk'; coming from common backgrounds and being based in the same geographical area meant that trust was more easily engendered. Indeed, this particular group had generated a high level of social capital and the 'moral resources' that are said to facilitate collective action (Hirschman, 1984; Putnam, 1993; Powell and Smith-Doerr, 1994).

Burt (1992) has contended that it is social, rather than human and financial resources, that is the final arbiter of competitive success. Although the empirical evidence cannot confirm or deny such a contention, it does indicate that social capital, or the 'social glue' (Rosenfeld, 1997a), sticking network members together was vital in generating sustainability. The success of the networks can be further related to the attitudes and pre-conceptions of the members. For instance, those members that had already developed their own strong socio-centric networks were more likely to be pre-disposed to acting, and valuing positively, the associations developed within the network initiatives. This finding is similar to much of the research undertaken on entrepreneurs and networking building, whereby the most innovative entrepreneurs are also seen to those that have large socio-centric networks and who are subsequently better at building 'professional' networks (Birley, 1985; Aldrich and Zimmer, 1986; Johannisson, 1995).

Within network initiatives, the energy, enthusiasm, and experience of the brokers and co-ordinators is instrumental in generating valid interaction and exchange between participants, particularly in the early stages of group formation before momentum is gathered and the relationships became to some degree institutionalised. Brokers of networks that had become sustainable played a key role in maintaining an equal distribution of power and dependency, in order to alleviate the potential for friction and animosity to emerge. In these cases, the brokers had successfully adopted the role of 'civic entrepreneurs' at an individual level. They encouraged and guided the network development process through deploying their own local knowledge resources and networks, within an environment that was conducive to mutual learning (Gibb, 1993; Wilson, 1995; Wilson, 1997). Conducive social environments and elements within the networks were closely related to furthering economic expectations and for sustaining collective action.

Collective action was best mobilised when there was a true and real sense of belonging to, and ownership of, the networks. This emphasis on mobilising social institutions in processes of organisational change is highlighted by evolutionary economic thinking to be a primary factor by which innovative firms overcome uncertainty and instability (Dosi et al., 1988; Freeman, 1994; Cooke, 1998). In other words, it is socio-economic factors, in the form of resource and institutional capital, that are the key to the success of both firms and the networks within which they interact (Amin and Thrift, 1995; Lado et al., 1997, Oliver, 1997). It is forward looking and progressive managing directors that are most aware of the potential to accrue economic gain through social exchange, particularly when they are motivated by both long-term and short-term objectives. These individuals represent the 'human network builders' of actor-network theory who understand and acknowledge the link between interaction and personal and/or business advancement (Callon, 1986; Knights et al., 1993).

The most valued exchanges took place after a degree of trust and empathy had emerged, and after potential 'free-loaders' and 'free-riders', who may have sought to gain from the network without any valid input, had been eliminated. As Granovetter (1985) suggests, in business situations there will necessarily be a variability in the 'degree of confidence' individuals have in one another, due to existing economic considerations. For network initiatives this confidence was highest when there was a relatively low level of direct market competition between the members, which facilitated the strengthening of personal relations. In the example of the failed formal network initiative - the Defence Contractors Network (DCN) - a significant lack of confidence by the members towards the broker occurred, as it emerged there was little foundation to the supposed economic expectations of the network. Furthermore, these high expectancy economic objectives were set without any real consideration being given to the value of social exchange in nurturing a network environment, or the manner in which social relations can evolve from minor transactions into major transactions via Blau's (1964) 'trying out' processes.

Instead of building trust among the participants, through interaction based on social exchange and adaptation (Hakansson, 1989; Forsgren et al., 1995; Mattsson, 1995), the DCN broker appeared to be operating within Marsden's (1982) concept of a 'restricted exchange network' whereby he controlled the passing of information. In essence, the broker was not 'plugging' what Burt (1992) refers to as the 'structural holes' that existed between the network members. In this case there were structural holes between the members because they did not all share the same information, and the broker continued to act in a manner that restricted its flow. Rather than constructively exploiting his position of power and centrality for the benefit of the members, he abused it by employing a strategy involving the members becoming over-reliant and over-dependent on his resource-base (Galaskiewicz, 1979; Mizruchi and Galaskiewicz, 1994). This was apparently in the expectancy of some 'social' and/or 'economic' profit, through the use of opportunistic means that were not part of his overall official remit.

A pattern has emerged whereby the smaller the number of participants involved in a network initiative the higher the chances are of achieving sustainability. This was primarily due to a lessening of the range of diverse interests and opinions that are required to be represented. This concurs with the 'logic of collective action' developed by Olson (1965), which contends that unless the membership of collective action groups remains quite small, not all individuals will act in a manner that seeks to achieve their common interests. Therefore, it is suggested that initiatives which seek to form inter-firm networks should, from a very early stage, attempt to ascertain whether or not the relationships and the exchanges that are expected to develop are potentially more effective than fulfilling what are essentially 'knowledge transactions' through Williamson's (1975; 1985) market or hierarchy approach. In other words, is the asset specificity and the investments required for the adoption of a networked approach justifiable from the point of view of either a social and/or economic rationality? Such situations appear to most appropriate when a relatively small group of SMEs can be identified that are facing some kind of common problem due to size constraints and a resulting lack of either resource and/or institutional capital (Oliver, 1997).

The ethos of co-operation and pooling is often most effective when there is a 'camaraderie' engendered by a common difficulty or weakness. These difficulties may lead to what Gibb (1997) refers to as intermittent and transactional relationships evolving into ongoing interactions that enable 'how to' and 'who with' learning needs to be addressed. Therefore, as evolutionary economists, such as Nelson and Winter (1982) and Dosi et al. (1988), suggest, the routinising of relationships through networks necessitates improvements in the effectiveness of the network itself and the individual participants. However, network builders should not attempt to routinise relationships via a process of formalised binding agreements before the 'ground rules' of the agreement are already being met implicitly in the general functioning of the groups. These ground rules will only be realised and assimilated if, as Storper (1993; 1994; 1995) contends, the evolutionary path-way of the relationships which generate untraded interdependencies form a valid and valued collective asset.

## Policy Recommendations

This book has sought to examine the extent to which TECs are attempting to embed a culture of competitiveness by co-operation in the UK. In particular, it has considered how TECs have practically undertaken the creation of inter-firm networks, through their role as facilitators of local economic development - as empowered by the previous Conservative Government. This final section looks at some of the policy conclusions and recommendations that can be made regarding the institutional position of those involved in economic development, and the fostering of inter-firm networks as a contributory tool for sustaining the regeneration of local business communities.

### TECs as Contributors to Economic Development

As TECs have increasingly taken a strategic role they have come to realise that their impact relies more and more in mobilising the activities of others, if economic development strategies are to be translated into effective support delivery mechanisms. This approach has emphasised the importance of networking and networks within this framework, with TECs increasingly focusing on trying to bring local businesses closer together through the building of inter-firm networks. Such an approach is, in itself, an innovative shift away from the 'traditional' concerns of economic development, such as area promotion and the provision of land and buildings, to policies more concerned with 'soft' support and business 'aftercare'. However, this type of intervention has not so far achieved much success and, as Bennett (1996) argues, public policy support of this kind can only be fully justified if it is either remedying market failure adversely affecting businesses or promoting an increase in the welfare of society as a whole. TECs have not contributed to either of these factors to any great extent; however, they have at least been important catalysts in pushing forward a new local economic development agenda, in which human resources are seen as being equally as important as more 'physical' assets. The future role of the Learning and Skill Councils, Small Business Service and RDAs in England, and their respective counterparts in Wales and Scotland, must continue to embrace both human and social capital as key drivers of economic development.

The economic development approach adopted by TECs has suffered in many circumstances due to the Governmental policy restrictions placed upon them. Firstly, there has been a necessity to constrict activities to arenas that were often seen by TECs as being overly localised. TECs considered that many of their more successful projects were those administered at a wider regional level, often based around industrial sectors that incorporated a common sense of regional identity. It would, therefore, appear advantageous for future policy intervention in this sphere to focus more on the development of regional, in addition to local, governance coalitions and networks. This is undoubtedly a key issue to be met by the RDAs, facilitated through partnerships with the Learning and Skill Councils and the Small Business Service. A starting point would be to ring-fence more funding into sector challenge-type initiatives that are delivered at a regional level.

However, the removal of spatial 'cramps' will do little to eliminate the friction, tension and subsequent 'turf wars' that have emerged, particularly between TECs and Business Links - as 'quasi' public-private bodies - and local authorities. This problem, which is innately related to funding issues, can only be alleviated by better co-ordination and closer collaboration with the bidding-related bureaucracy, in particular that surrounding the SRB, of the regional Government Offices. In future, these Offices, in tandem with RDAs, should take greater responsibility for funding projects based on sound and long-term objectives, rather than an over fascination with prescribing funds towards short-term 'flavour of the month' initiatives. This may be best achieved through the requirement for all the local and regional partners to participate in policy networks, co-ordinated through the Government Offices, focused on bidding issues processes that move beyond the superficial level.

Government Offices should also continue to strive to evolve more flexibility in the distribution of funding, so as to match the plethora of needs of local/regional economies and their agencies. That is, to undertake ongoing dialogue in order to produce synergies that reinforce, rather than detract from, the purposes of the proposals and projects at stake. There is a need to move away from satisfying the rigidities of national evaluation models and the accompanying arbitrary and short-sighted criteria as to what actually constitutes the success or failure of an initiative or project. As Storey (1993) has argued, success should not be judged on 'playing number games', such as the number of leaflets handed out or the number of companies visited speculatively, but by interacting and working with local businesses over a significant period of time that allows them to surmount particular hurdles. Policy changes in this area should concentrate on Government departments, in particular the DTI, dramatically reviewing their evaluation criteria in order to incorporate more 'softer' or qualitative criteria. An example of a precedent Government model is that operated by the Government's Schools Inspectorate, which involves the analysis of both 'hard' quantitative outputs as well as a significant degree of 'person-based' monitoring. Although such an approach could not be expected to be carried out on the level that it is for schools, a structured sample would nevertheless significantly add to the knowledge available to 'official evaluators'.

The shape of local and regional economic development in the UK is changing rapidly with the introduction of RDAs, Learning and Skills Councils, the Small Business Service in England, and related policy re-organisation and revamping in Wales and Scotland. Also, the local authorities, that were increasingly side-lined by the Conservative Government, are again becoming empowered to play a more active role in economic development networks that had increasingly become the domain of local business leaders on TEC and other quango-type boards (Coulson, 1997b). The Government's overall decentralisation strategy - through the introduction of a structured system of regional development - should, therefore, be geared towards constituting a positive effect on speeding up access to the decision making processes involved in large partner projects, thus reducing the time for underlying tensions between partners to emerge.

As Sabel (1995) contends, public entities that do no more than enable actors to draw lessons from common local experiences, or to assess the significance of developments for their own purposes, do at least provide encouragement and insight for purposeful restructuring. To some extent TECs have had an almost 'invisible hand' in shaping and administering economic development policy, with often the most minimal of resources. In this respect, the introduction of Business Links can be said to be a direct result of some of the more difficult encounters of TECs in delivering business and enterprise support. However, the dual existence of both TECs and Business Links has led not only to fuelling more anxieties and friction, but also a further fragmentation of an already confused, duplicative and counter-productive system of business support, in which Business Links have faced credibility problems in the business community, in a way similar to that confronted by TECs concerning their own integrity issues within the training sector. These experiences should be strongly drawn-upon by those policy makers responsible for operationalising the new system of economic development. In particular, they should not overlook the 'voices' and experiences of both TECs and Business Links, but listen to them very closely, especially with regard to the relationships between the Learning and Skills Councils and the Small Business Service.

Finally, as Blackburn and Jennings (1996) have argued, failure to achieve credibility in the minds of other business advisers and network intermediaries, including bankers, accountants and solicitors, will necessarily lead to serious weaknesses in the application of 'one-stop-shop' models and a subsequent breakdown in the network approach system. Therefore, if the Learning and Skills Councils and the Small Business Service are to become sustainable, in a way which the TEC-Business Link system was unable to achieve, there needs to be an emphasis on consolidating and introducing transparency to the business support system. This is an issue that must be met as one of the primary objectives of the RDAs, utilising the expertise that has been generated at a local level among some TEC and Business Link personnel, if there is to be cohesion between to what Chittenden et al. (1995) label a 'miscellany of cultures'; involving civil service paymasters, large company managers, small business consultants, higher education representatives and local authority officers.

*Inter-firm Network Policy*

TECs, as the key facilitators of inter-firm network initiatives in the UK, have faced a number of highly problematic barriers of both a supply (policy formulation) and demand (outlook of participating companies) nature. This has severely limited the number of firms that have benefited from participation, as well as the overall level of economic impact on growth and development. More positively, it has been shown that the initiatives have resulted in substantial gains for albeit a small number of participating companies. Also, it has been assessed that the cost of the jobs created through network initiatives have not been overly expensive to the public exchequer. The small number of companies achieving substantial benefits have most often been those involved in initiatives that have been able to formalise sustainable networks. The key policy problem is that this situation has occurred in only a very restricted number of circumstances, with formal network initiatives being subject to extremely high 'drop-out' rates.

Although formal initiatives have the potential to produce the most substantial economic growth it is informal initiatives, especially 'task-specific groups', that have generated the most widespread (in terms of numbers of firms) benefits for the highest proportion of firms, particularly in terms of learning and innovation capabilities. This relative 'success' has partly occurred due to these initiatives often being part of a wider business support strategy, within which the stimulation of inter-company contact has proven to be the most feasible method of action. The creation of this interaction during the early stages of these initiatives is closely related to embryonic network development, as barriers concerning compatibility are overcome. If some early positive outcomes are forthcoming through informal networks, participating companies are far more likely to commit increased time and effort to the initiatives. In such cases, the value they actually place on the initiatives increases and social capital, or 'social glue', is built-up. Therefore, increasing the time companies commit to initiatives has a positive effect on embeddedness, as trust between companies is secured.

Although the development of formalised and sustainable company groups should be the aim of business network policy, formal network initiatives are not in themselves the most effective way of catalysing them. It is recommended, almost paradoxically, that policies aimed at formal network initiatives should be abandoned as a mechanism for creating a critical mass of sustainable networks. Instead, the progression of policy models based on informal, and in particular task-specific, initiatives offer the most plausible means of catalysing inter-company contact. Such policy approaches should initially adopt a 'low pressure' expectancy environment, being aimed at developing sustainable networks that more closely resemble those networks that have emerged without such intervention. These models would necessarily require increased resourcing (part of which could be covered by that vired from formal initiatives) to develop a framework that would essentially need to 'formalise the informal' at some critical point. Also, they would require a structured monitoring approach to measure participant outcomes in both the short and long term.

Positive impacts may be limited during the informal period, but they should at least be spread over a wide range of participants. This would alleviate a significant degree of scepticism and enhance the possibility of transferring the arrangements to more binding agreements, whereby the potential to achieve discounts on transaction-costs and take advantage of 'spill-overs' would increase. Such initiatives should not be pursued on a stand-alone basis but should be integrated into a coherent business support policy framework facilitating economic development. As a Trade and Industry Select Committee (1998) report made clear, business support policies in the UK are still highly fragmented, resulting in a lack of defined and measurable objectives and targets. It is to be hoped that the new emphasis on developing networks through clusters (HM Government, 1998) will promote inter-firm interaction as an integral feature of business support policy.

Within inter-firm networks there is a crucial need to engage the right individuals, who are vested with a significant degree of personal autonomy and authority, and have the capacity to develop trustworthy relationships. As Lundvall and Johnson (1994) suggest, this implies that network participants must know 'how to communicate', in order to facilitate the processes of establishing respect and trust. Trust is the key issue in network formation, and as it cannot be bought its value is paramount when parties invest in specific assets locking them into a relationship (Arrow, 1971; Lorenz, 1991). The nurturing of trust, therefore, should not be rushed or forced but fostered gradually over a significant period of time, through regular and perceptible increases in the frequency and intensity of contact. This echoes the need to shift away from the present impatient political evaluation criteria, that demands almost instantaneous results from any form of public intervention (Rosenfeld, 1996).

The initial focus of projects should consist of expanding the 'stakeholder webs' (Jennings and Beaver, 1997) of SMEs through networks that focus on building the stock of social capital. As Rosenfeld (1997a) argues, social capital is often the least visible but most undervalued contributor to economic development. Therefore, gaining sufficient reserves should be considered prior to the planning of any formal 'dotted line' commercial or innovation-based relations. It is worth remembering that many informal structures may not initially even be consciously constituted by participants as 'networks' (Staber, 1996a). This is obviously particularly true during the early stages, or what Malecki and Tootle (1996) term the 'trial period' towards formalisation, which they consider invariably takes at least two years. This implies that the perception of those involved, from both the public and private sector, needs to be changed from one of short to long-term business development.

The networks TECs and their partners have facilitated, particularly those that have gained a degree of formality and sustainability through informal means, can - under the right conditions - form a valuable component of economic development strategies. This concurs with the fact that many other countries have also now recognised the value of developing of business networks and inter-firm organisations. In the UK, Joyce et al. (1995) found that membership of business and trade associations was strongly correlated with the development of further informal networks. Similarly, Chaston (1996a) has suggested that it is informal networks that have appeared as initially more compatible with the norms and practice of SMEs in the UK. Further afield, Silicon Valley is also seen to owe much of its success to an informal social infrastructure, catalysed by local 'socio-economic' associations and groups. For example, an informal group known as the Homebrew Computer Club eventually spun-out more than twenty new firms, including Apple Computer (Rosenfeld, 1997a).

The challenge in the UK is to further find the right conditions and most appropriate models for development within different localities and regions. It has been shown that there are advantages and disadvantages associated with different network-types. Therefore, any public policy approach must presume a deep understanding of the problems, tensions and contradictions involved in setting-up networks. For instance, cross-sector networks may bring together businesses at similar stages of development - sharing similar problems and priorities - but may reduce the cohesion and access to the expertise of successful comparable businesses, that are often a feature of sector-based groups (Perry, 1996; Sydow, 1996). This highlights the need for more local and regional 'market' research to be undertaken, identifying: the institutions most applicable to generating networks; the types of networks to be supported; as well as the firms and individuals that appear best suited for potential participation. Future research on inter-firm networks should incorporate the crucial distinction between 'organic' and 'implanted' structures, in terms of both theoretical discourse and empirical study, as their constituent characteristics need to be fully differentiated if more is to be found out about their functioning.

*Final Remarks*

The cumulative effect of the problems encountered by TECs and their partners has hindered attempts to further shift public policy measures from a 'grant-aid' mentality to the provision of support that is valued and subsequently co-financed by businesses. TECs have attempted to fill this credibility gap by securing the participation of successful and respected local companies as mentors of the learning processes involved in their initiatives and programmes, in a loose form of corporate community involvement. As Chittenden and Robertson (1993) argue, expertise of this kind is one of the most valued types of support among SMEs, and through private sector involvement has a far higher chance of being acceptable to business 'clients'. However, scepticism in the private sector will only be overcome on a wholesale level if initiatives and programmes gain a degree of self-sustainability in the market-place. The positive marketing of 'success stories' has made a small contribution to this end. However, it is far more necessary to change the 'mind-set' of SME owners and managers towards such programmes, so that they do not feel they are wasting their time. This should be approached by developing well managed and organised initiatives with the objectives, direction and potential - realistic - outputs being as transparent as possible, i.e. to prove that the initiatives do work. Therefore, there is a need to avoid 'industrial tourism' projects inhabited by 'network junkies', and to focus on the creation of worthwhile groups, such as the manufacturing performance improvement networks and cluster groups outlined in chapter 6.

The strength of network, particularly inter-firm, approaches to business support programme delivery is that they not only give participants the capacity to create their own synergy, but that they allow the evolution of projects to be demand rather than supply led. Participants can define their own needs in an 'organic', rather than an imposed, manner; the long-term - although admittedly difficult - aim of the intervention being for firms to administer and manage their own networks (Sabel, 1992; Fahrenkrog, 1994; Malecki and Tootle, 1996). As already indicated, such networks should not be seen as ends in themselves but part of comprehensive strategies to enhance economic competitiveness (Rosenfeld, 1996). Therefore, those responsible for developing and operating network policies need to give more attention to the quality of the networks they are facilitating. They should pursue policies that seek to instil exemplary networks, convincing the business community of their viability and capacity for genuine economic gain.

# References

Adam-Smith, D. and McGeever, M. (1995) Training and Enterprise Councils and Small- and Medium-Sized Enterprises: Not Meeting Needs or Just Not Meeting the Customer?, *Small Business and Enterprise Development*, Vol. 2, 149-157.

Aldrich, H. and Zimmer, C. (1986) Entrepreneurship through Social Networks, in Sexton, D. and Smilor, R. (eds.) *The Art and Science of Entrepreneurship*, Cambridge, MA, Ballinger.

Alter, C. and Hage, J. (1993) *Organizations Working Together*, Newbury Park, Sage.

Amin, A. (1992) Big firms versus the region on the Single European Market, in Dunford, M. and Kafkalas, G. (eds.) *Cities and regions in the new Europe: the global-local interplay and spatial development strategies*, London, Belhaven.

Amin, A. (1993) The globalization of the economy: An erosion of regional networks, in Grabher, G. (ed.) *The Embedded Firm: On the Socio-Economics of Industrial Networks*, London, Routledge.

Amin, A. (1994) The difficult transition from informal economy to Marshallian industrial district, *Area*, Vol. 26, 13-24.

Amin, A. and Robins, K. (1990) Industrial districts and regional development: Limits and possibilities, in Pyke, F., Becattini, G. and Sengenberger, W. (eds.) *Industrial districts and inter-firm co-operation in Italy*, Geneva, International Institute for Labour Studies.

Amin, A. and Thrift, N. (1995) Institutional issues for the European regions: from markets and plans to socioeconomics and powers of association, *Economy and Society*, Vol. 24, 41-66.

Anderson, J., Hakansson, H. and Johanson, J. (1994) Dyadic Business Relationships Within a Business Network Context, *Journal of Marketing*, Vol. 58, 1-15.

Antonelli, C. (1996) Localized knowledge percolation processes and information networks, *Journal of Evolutionary Economics*, Vol. 6, 281-295.

Appold, S. (1995) Agglomeration, Interorganizational Networks, and Competitive Performance in the U.S. Metalworking Sector, *Economic Geography*, Vol. 71, 27-54.

Arrow, K. (1971) Political and economic evaluation of social effects and externalities, in Intrilligator, M. (ed.) *Frontiers of Quantitative Economics*, Amsterdam, North Holland.

Arrow, K. (1974) *The Limits of Organisation*, New York, Norton.

Arthur, B. (1988) Self reinforcing mechanisms in economics, in Anderson, P. (ed.) *The Economy as an Evolving Complex System*, Reading, MA, Addison-Wesley.

Arthur, B. (1989) Competing technologies and lock-in by historical events: the dynamics of allocation under increasing returns, *Economic Journal*, Vol. 99, 116-131.

Asheim, B. (1996a) *Localised Learning, Inter-firm Cooperation and Endogenous Regional Development: Towards 'Learning Regions'*, Paper prepared for the EMOT Workshop on 'The Dynamics of Industrial Transformation', Turin, 15-16 November.

Asheim, B. (1996b) Industrial Districts as 'learning regions': a condition for prosperity, *European Planning Studies*, Vol. 4, 379-400.

Axelrod, R. (1984) *The Evolution of Cooperation*, New York, Basic Books.

Axelsson, B. and Easton, J. (eds.) (1992) *Industrial Networks: A New View of Reality*, London, Routledge.

Axford, N. and Pinch, S. (1994) Growth coalitions and local economic development strategy in southern England, *Political Geography*, Vol. 13, 344-360.

Baker, P. (1995) Small firms, industrial districts and power asymmetries, *International Journal of Entrepreneurial Behaviour & Research*, Vol. 1, 8-25.

Baker, W. (1992) The Network Organization in Theory and Practice, in Nohria, N. and Eccles, R. (eds.) *Networks and Organizations: Structure, Form and Action*, Boston, MA, Harvard Business School Press.

Baker, W. (1994) *Networking Smart: How to Build Relationships for Personal and Organizational Success*, New York, McGraw-Hill.

Ball, R. (1995) *Local Authorities and Regional Policy in the UK: Attitudes, Representations and the Local Economy*, London, Paul Chapman.

Barnes, J. (1954) Class and Committees in a Norwegian Island Parish, *Human Relations*, Vol. 7, 39-58.

Barney, J. (1986) Strategic factor markets: Expectations, luck and business strategy, *Management Science*, Vol. 21, 1231-1241.

Bazalgette, J., Armstrong, D., Hutton, J. and Quine, C. (1994) *The early use of local initiative funds by TECs: Evoking local prosperity*, Research Series No. 24, Sheffield, Employment Department.

Beck, U. (1992) *Risk Society*, London, Sage.

Bellone, C. and Goerl, G. (1992) Reconciling Public Entrepreneurship and Democracy, *Public Administration Review*, Vol. 52, 130-134.

Bennett, R. (1994) PICs, TECs and LECs: lessons to be learnt from the differences between the USA Private Industry Councils and Britain's Training and Enterprise Councils, *British Journal of Education and Work*, Vol. 7, 63-85.

Bennett, R. (1995a) The Re-focusing of Small Business Services in Enterprise Agencies: The Influence of TECs and LECs, *International Small Business Journal*, Vol. 13, 35-55.

Bennett, R. (1995b) *Meeting Business Needs in Britain: Engaging the Business Community through New Style Chambers*, London, British Chambers of Commerce.

Bennett, R. (1996) Can Transaction Cost Economics Explain Voluntary Chambers of Commerce?, *Journal of Institutional and Theoretical Economics*, Vol. 152, 654-680.

Bennett, R. and Krebs, G. (1991) *Local Economic Development Public-Private Partnership Initiatives in Britain and Germany*, London, Belhaven.

Bennett, R. and McCoshan, A. (1993) *Enterprise and Human Resource Development: Local capacity building*, London, Paul Chapman.

Bennett, R., Wicks, P. and McCoshan, A. (1994) *Local empowerment and business services, Britain's experiment with Training and Enterprise Councils*, London, UCL Press.

Bergman, E., Maier, G. and Tödtling, F. (1991) Reconsidering Regions, in Bergman, E., Maier, G. and Tödtling, F. (eds.) *Regions Reconsidered: Economic Networks, Innovation and Local Development in Industrialised Countries*, London, Mansell.

Bessant, J. (1995) Networking as a mechanism for enabling organisational innovations: the case for continuous improvement, in Kaplinsky, R., Coriat, B. and Hertog, F. den (eds.) *Europe's Next Step*, Ilford, Essex, Frank Cass.

Biggart, N. and Hamilton, G. (1992) On the Limits of a Firm-Based Theory to Explain Business Networks: The Western Bias of Neoclassical Economics, in Nohria, N. and Eccles, R. (eds.) *Networks and Organizations: Structure, Form and Action*, Boston, MA, Harvard Business School Press.

Birley, S. (1985) The Role of Networks in the Entrepreneurial Process, *Journal of Business Venturing*, Vol. 1, 107-118.

Birley, S. and Cromie, S. (1988) *Social Networks and Entrepreneurship in Northern Ireland*, Paper presented at Conference on 'Enterprise in Action', Belfast, September.

Blackburn, R. and Jennings, P. (1996) Introduction: The Contribution of Small Firms to Economic Regeneration, in Blackburn, R. and Jennings, P. (eds.) *Small Firms: Contributions to Economic Regeneration*, London, Paul Chapman.

Blackburn, R., Curran, J. and Jarvis, R. (1990) *Small firms and local networks: some theoretical and conceptual explorations*, Proceedings of the 13th National UK Small Firms Policy and Research Conference, Leeds, November.

Blackler, F. (1993) Knowledge and the theory of organizations: Organizations as activity systems and the reframing of management, *Journal of Management Studies*, Vol. 30, 863-884.

Blau, P. (1964) *Exchange and Power in Social Life*, New York, John Wiley.

Blau, P. (1977) *Inequality and Heterogeneity*, New York, The Free Press.

Bolton, J. (1971) *Report of the Committee of Enquiry on Small Firms*, London, HMSO.

Borch, O. and Arthur, M. (1995) Strategic Networks among Small Firms: Implications for Strategy Research Methodology, *Journal of Management Studies*, Vol. 32, 419-441.

Bosworth, B. (1995) Interfirm Cooperation: The Points of Intervention, *Firm Connections*, Vol. 3, No. 1, 2-5.

Bosworth, B. (1997) Great Expectations: USNet, Start to Finish, *Firm Connections*, Vol. 5, No. 6, 2-3.

Bosworth, B. and Rosenfeld, S. (1993) *Significant Others: Exploring the Potential of Manufacturing Networks*, Chapel Hill, NC, RTS Inc.

Bott, E. (1957) *Family and Social Network*, London, Tavistock.

Braczyk, H., Cooke, P. and Heidenreich, M. (eds.) (1998) *Regional Innovation Systems: The role of governances in a globalized world*, London, UCL Press.

Bradach, J. and Eccles, R. (1991) Price, authority and trust: from ideal types to plural forms, in Thompson, G., Frances, J., Levacic, R. and Mitchell, J. (eds.) *Markets, Hierarchies and Networks: The Coordination of Social Life*, London, Sage.

Brown, B. and Butler, J. (1993) Networks and entrepreneurial development: the shadow of borders, *Entrepreneurship and Regional Development*, Vol. 5, 101-116.

Brusco, S. (1992) Small firms and the provision of real services, in Pyke, F. and Sengenberger, W. (eds.) *Industrial districts and local economic regeneration*, Geneva, International Institute for Labour Studies.

Brusco, S. (1996) Trust, Social Capital and Local Development: Some Lessons from the Experience of the Italian Districts, in OECD (eds.) *Networks of Enterprises and Local Development: Competing and Co-operating in Local Productive Systems*, Paris, Organisation for Economic Co-operation and Development.

Bryson, J. (1997) Small and Medium-Sized Enterprises, Business Link and the New Knowledge Workers, *Policy Studies*, Vol. 18, 67-80.

Bryson, J., Wood, P. and Keeble, D. (1993) Business networks, small firm flexibility and regional development in the UK business services, *Entrepreneurship and Regional Development*, Vol. 5, 265-277.

Burrows, R. (1991) The discourse of the enterprise culture and the restructuring of Britain: a polemical contribution, in Curran, J. and Blackburn, R. (eds.) *Paths of enterprise: The future of the small business*, London, Routledge.

Burt, R. (1992) *Structural Holes: The Social Structure of Competition*, Cambridge, MA, Harvard University Press.

Cable, D. and Shane, S. (1997) A Prisoner's Dilemma Approach to Entrepreneur-Venture Capitalist Relationships, *Academy of Management Review*, Vol. 22, 142-176.

Callon, M. (1986) Some elements of a sociology of translation, in Law, J. (ed.) *Power, Action and Belief*, London, Routledge.

Callon, M. (1991) Techno-economic networks and irreversibility, in Law, J. (ed.) *A Sociology of Monsters: Essays on Power, Technology and Domination*, London, Routledge.

Camagni, R. (ed.) (1991) *Innovation Networks: Spatial Perspectives*, London, Belhaven.

Carlisle, R. (1993) *Entrepreneurial Policies: Can Collaborative Behavior Among Firms Help Generate More Start-Up Companies*, Paper to Conference on 'Interfirm Cooperation - a means towards SME Competitiveness', Lisbon, 6-8 October.

Castells, M. (1996) *The Rise of the Network Society*, Oxford, Blackwell.

Castells, M. and Hall, P. (1994) *Technopoles of the World: The making of twenty-first-century industrial complexes*, London, Routledge.

Chaston, I. (1996a) Critical Events and Process Gaps in the Danish Technological Institute SME Structured Networking Model, *International Small Business Journal*, Vol. 14, 71-84.

Chaston, I. (1996b) *Small Business Networking: Evolving an Appropriate UK National Process Model*, Paper presented at the 19th ISBA 'National Small Firms Policy and Research Conference', November.

Chittenden, F. and Robertson, M. (1993) Small Firms: Public Policy Issues in Recession and Recovery, in Chittenden, F., Robertson, M. and Watkins, D. (eds.) *Small Firms: Recession and Recovery*, London, Paul Chapman.

Chittenden, F., Robertson, M. and Marshall, I. (1995) Small Firms: Public Policy Issues in Partnerships for Growth, in Chittenden, F., Robertson, M. and Marshall, I. (eds.) *Small Firms: Partnerships for Growth*, London, Paul Chapman.

Cho, M. (1997) Large-small firm networks: a foundation of the new globalizing economy in South Korea, *Environment and Planning A*, Vol. 29, 1091-1108.

Christensen, P., Eskelinen, H., Forström, B., Lindmark, L. and Vatne, E. (1990) Firms in Networks: Concepts, Spatial Impacts and Policy Implications, in S. Illeris and L. Jakobsen (eds.) *Networks and Regional Development*, Copenhagen, University Press Copenhagen.

CIHE (1996) *Colleges and Companies Sharing Great Expectations*, London, Council for Industry and Higher Education.

Clark, P. and Staunton, N. (1989) *Innovation in Technology and Organization*, London, Routledge.

Clarke, S. and Gaile, G. (1997) Local Politics in a Global Era: Thinking Locally, Acting Globally, *Annals of the American Academy of Political and Social Science*, Vol. 551, 28-43.

Coase, R. (1937) The nature of the firm, *Economica*, Vol. 4, 386-405.

Collins, R. (1994) *Four Sociological Traditions*, Oxford, Oxford University Press.

Cook, K. (1977) Exchange and power in networks of interorganizational relations, *Sociological Quarterly*, Vol. 18, 62-82.

Cook, K. (1982) Network Structures from an Exchange Perspective, in Nohria, N. and Eccles, R. (eds.) *Networks and Organizations: Structure, Form and Action*, Boston, MA, Harvard Business School Press.

Cooke, P. (1994) *The Co-operative Advantage of Regions*, paper presented to conference on 'Regions, Institutions and Technology: Reorganizing Economic Geography in Canada and the Anglo-American World', University of Toronto, September.

Cooke, P. (1998) Introduction: origins of the concept, in Braczyk, H., Cooke, P. and Heidenreich, M. (eds.) *Regional Innovation Systems: The role of governances in a globalized world*, London, UCL Press.

Cooke, P. and Morgan, K. (1993) The network paradigm: new departures in corporate and regional development, *Environment and Planning D: Society and Space*, Vol. 11, 543-564.

Cooke, P. and Morgan, K. (1994a) The Creative Milieu: A Regional Perspective on Innovation, in Dodgson, M. and Rothwell, R. (eds.) *The Handbook of Industrial Innovation*, Aldershot, Hants, Edward Elgar.

Cooke, P. and Morgan, K. (1994b) The regional innovation system of Baden-Wurttemberg, *International Journal of Technology Management*, Vol. 9, 394-429.

Cooke, P. and Morgan, K. (1998) *The Associational Economy: Firms, Regions, and Innovation*, Oxford, Oxford University Press.

Cooke, P., Huggins, R. and Davies, S. (1995) *South Wales Technopole Project: Customer Survey and Design of Network*, 2nd Interim Report to the Commission of the European Communities DGXIII SPRINT-RITTS Programme, Cardiff, Centre for Advanced Studies.

Coopers and Lybrand (1994) *TEC Baseline Follow-up Studies: Final Overall Report*, London, Employment Department.

Coopers and Lybrand (1995) *TECs as Market Makers: Approaches to TEC/Employer Relations*, Moorfoot, Sheffield, Department for Education and Employment.

Coulson, A. (1997) 'Transaction Cost Economics' and its Implications for Local Governance, *Local Government Studies*, Vol. 23, 107-113.

Crewe, L. (1996) Material culture: embedded firms, organizational networks and the local economic development of a fashion quarter, *Regional Studies*, Vol. 30, 257-272.

Cromie, S., Birley, S. and Callaghan, I. (1993) Community brokers: Their Role in the formation and development of business ventures, *Entrepreneurship and Regional Development*, Vol. 5, 247-264.

Crowley-Bainton, T. (1993) *TECs & Employers, Developing effective links, Part 2: TEC-employer links in six TEC areas*, Research Series No. 13, Sheffield, Employment Department.

Crowley-Bainton, T. and Wolf, A. (1994) *Access to assessment initiative*, Sheffield, Employment Department.

Curran, J. (1993) *TECs and Small Firms: Can TECs Reach The Small Firms Other Strategies Have Failed to Reach*, Paper presented to the All Party Social Science and Policy Group, House of Commons, April.

Curran, J. and Blackburn, P. (1991) Changes in the context of enterprise: some socio-economic and environmental factors facing small firms in the 1990s, in Curran, J. and Blackburn, R. (eds.) *Paths of enterprise: The future of the small business*, London, Routledge

Curran, J. and Blackburn, R. (1993) Local Economies and Small Firms: A View from the Ground, in Chittenden, F., Robertson, M. and Watkins, D. (eds.) *Small Firms: Recession and Recovery*, London, Paul Chapman.

Curran, J. and Blackburn, R. (1994) *Small Firms and Local Economic Networks: The Death of the Local Economy*, London, Paul Chapman.

Curran, J., Jarvis, R., Blackburn, R. and Black, S. (1993) Networks and Small Firms: Constructs, Methodological Strategies and Some Findings, *International Small Business Journal*, Vol. 11, 13-25.

Dahms, H. (1995) Creative Action to the Social Rationalization of the Economy, *Sociological Theory*, Vol. 13, 1-13.

de Leon, L. (1996) Ethics and Entrepreneurship, *Policy Studies Journal*, Vol. 24, 495-510.

de Toni, A. and Nassimbeni, G. (1995) Supply Networks: Genesis, Stability and Logistics Implications. A Comparative Analysis of Two Districts, Omega, Vol. 23, 403-418.

de Vet, J. (1993) Globalisation and Local and Regional Competitiveness, *STI Review*, Vol. 13, 89-122.

Dean, J. and Frost, M. (1997) Some Contrasts - US and Australian Networks, *Firm Connections*, Vol. 5, No. 6, 13.

DeBresson, C. and Amesse, F. (1991) *Networks of innovators: A review and introduction to the issue*, Research Policy, Vol. 20, 363-379.

Dei Ottati, G. (1994) Trust, interlinking transactions and credit in the industrial district, *Cambridge Journal of Economics*, Vol. 18, 529-546.

DFEE (1995a) *Enterprise and the TEC: Partnerships for Economic Development*, Sheffield, Department for Education and Employment.

DFEE (1995b) *Enterprise and the TEC: Effective TEC/Employer Relationships*, Sheffield, Department for Education and Employment.

Dickson, K. (1996) How informal can you be? Trust and reciprocity within co-operative and collaborative relationships, *International Journal of Technology Management*, Vol. 11, 129-139.

DiMaggio, P. and Powell, W. (1991) Introduction, in Powell, W. and DiMaggio, P. (eds.) *The New Institutionalism in Organizational Analysis*, Chicago, University of Chicago Press.

Dodgson, M. and Rothwell, R. (eds.) (1994) *The Handbook of Industrial Innovation*, Aldershot, Hants, Edward Elgar.

DoE (1992) *Small Business in Britain*, Department of Employment, London, HMSO.

Donckels, R. and Lambrecht, J. (1995) Networks and Small Business Growth: An Explanatory Model, *Small Business Economics*, Vol. 7, 273-289.

Dosi, G. (1988) Sources, Procedures and Microeconomic Effects of Innovation, *Journal of Economic Literature*, Vol. 26, 1120-1171.

Dosi, G., Freeman, C., Nelson, R., Silverberg, G. and Soete, L. (eds.) (1988) *Technical Change and Economic Theory*, London, Pinter.

Easton, G. and Araujo, L. (1992) Non-economic exchange in industrial networks, in Axelsson, B. and Easton, J. (eds.) *Industrial Networks: A New View of Reality*, London, Routledge.

Eisinger, P. (1988) *The Rise of the Entrepreneurial State: State and Local Development Policy in the United States*, Wisconsin, University of Wisconsin Press.

Eisinger, P. (1995) State Economic Development in the 1990s: Politics and Policy Learning, *Economic Development Quarterly*, Vol. 9, 146-158.

Emerson, R. (1962) *Power-dependence relations*, American Sociological Review, Vol. 27, 31-41.

Employment Committee (1991) *Training and Enterprise Councils and Vocational Training*, Fifth Report of the Employment Committee to the House of Commons, Volume 2, London, HMSO.

Employment Committee (1996) *The Work of TECs*, First Report of the Employment Committee to the House of Commons, London, HMSO.

Employment Department (1988) *Employment for the 1990s*, London, HMSO.

Enright, M. (1996) Regional Clusters and Economic Development: A Research Agenda, in Staber, U., Schaefer, N. and Sharma, B. (eds.) *Business Networks: Prospects for Regional Development*, Berlin, Walter de Gruyter.

Ernst and Young (1996) *Evaluation of Business Links*, A Report on behalf of the Department of Trade and Industry, London, Department of Trade and Industry.

Ettlinger, N. (1997) An assessment of the small-firm debate in the United States, *Environment and Planning A*, Vol. 29, 419-442.

Evans, R. and Harding, A. (1997) Regionalisation, regional institutions and economic development, *Policy and Politics*, Vol. 25, 19-30.

Fahrenkrog, G. (1994) *Clusters and networks of innovative SMEs: An inventory of policy instruments in the European Union*, Paper to the 'Six Countries Programme', London, May.

Fasenfest, D. (1993) *Community Economic Development: Policy Formation in the US and UK*, London, Macmillan.

Felstead, A. (1994) Funding Government Training Schemes: Mechanisms and Consequences, *British Journal of Education and Work*, Vol. 7, 21-42.

Field, P., Moore, J., Dickinson, P., Elgar, J. and Gray, P. (1995) *Local development partnerships and investments in people*, Research Series No. 51, Sheffield, Employment Department.

Fligstein, N. and Freeland, R. (1995) Theoretical and Comparative Perspectives on Corporate Organization, *Annual Review of Sociology*, Vol. 21, 21-43.

Flora, C. and Flora, J. (1993) Entrepreneurial Social Infrastructures: A Necessary Ingredient, *Annals of the American Academy of Political and Social Science*, Vol. 529, 48-58.

Florida, R. (1995) Toward the learning region, *Futures*, Vol. 27, 527-536.

Ford, D. (1994) Looking Forward, in Johanson, J. and Associates (eds.) *Internationalization, Relationships and Networks*, Uppsala, Uppsala University.

Forsgren, M., Hagg, I., Hakansson, H., Johanson, J. and Mattsson, L. (1995) Firms in Networks: A New Perspective on Competitive Power, *Studia Oeconomiae Negotiorum 38*, Uppsala, Uppsala University.

Freeman, C. (1994) Critical survey: the economics of technical change, *Cambridge Journal of Economics*, Vol. 18, 463-512.

Fukuyama, F. (1995) *Trust: The Social Virtues and the Creation of Prosperity*, London, Hamish Hamilton.

Galaskiewicz, J. (1979) *Exchange networks and community politics*, Beverly Hills, Sage.

Gallagher, C., Graves, A. and Miller, P. (1994) *TEC Performance and Firm Demographics*, Newcastle-upon-Tyne, Trends Business Research Ltd.

Gambetta, D. (ed.) (1988) *Trust: Making and Breaking Cooperative Relations*, Oxford, Basil Blackwell.

Garnsey, E. and Cannon-Brookes, A. (1993) Small high technology firms in an era of rapid change: evidence from Cambridge, *Local Economy*, Vol. 7, 318-33.

Gelsing, L. (1992) *Evaluating Programmes Promoting Networks: Measures of Success and Evaluation Methods*, Paper to Conference on 'Interfirm Linkages and Cooperation Among SMEs', Aspen Institute, Colorado, July.

Gelsing, L. and Knop, P. (1991) *Status of the network programme: The results from a questionnaire survey*, Report prepared for the National Agency for Industry and Trade, Copenhagen, October.

Gertler, M. (1995) 'Being There': Proximity, Organization, and Culture in the Development and Adoption of Advanced Manufacturing Technologies, *Economic Geography*, Vol. 71, 1-26.

Gertler, M. and Rutherford, T. (1996) Regional-Industrial Networks and the Role of Labour, in Staber, U., Schaefer, N. and Sharma, B. (eds.) *Business Networks: Prospects for Regional Development*, Berlin, Walter de Gruyter.

GHK (1995) *Learning for Experience: TECs and Local Economic Development Partnerships*, GHK Economics and Management, Birmingham.

Giaoutzi, M., Nijkamp, P. and Storey, D. (1988) Small is Beautiful - The Regional Importance of Small Scale Activities, in Giaoutzi, M., Nijkamp, P. and Storey, D. (eds.) *Small and Medium Size Enterprises and Regional Development*, London, Routledge.

Gibb, A. (1993) Key factors in the design of policy support from the small and medium enterprise (SME) development process: an overview, *Entrepreneurship and Regional Development*, Vol. 5, 1-24.

Gibb, A. (1997) Small Firms' Training and Competitiveness: Building Upon the Small Business as a Learning Organisation, *International Small Business Journal*, Vol. 15, 13-29.

Gibb, A. and Manu, G. (1990) Design of Extension and Support Services for Small-Scale Enterprise Development, *International Small Business Journal*, Vol. 8, 10-27.

Giddens, A. (1990) *The Consequence of Modernity*, Oxford, Polity Press.

Gittell, R. and Kaufman, A. (1996) State Government Efforts in Industrial Modernization: Using Theory to Guide Practice, *Regional Studies*, Vol. 30, 477-492.

Goss, D. (1991) *Small Business and Society,* London, Routledge.

Grabher, G. (1993) Rediscovering the social in the economics of interfirm relations, in G. Grabher (ed.) *The Embedded Firm: On the Socio-Economics of Industrial Networks*, London, Routledge.

Grabher, G. and Stark, D. (1997) Organizing Diversity: Evolutionary Theory, Network Analysis and Postsocialism, *Regional Studies*, Vol. 31, 533-544.

Grandori, A. and Soda, G. (1995) Inter-firm Networks: Antecedents, Mechanisms and Forms, *Organization Studies*, Vol. 16, 183-214.

Granovetter, M. (1973) The Strength of Weak Ties, *American Journal of Sociology*, Vol. 78, 1360-1380.

Granovetter, M. (1982) The Strength of Weak Ties: A Network Theory Revisited, in Marsden, P. and Lin, N. (eds.) *Social Structure and Network Analysis*, Beverly Hills, Sage.

Granovetter, M. (1985) Economic Action and Social Structure: The Problem of Embeddedness, *American Journal of Sociology*, Vol. 91, 481-510.

Granovetter, M. (1992) Problems of Explanation in Economic Sociology, in Nohria, N. and Eccles, R. (eds.) *Networks and Organizations: Structure, Form and Action*, Boston:MA, Harvard Business School Press.

Granovetter, M. (1994) Business Groups, in Smelser, N. and Swedberg, R. (eds.) *The Handbook of Economic Sociology*, Princeton, Princeton University Press.

Grant, R. (1996) Toward a Knowledge-Based Theory of the Firm, *Strategic Management Journal*, Vol. 17, 109-122.

Gray, A. (1997) Contract culture and target fetishism: The distortive effects of output measures in local regeneration programmes, *Local Economy*, Vol. 11, 343-357.

Grayson, D. (1994) Community Regeneration: Is It the Business of Business?, *Policy Studies*, Vol. 15, 37-51.

Gregersen, B. and Johnson, B. (1997) Learning Economies, Innovation Systems and European Integration, *Regional Studies,* Vol. 31, 479-490.

Greve, A. (1995) Networks and entrepreneurship - an analysis of social relations, occupational background and use of contacts during the establishment process, *Scandinavian Journal of Management*, Vol. 11, 1-24.

Grotz, R. and Braun, B. (1993) Networks, Milieux and Individual Firm Strategies: Empirical Evidence of an Innovative SME Environment, *Geografiska Annaler*, Vol. 75B, 149-162.

Gunasekaran, A., Okko, P., Martikainen, T. and Yli-Olli, P. (1996) Improving Productivity and Quality in Small and Medium Enterprises: Cases and Analysis, *International Small Business Journal*, Vol. 15, 59-72.

Hakansson, H. (1989) *Corporate Technological Behaviour: Co-operation and Networks*, London, Routledge.

Hakansson, H. (ed.) (1982) *International Marketing and Purchasing of Industrial Goods - An Interaction Approach*, London, Wiley.

Hakansson, H. and Johanson, J. (1993) The network as a governance structure: interfirm cooperation beyond markets and hierarchies, in Grabher, G. (ed.) *The Embedded Firm: On the Socio-Economics of Industrial Networks*, London, Routledge.

Hall, T. and Hubbard, P. (1996) The entrepreneurial city: new urban politics, new urban geographies?, *Progress in Human Geography*, Vol. 20, 153-174.

Hallen, L., Johanson, J. and Syed-Mohamed, N. (1991) Interfirm Adaptation in Business Relationships, *Journal of Marketing*, Vol. 55, 29-37.

Hara, G. and Kanai, T. (1994) Entrepreneurial Networks Across Oceans to Promote International Strategic Alliances for Small Businesses, *Journal of Business Venturing*, Vol. 9, 489-507.

Hardill, I., Fletcher, D. and Montagné-Villette, S. (1995) Small firms' 'distinctive capabilities' and the socio-economic milieu: findings from case studies in Le Choletais (France) and the East Midlands (UK), *Entrepreneurship and Regional Development*, Vol. 7, 167-186.

Harrison, B. (1994) *Lean and Mean: The Changing Landscape of Corporate Power in the Age of Flexibility*, New York, Basic Books.

Harrison, R. and Mason, C. (1996) Developing the Informal Venture Capital Market: A Review of the Department of Trade and Industry's Informal Investment Demonstration Projects, *Regional Studies,* Vol. 30, 765-771.

Hart, M. and Scott, R. (1994) Measuring the Effectiveness of Small Firm Policy: Some Lessons from Northern Ireland, *Regional Studies,* Vol. 28, 849-858.

Hart, T., Haughton, G. and Peck, J. (1996) Accountability and the Non-elected Local State: Calling Training and Enterprise Councils to Local Account, *Regional Studies*, Vol. 30, 429-441.

Harvey, D. (1989) From Managerialism to Entrepreneurialism: The Transformation in Urban Governance in Late Capitalism, *Geografiska Annaler*, Vol. 71B, 3-17.

Hassink, R. (1992) *Regional Innovation Policy: case studies from the Ruhr area, Baden-Wurttemberg and the North East of England*, Utrecht, NGS.

Haughton, G., Peck, J., Hart, T., Strange, I., Tickell, A. and Williams, C. (1995a) *TECs and their Boards*, Research Series No. 64, Sheffield, Department for Education and Employment.

Haughton, G., Hart, T., Strange, I. and Thomas, K. (1995b) *TECs and their non-employer stakeholders*, Research Series No. 46, Sheffield, Employment Department.

Haughton, G., Peck, J. and Strange, I. (1997) Turf Wars: The Battle for Control over English Local Economic Development, *Local Government Studies*, Vol. 23, 88-106.

Hirschman, A. (1984) *Getting ahead collectively: grassroots experiences in Latin America*, New York, Pergamon Press.

Hirst, P. and Zeitlin, J. (eds.) (1989) *Reversing Industrial Decline? Industrial Structure and Policy in Britain and Her Competitors*, Oxford, Berg.

HM Government (1994a) *TECs: Towards 2000, The Government's Strategic Guidance to TECs*, London, Crown Copyright.

HM Government (1994b) *Competitiveness: Helping Business to Win*, London, HMSO.

HM Government (1995) *Competitiveness: Forging Ahead*, London, HMSO.

HM Government (1996) *TECs: Beyond 2000, The Government's Strategic Guidance to TECs*, London, Crown Copyright.

HM Government (1998) *Our Competitive Future: Building the Knowledge Driven Economy*, London, HMSO.

Hobday, M. (1991) Dynamic Networks, Technology Diffusion and Complementary Assets: Explaining US Decline in Semiconductors, *DRC Discussion Paper 78*, University of Sussex, Science Policy Research Unit.

Hobday, M. (1994) The Limits of Silicon Valley: A Critique of Network Theory, *Technology Analysis & Strategic Management*, Vol. 6, 231-244.

Hudson, R., Dunford, M., Hamilton, D. and Kotter, R. (1997) Developing Regional Strategies for Economic Success: Lessons from Europe's Economically Successful Regions?, *European Urban and Regional Studies*, Vol. 4, 365-373.

Huggins, R. (1996) Technology Policy, Networks and Small Firms in Denmark, *Regional Studies*, Vol. 30, 523-526.

Huggins, R. (1997) Competitiveness and the Global Region: The Role of Networking, in Simmie, J. (ed.) *Innovation, Networks and Learning Regions?*, London, Jessica Kingsley.

Huggins, R. (1998a) Local Business Co-operation and Training and Enterprise Councils: The Development of Inter-firm Networks, *Regional Studies*, Vol. 32, 813-826.

Huggins, R. (1998b) Building and Sustaining Inter-firm Networks: Lessons from Training and Enterprise Councils, *Local Economy*, Vol. 13, 133-150.

Huggins, R. (1998c) An Evaluation of European Union Objective 2 Programmes in Industrial South Wales 1989-93, *European Urban and Regional Studies*, Vol. 5, 291-303.

Huggins, R. and Thomalla, R. (1995) Promoting innovation through technology networks in North-Rhine-Westphalia, in Cooke, P. (ed.) *The Rise of the Rustbelt*, London, UCL Press.

Humphries, C. (1996) The Territorialisation of Public Policies: The Role of Public Governance and Funding, in OECD (eds.) *Networks of Enterprises and Local Development: Competing and Co-operating in Local Productive Systems*, Paris, Organisation for Economic Co-operation and Development.

Hutchinson, J., Foley, P. and Oztel, H. (1996) From Clutter to Collaboration: Business Links and the Rationalization of Business Support, *Regional Studies*, Vol. 30, No. 5, 516-522.

Ibarra, H. (1992) Structural Alignments, Individual Strategies, and Managerial Action: Elements Toward a Network Theory of Getting Things Done, in Nohria, N. and Eccles, R. (eds.) *Networks and Organizations: Structure, Form and Action*, Boston, MA, Harvard Business School Press.

Indergaard, M. (1996) Making Networks, Remaking the City, *Economic Development Quarterly*, Vol. 10, 172-187,

Izushi, H. (1997) Conflict Between Two Industrial Networks: Technological Adaptation and Inter-firm Relationships in the Ceramics Industry in Seto, Japan, *Regional Studies*, Vol. 31, 117-129.

Jacobs, B. (1997) Networks, partnerships and European Union regional economic development initiatives in the West Midlands, *Policy and Politics*, Vol. 25, 39-50.

Jakobsen, L. and Martinussen, J. (1991) *A national incentive scheme for establishing cooperation networks between small firms*, Paper to 'ICSB 36th Annual Conference', Vienna, June.

Jennings, P. and Beaver, G. (1997) The Performance and Competitive Advantage of Small Firms: A Management Perspective, *International Small Business Journal*, Vol. 15, 63-75.

Jessop, B. (1991) Thatcherism and flexibility: the white heat of a post-Fordist revolution, in Jessop, B., Kastendiek, H., Nielsen, K., Pedersen, O. (eds.) *The Politics of Flexibility*, Aldershot, Hants, Edward Elgar.

Johannisson, B. (1995) Paradigms and entrepreneurial networks - some methodological challenges, *Entrepreneurship and Regional Development*, Vol. 7, 215-231.

Johanson, J. and Mattsson, L. (1985) Marketing Investments and Market Investments in Industrial Networks, *International Journal of Research in Marketing*, Vol. 2, 185-195.

Johanson, J. and Mattsson, L. (1987) Interorganizational relations in industrial systems: a network approach compared with the transaction-cost approach, *International Studies of Management and Organization*, Vol. 17, 34-48.

Jones, M. (1996) Business Link: A critical commentary, *Local Economy*, Vol. 11, 71-78.

Jones, M. (1997) Skills Revolution? Sorry, Wrong Number, *Local Economy*, Vol. 11, 290-298.

Joyce, P., Woods, A. and Black, S. (1995) Networks and partnerships: Managing change and competition, *Small Business and Enterprise Development*, Vol. 2, 11-18.

Karlsson, C. (1994) From Knowledge and Technology Networks to Network Technology, in B. Johansson, C. Karlsson and L. Westin (eds.) *Patterns of a Network Economy*, Berlin, Springer-Verlag.

Karlsson, C. and Westin, L. (1994) Patterns of a Network Economy - An Introduction, in Johansson, B., Karlsson, C. and Westin, L. (eds.) *Patterns of a Network Economy*, Berlin, Springer-Verlag.

Keeble, D. and Bryson, J. (1996) Small firm creation and growth, regional development and the North-South divide in Britain, *Environment and Planning A*, Vol. 28, 909-934.

Kingsley, G. and Klein, H. (1998) Interfirm Collaboration as a Modernization Strategy: A Survey of Case Studies, *Journal of Technology Transfer*, Vol. 23, 65-74.

Knights, D., Murray, F. and Wilmott, H. (1993) Networking as Knowledge Work: A Study of Strategic Interorganization Development in the Financial Services Industry, *Journal of Management Studies*, Vol. 30, 975-995.

Knoke, D. and Kuklinski, J. (1982) *Network Analysis*, Beverley Hills, Sage.

Kobrak, P. (1996) The Social Responsibilities of a Public Entrepreneur, *Administration and Society*, Vol. 28, 205-237.

Kogut, B. and Zander, U. (1996) What Firms Do? Coordination, Identity, and Learning, *Organization Science*, Vol. 7, 502-519.

Kogut, B., Shan, W. and Walker, G. (1993) Knowledge in the network and the network as knowledge: the structuring of new industries, in G. Grabher (ed.) *The Embedded Firm: On the Socio-Economics of Industrial Networks*, London, Routledge.

Krugman, P. (1995) *Development, Geography and Economic Theory*, Cambridge, MIT Press.

Lado, A., Boyd, N. and Hanlon, S. (1997) Competition, Cooperation, and the Search for Economic Rents: A Syncretic Model, *Academy of Management Review*, Vol. 22, 110-141.

Larson, A. (1992) Network Dyads in Entrepreneurial Settings: A Study of the Governance of Exchange Relationships, *Administrative Science Quarterly*, Vol. 37, 76-104.

Latour, B. (1986) The powers of association, in Law, J. (ed.) *Power, Action and Belief*, London, Routledge.

Latour, B. (1991) Materials and power: technology is society made durable, in Law, J. (ed.) *A Sociology of Monsters: Essays on Power, Technology and Domination*, London, Routledge.

Law, J. (1994) *Organising Modernity*, Oxford, Blackwell.

Law, J. (ed.) (1991) *A Sociology of Monsters: Essays on Power, Technology and Domination*, London, Routledge.

Leicht, K. and Jenkins, C. (1994) Three Strategies of State Economic Development: Entrepreneurial, Industrial Recruitment, and Deregulation Policies in the American States, *Economic Development Quarterly*, Vol. 8, 256-269.

Leonardi, R. and Nanetti, R. (eds.) (1990) *The Regions and European Integration: The Case of Emilia-Romagna*, London, Pinter.

Lichtenstein, G. (1990) *The Ecology of Enterprise in a Business Incubator: A Case Study of Networking Among Entrepreneurial Firms in the Fulton-Carroll Center*, Wharton School, University of Pennsylvania, Philadelphia, PA.

Lincoln, J., Gerlach, M. and Takahashi, P. (1992) Keiretsu Networks in the Japanese Economy: A Dyad Analysis of Intercorporate Ties, *American Sociological Review*, Vol. 57, 561-585.

Lipparini, A. and Sobrero, M. (1994) The Glue and the Pieces: Entrepreneurship and Innovation in Small-Firm Networks, *Journal of Business Venturing*, Vol. 9, 125-140.

Lloyd, P. and Meegan, R. (1996) Contested Governance: European Exposures in the English Regions, in Alden, J. and Boland, P. (eds.) *Regional Development Strategies: A European Perspective*, London, Jessica Kingsley.

Lorenz, E. (1991) Neither friends nor strangers: informal networks of subcontracting in French industry, in Thompson, G., Frances, J., Levacic, R. and Mitchell, J. (eds.) *Markets, Hierarchies and Networks*, London, Sage.

Lorenz, E. (1992) Trust, community, and cooperation: Toward a theory of industrial districts, in Storper, M. and Scott, A. (eds.) *Pathways to Industrialization and Regional Development*, London, Routledge.

Lowndes, V., Nanton, P., McCabe, A. and Skelcher, C. (1997) Networks, Partnerships and Urban Regeneration, *Local Economy*, Vol. 11, 333-342.

Luhmann, N. (1988) Familiarity, confidence, trust: problems and alternatives: in Gambetta, D. (ed.) *Trust: Making and Breaking Cooperative Relations*, Oxford, Basil Blackwell.

Lundvall, B. (1993) Explaining interfirm cooperation and innovation: Limits of the transaction-cost approach, in Grabher, G. (ed.) *The Embedded Firm: On the Socio-Economics of Industrial Networks*, London, Routledge.

Lundvall, B. (1994) The Global Unemployment Problem and National Systems of Innovation, in O'Doherty, D. (ed.) *Globalisation, Networking and Small Firm Innovation*, London, Graham & Trotman.

Lundvall, B. and Johnson, B. (1994) The Learning Economy. *Journal of Industry Studies*, Vol. 1, 23-42.

MacLeod, G. (1996) The Cult of Enterprise in a Networked Learning Region? Governing Business and Skills in Lowland Scotland, *Regional Studies*, Vol. 30, 749-755.

Maillat, D. (1998) Innovative milieux and new generations of regional policies, *Entrepreneurship and Regional Development*, Vol. 10, 1-16.

Malecki, E. and Tootle, D. (1996) The role of networks in small firm competitiveness, *International Journal of Technology Management*, Vol. 11, 43-57.

Malecki, E. and Tootle, D. (1997) Networks of small manufacturers in the USA: creating embeddedness, in Taylor, M. and Conti, S. (eds.) *Interdependent and Uneven Development: Global-local perspectives*, Aldershot, Ashgate.

Malecki, E. and Veldhoen, M. (1993) Network Activities, Information and Competitiveness in Small Firms, *Geografiska Annaler*, Vol. 75B, 131-147.

Markusen, A. (1994) Sticky Places in Slippery Space: A Typology of Industrial Districts, *Economic Geography*, Vol. 72, 293-313.

Marsden, P. (1982) Brokerage Behavior in Restricted Exchange Networks, in Nohria, N. and Eccles, R. (eds.) *Networks and Organizations: Structure, Form and Action*, Boston, MA, Harvard Business School Press.

Marshall, J., Alderman, N., Wong, C. and Thwaites, A. (1995) The Impact of Management Training and Development on Small and Medium-sized Enterprises, *International Small Business Journal*, Vol. 13, 73-90.

Martin, R. and Sunley, P. (1996) Paul Krugman's Geographical Economics and Its Implications for Regional Development Theory: A Critical Assessment, *Economic Geography*, Vol. 72, 259-292.

Martin, S. and Oztel, H. (1996) The business of partnership: Collaborative-competitive partnerships in the development of Business Links, *Local Economy*, Vol. 11, 131-142.

Maskell, P. and Malmberg, A. (1995) Localised learning and industrial competitiveness, paper to Regional Studies Association Conference on 'Regional Futures', Gothenburg, May.

Mason, C. and Harrison, R. (1997) Business Angel Networks and the Development of the Informal Venture Capital Market in the UK: Is There Still a Role for the Public Sector, *Small Business Economics*, Vol. 9, 111-123.

Mattsson, L. (1995) Firms, 'Megaorganizations' and Markets: A Network View, *Journal of Institutional and Theoretical Economics*, Vol. 151, 760-766.

Mawson, J. (1995) The re-emergence of the regional agenda in the English regions: new patterns of urban and regional governance, *Local Economy*, Vol. 10, 300-326.

Mawson, J. and Spencer, K. (1997) The government offices for the English regions: towards regional governance, *Policy and Politics*, Vol. 25, 71-84.

McGuiness, T. (1991) Markets and managerial hierarchies, in Thompson, G., Frances, J., Levacic, R. and Mitchell, J. (eds.) *Markets, Hierarchies and Networks: The Coordination of Social Life*, London, Sage.

Meyerson, D., Weick, K. and Kramer, R. (1996) Swift Trust and Temporary Groups, in Kramer, R. and Tyler, T. (eds.) *Trust in Organizations: Frontiers of Theory and Research*, Thousand Oaks, CA, Sage.

Meyerson, E. (1994) Human Capital, Social Capital and Compensation: The Relative Contribution of Social Contacts to Managers' Incomes, *Acta Sociologica,* Vol. 37, 383-399.

Miles, R. and Snow, C. (1992) Causes of Failure in Network Organizations, *California Management Review*, Vol. 34, 53-72.

Mintrom, M. (1997) Policy Entrepreneurs and the Diffusion of Innovation, *American Journal of Political Science*, Vol. 41, 738-770.

Mitchell, J. (1969) The concept and use of networks, in Mitchell, J. (ed.) *Social Networks in Urban Situations*, Manchester, Manchester University Press.

Mitchell, J. (1973) Networks, norms and institutions, in Boissevain, J. and Mitchell, J. (eds.) *Network Analysis: Studies in Human Interaction*, The Hague, Mouton,

Mizruchi, M. and Galaskiewicz, J. (1994) Networks of Interorganizational Relations, in Wasserman, S. and Galaskiewicz, J. (eds.) *Advances in Social Network Analysis*, London, Sage.

Miztal, B. (1996) *Trust in Modern Societies: The Search for the Bases of Social Order*, Cambridge, Polity Press.

Monsted, M. (1991) *Different Types of Regional Networks: Methodological Considerations*, Paper to 'ICSB 36th Annual Conference', Vienna, June.

Monsted, M. (1995) Processes and structures of networks: reflections on methodology, *Entrepreneurship and Regional Development*, Vol. 7, 193-213.

Morgan, K. (1997) The Learning Region: Institutions, Innovation and Regional Renewal, *Regional Studies*, Vol. 31, 491-503.

Mowery. D., Oxley, J. and Silverman, B. (1996) Strategic Alliances and Interfirm Knowledge Transfer, *Strategic Management Journal*, Vol. 17, 77-91.

Murdoch, J. (1995) Actor-networks and the evolution of economic forms: combining description and explanation in theories of regulation, flexible specialization, and networks, *Environment and Planning A*, Vol. 27, 731-757.

Murdoch, J. (1997) Inhuman/nonhuman/human: actor-network theory and the prospects for a nondualistic and symmetrical perspective on nature and society, *Environment and Planning D: Society and Space*, Vol. 15, 731-756.

Nelson, R. and Winter, S. (1982) *An Evolutionary Theory of Change*, Cambridge, MA, Harvard University Press.

New, S. and Mitropoulos, I. (1995) Strategic networks: morphology, epistemology and praxis, *International Journal of Operations and Production Management*, Vol. 15, 53-61.

Nielsen, N. (1994) *The Concept of a Technological Service Infrastructure: Innovation and the Creation of Good Jobs*, paper to OECD Conference on 'Employment and Growth in the Knowledge-Based Economy', Copenhagen, November.

Nijkamp, P., van Oirscoht, G. and Oosterman, A. (1994) Knowledge networks, science parks and regional development: An international comparative analysis of critical success factors, in Cuadrado-Roura, J., Nijkamp, P. and Salva, P. (eds.) *Moving Frontiers: Economic Restructuring, Regional Development and Emerging Networks*, Aldershot, Avebury.

North, D. (1990) *Institutions, Institutional Change and Economic Performance*, Cambridge, Cambridge University Press.

OECD (1992) *Technology and the Economy: The Key Relationships*, Paris, Organisation for Economic Co-operation and Development.

Office for National Statistics (1996) *Regional Trends*, London, HMSO.

Oliver, C. (1997) Sustainable Competitive Advantage: Combining Institutional and Resource-Based Views, *Strategic Management Journal*, Vol. 18, 697-713.

Olson, M. (1965) *The Logic of Collective Action*, Cambridge, MA, Harvard University Press.

Osborne, D. and Gaebler, T. (1992) *Reinventing Government: How the Entrepreneurial Spirit is Transforming the Public Sector*, Reading, Mass, Addison-Wesley.

Ostgaard, T. and Birley, S. (1996) New Venture Growth and Personal Networks, *Journal of Business Research*, Vol. 36, 37-50.

PACEC (1995) *Evaluation of DTI funded TEC services in support of small and medium-sized businesses*, A report prepared by PA Cambridge Economic Consultants on behalf of the Department of Trade and Industry, London, HMSO.

Parker, K. and Vickerstaff, S. (1996) TECs, LECs, and small firms: differences in provision and performance, *Environment and Planning C: Government and Policy*, Vol. 14, 251-267.

Peck, J. (1993) The Trouble With TECs: a critique of the Training and Enterprise Councils initiative, *Policy and Politics*, Vol. 21, 289-305.

Peck, J. and Emmerich, M. (1993) Training and Enterprise Councils: Time for a Change, *Local Economy*, Vol. 8, 4-21.

Peck, J. and Jones, M. (1995) Training and Enterprise Councils: Schumpeterian workfare state, or what?, *Environment and Planning A*, Vol. 27, 1361-1396.

Penn, R. (1992) Contemporary Relationships Between Firms in a Classic Industrial Locality: Evidence from the Social Change and Economic Life Initiative, *Work, Employment & Society*, Vol. 6, 209-227.

Penrose, E. (1959) *The Theory of the Growth of the Firm*, Oxford, Blackwell.

Perroux, F. (1970) Note on the concept of 'growth poles', in McKee, D., Dean, R. and Leahy, W. (eds.) *Regional Economics: Theory and Practice*, New York, The Free Press.

Perry, M. (1995) Industry structures, networks and joint action groups, *Regional Studies*, Vol. 29, 208-217.

Perry, M. (1996) Network Intermediaries and Their Effectiveness, *International Small Business Journal*, Vol. 14, 72-80.

Perry, M. and Goldfinch, S. (1996) Business Networks Outside and Industrial District, *Tijdschrift voor Economische en Sociale Geografie*, Vol. 87, 222-236.

Pfeffer, J. and Salancik, G. (1978) *The External Control of Organizations*, New York, Harper and Row.

Piore, M. and Sabel, C. (1984) *The Second Industrial Divide*, New York, Basic Books.

Pitt, M. (1998) A Tale of Two Gladiators: 'Reading' Entrepreneurs as Texts, *Organization Studies*, Vol. 19, 387-414.

Ploszajska, T. (1994) Training and Enterprise in England and Wales: A Critical Review, *British Journal of Education and Work*, Vol. 7, 43-62.

Podolny, J. and Baron, J. (1997) Resources and Relationships: Social Networks and Mobility in the Workplace, *American Sociological Review*, Vol. 62, 673-693.

Porter, M. (1990) *The Competitive Advantage of Nations*, London, Macmillan.

Powell, W. (1990) Neither Market Nor Hierarchy: Network Forms of Organization, in Cummings, L. and Straw, B. (eds.) *Research in Organizational Behaviour*, Greenwich: CT, JAI Press.

Powell, W. (1996) Trust-Based Forms of Governance, in Kramer, R. and Tyler, T. (eds.) *Trust in Organizations: Frontiers of Theory and Research*, Thousand Oaks, CA, Sage.

Powell, W. and Smith-Doerr, L. (1994) Networks and Economic Life, in Smelser, N. and Swedberg, R. (eds.) *The Handbook of Economic Sociology*, Princeton, Princeton University Press.

Powell, W., Koput, K. and Smith-Doerr, L. (1996) Interorganization Collaboration and the Locus of Innovation: Networks of Learning in Biotechnology, *Administrative Science Quarterly*, Vol. 41, 116-145.

Putnam, R. (1993) *Making Democracy Work: Civic Traditions in Modern Italy*, Princeton, Princeton University Press.

Putnam, R. (1995) Bowling Alone: America's Declining Social Capital, *Journal of Democracy*, Vol. 6, 65-78.

Pyke, F. (1992) *Industrial development through small-firm cooperation: Theory and practice*, Geneva, ILO.

Pyke, F. (1994) *Small firms, technical services and inter-firm cooperation*, Geneva, International Institute for Labour Studies.

Pyke, F. and Sengenberger, W. (eds.) (1992) *Industrial districts and local economic regeneration*, Geneva, International Institute for Labour Studies.

Pyke, F., Becattini, G. and Sengenberger, W. (eds.) (1990) *Industrial Districts and inter-firm co-operation in Italy*, Geneva, International Institute for Labour Studies.

QAD (1995) *TEC Delivery of Investors in People*, Moorfoot, Sheffield, Quality Assurance Division, Employment Department.

QPID (1996a) Review of 1995/96 Contracting Round with TECs, *QPID Study Report No. 45*, Moorfoot, Sheffield, Quality and Performance Improvement Division, Department for Education and Employment.

QPID (1996b) Improving the Responsiveness of FE Colleges to Labour Market Needs: The Effectiveness of the 1994 Competitiveness White Paper Arrangements, *QPID Study Report No. 50*, Moorfoot, Sheffield, Quality and Performance Improvement Division, Department for Education and Employment.

Rajan, A. (1993) *The Role of TECs in Local Economic Development*, London, TEC National Council.

Rawlinson, S. and Connor, H. (1996) *Developing Responsiveness: College-Employer Interaction*, Report 300, Brighton, Institute for Employment Studies.

Reese, L. and Malmer, A. (1994) The Effects of State Enabling Legislation on Local Economic Development Policies, *Urban Affairs Quarterly*, Vol. 30, 114-135.

Rhodes, R. (1997) *Understanding Governance: Policy Networks, Governance, Reflexivity and Accountability*, Buckingham, Open University Press.

Ring, P. and Van de Ven, A. (1994) Developmental Processes of Cooperative Interorganizational Relationships, *Academy of Management Review*, Vol. 19, 90-118.

Roberston, M., Swan, J. and Newell, S. (1996) The Role of Networks in the Diffusion of Technological Innovation, *Journal of Management Studies*, Vol. 33, 333-359.

Robertson, M. (1996a) Strategic Issues Impacting on Small Firms, in Blackburn, R. and Jennings, P. (eds.) *Small Firms: Contributions to Economic Regeneration*, London, Paul Chapman.

Robertson, M. (1996b) *Do Business Link Boards of Directors Provide Strategic Orientation*, Paper to Conference on 'Small Business and Enterprise Development', University of Leeds, 25-26 March.

Robertson, P. and Langlois, R. (1995) Innovation, networks, and vertical integration, *Research Policy*, Vol. 24, 543-562.

Rosenfeld, S. (1996) Does cooperation enhance competitiveness? Assessing the impacts of inter-firm collaboration, *Research Policy*, Vol. 25, 247-263.

Rosenfeld, S. (1997a) Bringing Clusters into the Mainstream of Economic Development, *European Planning Studies*, Vol. 5, 3-23.

Rosenfeld, S. (1997b) USNet- with Benefit of Hindsight, *Firm Connections*, Vol. 5, No. 6, 3-4.

Sabel, C. (1992) Studied trust: Building new forms of co-operation in a volatile economy, in Pyke, F. and Sengenberger, W. (eds.) *Industrial districts and local economic regeneration*, Geneva, International Institute for Labour Studies.

Sabel, C. (1994) Learning by Monitoring: the institutions of economic development, in Smelser, N. and Swedberg, R. (eds.) *The Handbook of Economic Sociology*, Princeton, Princeton University Press.

Sabel, C. (1995) *Experimental Regionalism and the Dilemmas of Regional Economic Policy in Europe*, Paper to OECD Seminar on 'Local Systems of Small Firms and Job Creation', Paris, 1-2 June.

Sako, M. (1992) *Prices, quality and trust: Inter-firm relations in Britain and Japan*, Cambridge, Cambridge University Press.

Saxenian, A. (1990) Regional Networks and the Resurgence of Silicon Valley, *California Management Review*, Vol. 33, 89-112.

Saxenian, A. (1994) *Regional Advantage: Culture and Competition in Silicon Valley and Route 128*, Cambridge, MA, Harvard University Press.

Sayer, A. and Walker, R. (1992) *The New Social Economy: Reworking the Division of Labor*, Cambridge, MA, Blackwell.

Schneider, M. and Teske, P. (1995) *Public Entrepreneurs: Agents for Change in American Government*, Princeton, Princeton University Press.

Schumpeter, J. (1934) *The Theory of Economic Development*, Cambridge, MA, Harvard University Press.

Scott, A. (1988) *New Industrial Spaces: Flexible Production Organisation and Regional Development in North America and Europe*, London, Pion.

Scott, A. (1994) *Technopolis: High-Technology Industry and Regional Development in Southern California*, Los Angeles, University of California Press.

Scott, A. (1998) *Regions and the World Economy: The coming shape of global production, competition, and political order*, Oxford, Oxford University Press.

Scott, A. and Storper, M. (1992) Regional development reconsidered, in Ernste, H. and Meier, V. (eds.) *Regional Development and Contemporary Industrial Response: Extending Flexible Specialisation*, London, Belhaven.

Scott, P., Jones, B., Bramley, A. and Bolton, B. (1996) Enhancing Technology and Skills in Small- and Medium-sized Manufacturing Firms: Problems and Prospects, *International Small Business Journal*, Vol. 14, 83-97.

Semlinger, K. (1993) Economic Development and Industrial Policy in Baden-Wurttemberg: Small Firms in a Benevolent Environment, *European Planning Studies*, Vol. 1, 435-464.

Sengenberger, W. and Pyke, F. (1992) Industrial districts and local economic regeneration: Research and policy issues, in Pyke, F. and Sengenberger, W. (eds.) *Industrial districts and local economic regeneration*, Geneva, International Institute for Labour Studies.

Shapira, P. (1993) *Public infrastructures supporting small firm industrial modernization in the United States*, Paper to Conference on 'Interfirm Cooperation - a means towards SME Competitiveness', Lisbon, 6-8 October.

Shapira, P. (1997) Evaluation as a Learning Strategy: Building Assessment In, *Firm Connections*, Vol. 5, No. 6, 6-7.

Shutt, J. (1996) Appraising Europe in the Regions 1994-1999: A Case Study of Recent Experiences in Yorkshire and Humberside, UK, in Alden, J. and Boland, P. (eds.) *Regional Development Strategies: A European Perspective*, London, Jessica Kingsley.

Simmie, J. (1997) The Origins and Characteristics of Innovation in Highly Innovative Areas, in Simmie, J. (ed.) *Innovation, Networks and Learning Regions?*, London, Jessica Kingsley.

Smits, S. and Rushing, F. (1997) *Great Britain: A Case Study of the Role of Workforce Development in the Global Competition for Jobs*, Policy Research Center, Georgia State University.

Smits, S., Rushing, F. and Hind, D. (1996) Human Resource and Enterprise Development at the Community Level in Great Britain: A Strategic Constituencies Assessment, *Research Paper No. 62*, Policy Research Center, Georgia State University.

Staber, U. (1996a) Networks and Regional Development: Perspectives and Unresolved Issues, in Staber, U., Schaefer, N. and Sharma, B. (eds.) *Business Networks: Prospects for Regional Development*, Berlin, Walter de Gruyter.

Staber, U. (1996b) The Social Embeddedness of Industrial Districts, in Staber, U., Schaefer, N. and Sharma, B. (eds.) *Business Networks: Prospects for Regional Development*, Berlin, Walter de Gruyter.

Staber, U. (1996c) Accounting for Variation in the Performance of Industrial Districts: The Case of Baden-Wurttemberg, *International Journal of Urban and Regional Research*, Vol. 20, 299-316.

Staber, U. and Aldrich, H. (1995) Cross-National Similarities in the Personal Networks of Small Business Owners: A Comparison of Two Regions in North America, *Canadian Journal of Sociology*, Vol. 20, 441-467.

Stockport, G. and Kakabadse, A. (1994) New Technology-Based Firms (NTBFs) and Interorganisation Networks: Developing a Conceptual Framework, in Oakey, R. (ed.) *New Technology-Based Firms in the 1990s*, London, Paul Chapman.

Storey, D. (1993) Should We Abandon Support to Start-Up Businesses?, in Chittenden, F., Robertson, M. and Watkins, D. (eds.) *Small Firms: Recession and Recovery*, London, Paul Chapman.

Storey, D. (1994) *Understanding the small business sector*, London, Routledge.

Storey, D. and Strange, A. (1992) New Players in the 'Enterprise Culture', in Caley, K., Chell, E., Chittenden, F. and Mason, C. (eds.) *Small Enterprise Development: Policy and Practice in Action*, London, Paul Chapman.

Storper, M. (1992) The limits to globalization: technology districts and international trade, *Economic Geography*, Vol. 68, 60-93.

Storper, M. (1993) Regional 'Worlds' of Production: Learning and Innovation in the Technology Districts of France, Italy and the USA, *Regional Studies*, Vol. 27, 433-455

Storper, M. (1994) *Institutions in a learning economy*, paper presented to OECD-conference on 'Employment and Growth in a Knowledge-Based Economy', Copenhagen, November.

Storper, M. (1995) The resurgence of regional economies, ten years later: the region as a nexus of untraded interdependencies, *European Urban and Regional Studies*, Vol. 2, 191-221.

Storper, M. (1997) *The Regional World: Territorial development in a global economy*, New York, Guilford Press.

Storper, M. and Scott, A. (1995) The Wealth of Regions: Market forces and policy imperatives in local and global context, *Futures*, Vol. 27, 505-526.

Strambach, S. (1994) Knowledge-Intensive Business Services in the Rhine-Neckar Area, *Tijdschrift voor Economische en Sociale Geografie*, Vol. 85, 354-365.

Strange, I. (1997) Directing the show? Business leaders, local partnership, and economic regeneration in Sheffield, *Environment and Planning C: Government and Policy*, Vol. 15, 1-17.

Sverisson, A. (1994) Making Sense of Chaos: Socio-technical Networks, Careers and Entrepreneurs, *Acta Sociologica*, Vol. 37, 401-417.

Sweeney, G. (1996) Learning efficiency, technological change and economic change, *International Journal of Technology Management*, Vol. 11, 5-27.

Sweeting, R. (1995) Competition, co-operation and changing the manufacturing infrastructure, *Regional Studies*, Vol. 29, 87-94.

Sydow, J. (1996) Flexible Specialization in Regional Networks, in Staber, U., Schaefer, N. and Sharma, B. (eds.) *Business Networks: Prospects for Regional Development*, Berlin, Walter de Gruyter.

Szarka, J. (1990) Networking and Small Firms, *International Small Business Journal*, Vol. 8, 10-22.

TEC National Council (1995) Local Authorities and TECs Plan Closer Working, London, TEC National Council Press Release.

TEC National Council (1997) *The role of the business community in local economic development*, London, TEC National Council.

Telser, L. (1987) *A Theory of Efficient Cooperation and Competition*, Cambridge, Cambridge University Press.

Teske, P. and Schneider, M. (1994) The Bureaucratic Entrepreneur: The Case of City Managers, *Public Administration Review*, Vol. 54, 331-340.

Thorelli, H. (1986) Networks: Between Markets and Hierarchies, *Strategic Management Journal*, Vol. 7, 37-51.

Tilson, B., Mawson, J., Beazley, M., Burfitt, A., Collinge, C., Hall, S., Loftman, P., Nevin, B. and Janin, A. (1997) Partnerships for Regeneration: The Single Regeneration Budget Challenge Fund Round One, *Local Government Studies*, Vol. 23, 1-15.

Tödtling, F. (1994) The Uneven Landscape of Innovation Poles: Local Embeddedness and Global Networks, in Amin, A. and Thrift, N. (eds.) *Globalization, Institutions, and Regional Development in Europe*, Oxford, Oxford University Press.

Trade and Industry Select Committee (1998) *Small and Medium Sized Enterprises*, Sixth Report to the House of Commons, London, Stationery Office.

Tyler, T. and Kramer, R. (1996) Whither Trust?, in Kramer, R. and Tyler, T. (eds.) *Trust in Organizations: Frontiers of Theory and Research*, Thousand Oaks, CA, Sage.

Uzzi, B. (1996) The Sources and Consequences of Embeddedness for the Economic Performance of Organizations: The Network Effect, *American Sociological Review*, Vol. 61, 674-698.

Vaessen, P. and Keeble, D. (1995) Growth-oriented SMEs in Unfavourable Regional Environments, *Regional Studies*, Vol. 29, 489-505.

Varaldo, R. and Ferrucci, L. (1996) The Evolutionary Nature of the Firm within Industrial Districts, *European Planning Studies*, Vol. 4, 27-34.

Vatne, E. (1995) Local resource mobilisation and internationalisation strategies in small and medium sized enterprises, *Environment and Planning A*, Vol. 27, 63-80.

Vaughan, P. (1993) *TECs & Employers, Developing effective links, Part 1: a survey*, Research Series No. 12, Sheffield, Employment Department.

Vere, D. (1993) Training and Enterprise Councils: Putting Business in the Lead, in Harrison, A. (ed.) *From Hierarchy to Contract*, Newbury, Berks, Policy Journals.

Vickerstaff, S. and Parker, K. (1995) Helping Small Firms: The Contribution of TECs and LECs, *International Small Business Journal*, Vol. 13, 56-72.

von Hippel, E. (1988) *The Sources of Innovation*, New York, Oxford University Press.

Ward, K. (1997) The Single Regeneration Budget and the Issues of Local Flexibility, *Regional Studies*, Vol. 31, 78-81.

Welch, D., Oldsman, E., Shapira, P., Youtie, J. and Lee, J. (1997) *Net Benefits: An assessment of a set of manufacturing business networks and their impacts on member companies*, USNet Evaluation Working Paper 9701, Georgia, Georgia Institute of Technology.

Wilkinson, J. (1997) A new paradigm for economic analysis, *Economy and Society*, Vol. 26, 305-339.

Williamson, O. (1975) *Markets and Hierarchies*, New York, The Free Press.

Williamson, O. (1985) *The Economic Institutions of Capitalism*, New York, The Free Press.

Williamson, O. (1991) Comparative economic organization: the analysis of discrete structural alternatives, *Administrative Science Quarterly*, Vol. 36, 269-296.

Williamson, O. (1993) Calculativeness, trust, and economic organization, *Journal of Law and Economics*, Vol. 34, 453-502.

Williamson, O. (1994) Transaction Cost Economics and Organization Theory, in Smelser, N. and Swedberg, R. (eds.) *The Handbook of Economic Sociology*, Princeton, Princeton University Press.

Wilson, P. (1995) Embracing Locality in Local Economic Development, *Urban Studies*, Vol. 32, 645-658.

Wilson, P. (1996) Empowerment: Community Economic Development from the Inside Out, *Urban Studies*, Vol. 33, 617-630.

Wilson, P. (1997) Building Social Capital: A Learning Agenda for the Twenty-first Century, *Urban Studies*, Vol. 34, 745-760.

Zhou, Y. (1996) Inter-firm Linkages, Ethnic Networks, and Territorial Agglomeration: Chinese Computer Firms in Los Angeles, *Papers in Regional Science*, Vol. 75, 265-291.

# Index

For Product Safety Concerns and Information please contact our EU representative GPSR@taylorandfrancis.com Taylor & Francis Verlag GmbH, Kaufingerstraße 24, 80331 München, Germany

Printed and bound by CPI Group (UK) Ltd, Croydon, CR0 4YY
01/05/2025
01858351-0002